Read 12.2.18

Ted Clarke

BUILDING BOSTON

Stories of Architectural and Engineering Feats

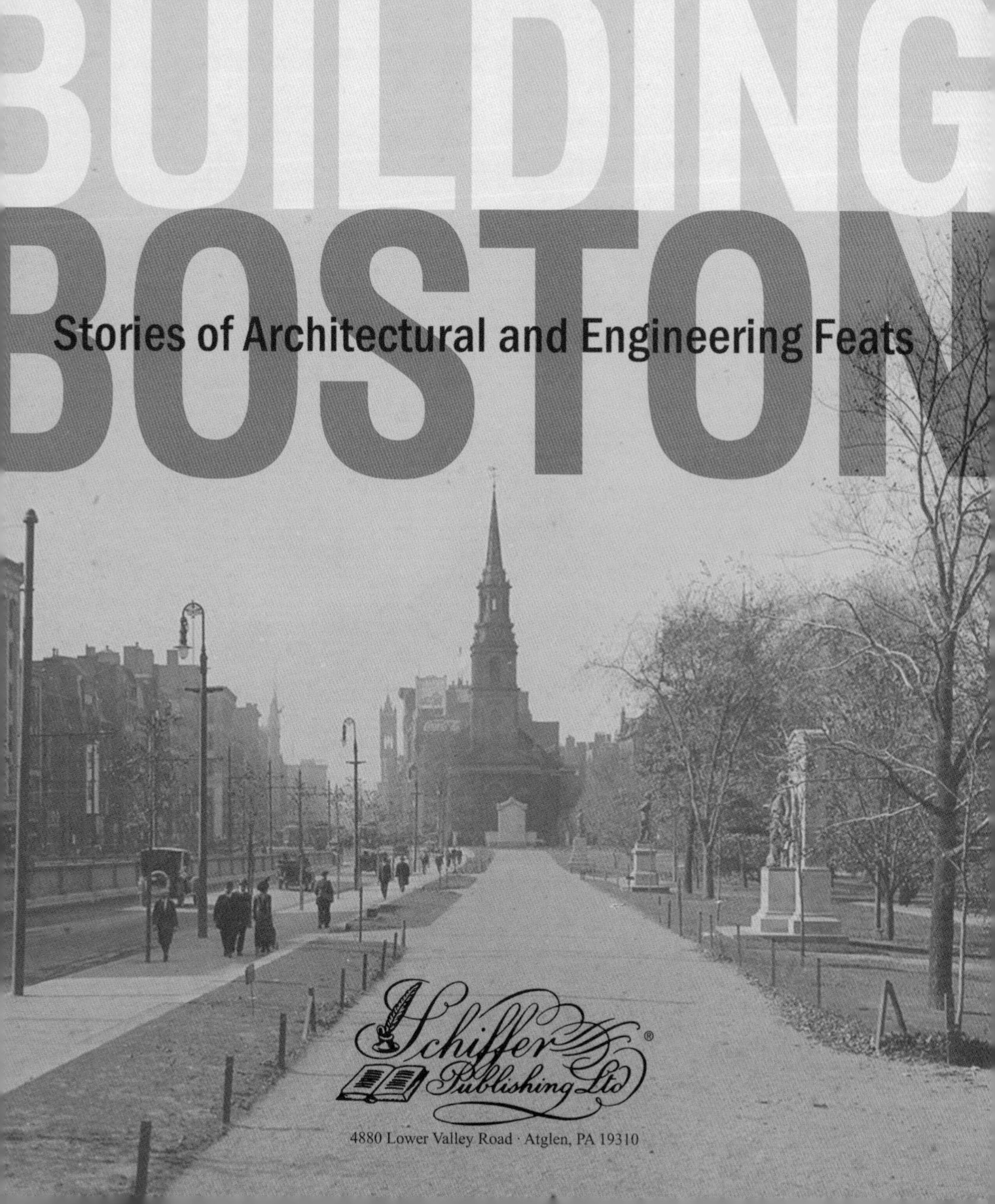

Schiffer Publishing Ltd®
4880 Lower Valley Road · Atglen, PA 19310

Other Schiffer Books by the Author:

North Shore Lore: Stories of the Massachusetts Coast. ISBN: 978-0-7643-4506-7

The Charles River: A History of Greater Boston's Waterway. ISBN: 978-0-7643-4154-0

Other Schiffer Books on Related Subjects:

Boston Below. Joseph R. Votano and Karen E. Hosking. ISBN: 978-0-7643-4542-5

Boston Wide. Arthur P. Richmond. ISBN: 978-0-7643-3273-9

Contemporary Boston Architects. E. Ashley Rooney with Gary Johnson and Maryann Thompson. ISBN: 978-0-7643-4221-9

Boston: Past & Present. Mary L. Martin and E. Ashley Rooney. ISBN: 978-0-7643-3058-2

Published by Schiffer Publishing, Ltd.
4880 Lower Valley Road
Atglen, PA 19310
Phone: (610) 593-1777 | Fax: (610) 593-2002
E-mail: Info@schifferbooks.com
Web: www.schifferbooks.com

Library of Congress Control Number: 2016931398

Cover design by Brenda McCallum
Type set in Helvetica/Minion
ISBN: 978-0-7643-5112-9
Printed in China

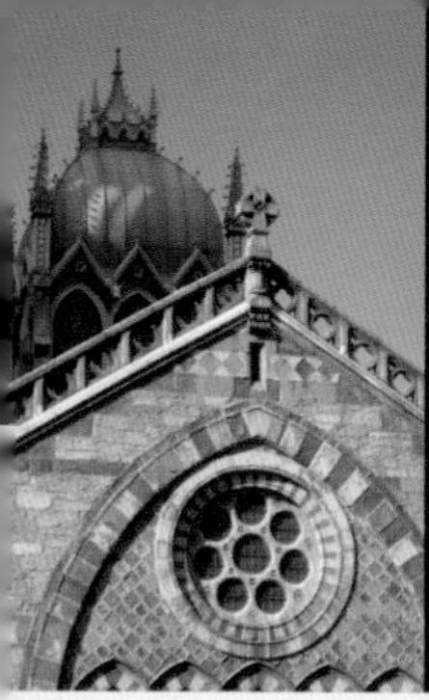
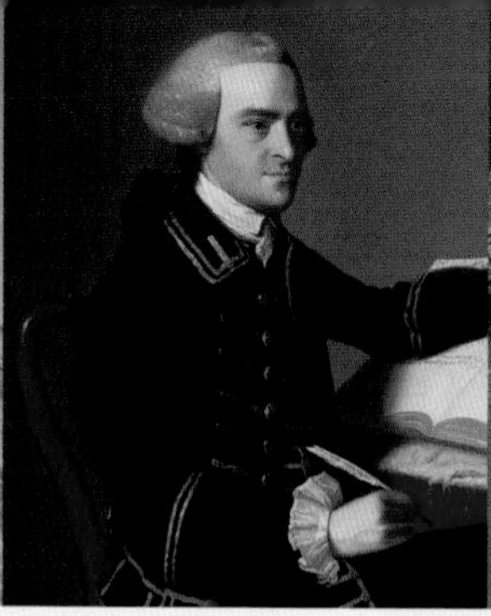
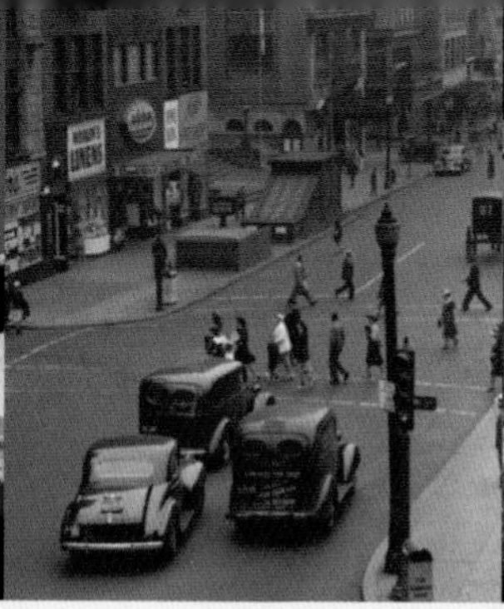
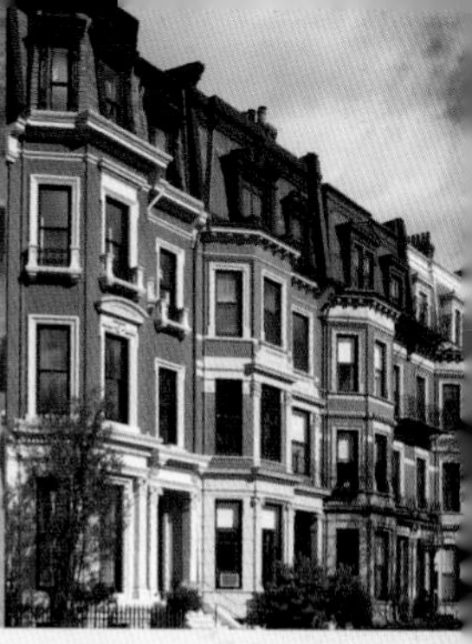

Contents

CHAPTER ONE

This Hallowed Ground

Since the "Marathon Bombings" of April 2013 and the heroic response of the people of Boston, Copley Square has become the center of an almost religious focus, in that it joins places, like the World Trade Center in New York, or Dealey Plaza in Dallas, as iconic urban locations that represent historic but tragic moments in American history.

That focus garnered national attention, but the heroics it represents and the exceptionalism that Boston's citizens displayed are not a new thing in what Oliver Wendell Holmes Jr. called "The Hub of the Universe." Boston has taken that kind of fame in its stride and has integrated each outstanding event or experience into its native character. Historical significance has simply become part of the "fabric" of Boston.

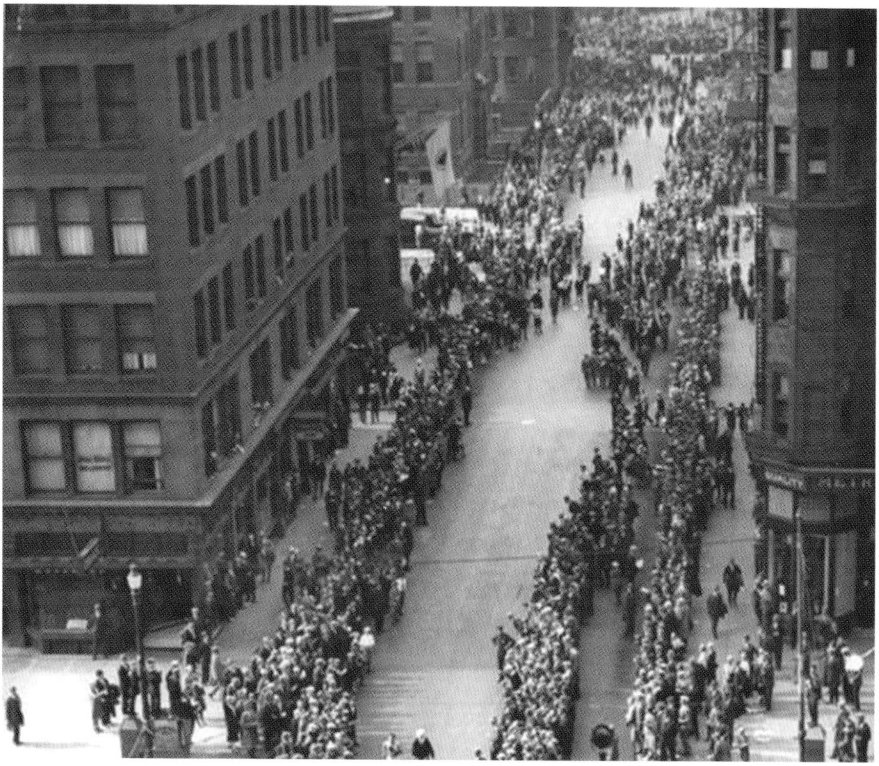

BOSTON MARATHON, 1910
COURTESY BOSTON PUBLIC LIBRARY

The Marathon itself, commonly called the "Boston Marathon," is the oldest race of its kind in the world. It was first run in 1897, on Patriot's Day, the day being chosen to link the Athenian and American struggles for liberty. (The initial marathons were run in honor of an earlier run by an Athenian from Marathon, Greece, to Athens, to tell the populace about a historic victory.)

The race was initiated and managed by the Boston Athletic Association (BAA), the club building standing on Exeter Street near Boylston where the Marathon ends and also near the spot where the Boston Public Library's Johnson Building is located today.

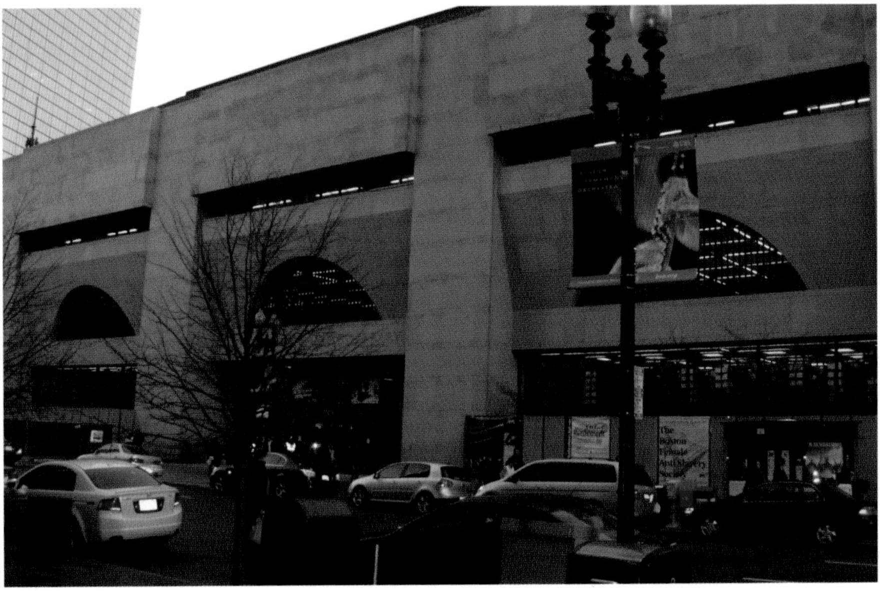

FINISH LINE, OPPOSITE BOSTON PUBLIC LIBRARY
COURTESY AUTHOR

The Boston Marathon is still held on Patriot's Day, a holiday in Massachusetts and Maine (which was once part of Massachusetts) and commemorates the Battles of Lexington and Concord on April 19, 1775. The race, itself, was held on the nineteenth until the holiday was moved to the third Monday in April in 1969. On each Patriot's Day, re-enactments are held at the battle sites on Lexington Green and at North Bridge in Concord, and there are also re-enactments of the storied rides by Paul Revere and William Dawes over their original routes. But the widest interest is in the marathon, on the day that many call "Marathon Monday."

Since 1959, the Red Sox have played a home game at Fenway Park on that day. For years, the game began in the morning and would end at about the time the marathon leaders were passing through nearby Kenmore Square, where the Citgo sign announced that they had one mile to go. The baseball crowds could catch that final part of the marathon as the leading runners made their way down Beacon Street to Kenmore Square and Commonwealth Avenue after the fans had filed out of Fenway. Game over, game on!

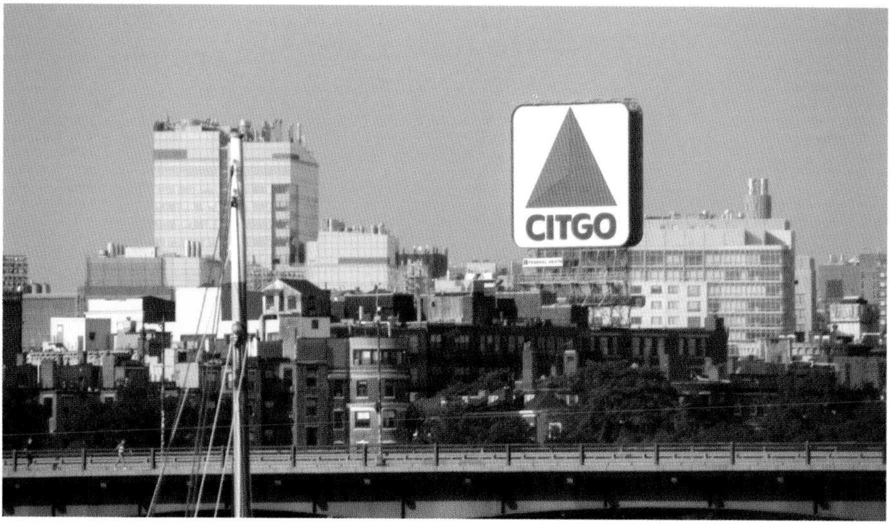

CITGO SIGN FROM CHARLES RIVER
COURTESY AUTHOR

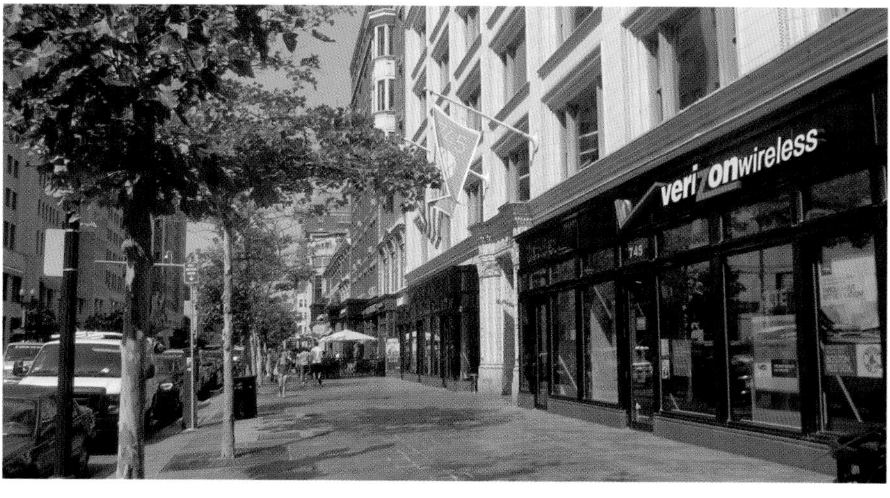

CURRENT SCENE NEAR BOMB SITES
COURTESY AUTHOR

The exploding of two bombs by terrorists near the finish line at the 2013 race changed the placid nature of the event and the way Bostonians viewed the event. But most notably, the rescue efforts made by first responders, medical people, and ordinary people showed a gritty determination that Bostonians decided represented the character of their city, a determination that has been carried on. It was shown and publicized in a big way by the Boston Red Sox.

An earlier start to the race since 2007 has not diminished the fervor of the fans. The Red Sox became even more closely tied to the marathon after a special observance at the next home game after the bombing. At that time the team helped to galvanize Boston's fortitude to overcome the tragedy. A sellout crowd at Fenway was visually stirred by the tribute to Bostonians affected by the bombings and by the defiant words of some Red Sox players to remain strong in the face of adversity. After that, when the Sox went on to win the World Series, it was said that this was a "divine balm" to help Boston heal the wounds inflicted earlier that spring.

Even before that Red Sox event, and within hours of the bombing, two Emerson College students came up with a design for blue T-shirts with gold lettering showing the slogan "Boston Strong." It seems to have first appeared on Twitter in a post by Curtis Cough, followed by one by Red Sox player Will Middleton. Later came the "One Fund Boston" to help survivors with their medical expenses.

The race in April 21, 2014 drew record crowds and more than 36,000 entrants, huge numbers, and as a special bonus to the spectators, the men's race was won by an American for the first time since 1983. Naturally the city went all-out to provide the tightest security possible while still allowing spectators to enjoy watching the race. The improved security at the event didn't diminish the fervor of the fans or runners, and was seen as a major civic victory, as the spirit of the city was affirmed by the overwhelming participation and jubilation.

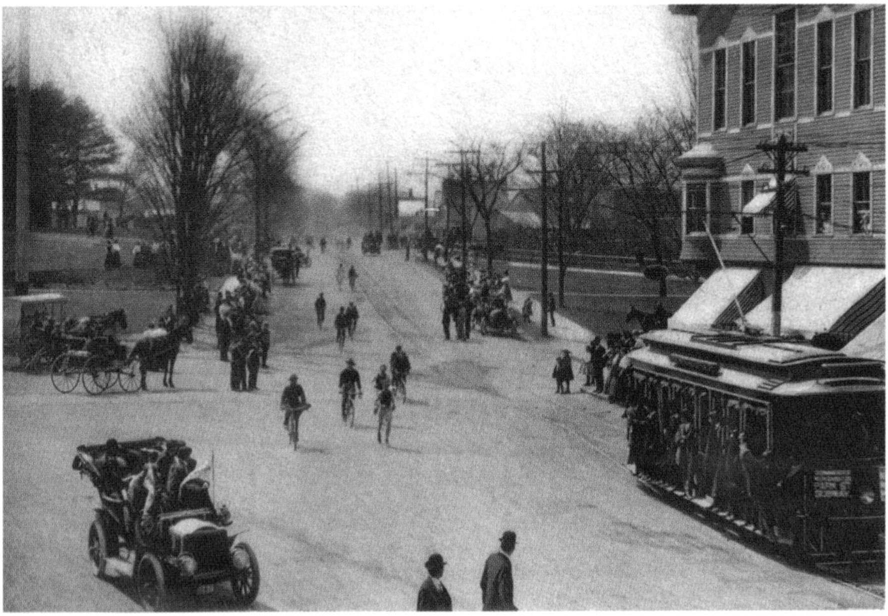

1906 MARATHON, WELLESLEY

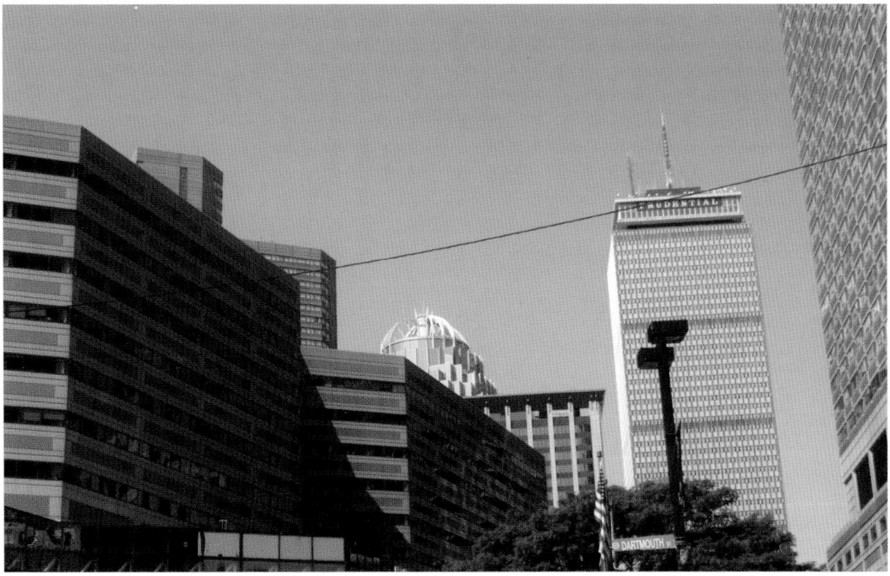

PRU HOVERS OVER LENOX
COURTESY AUTHOR

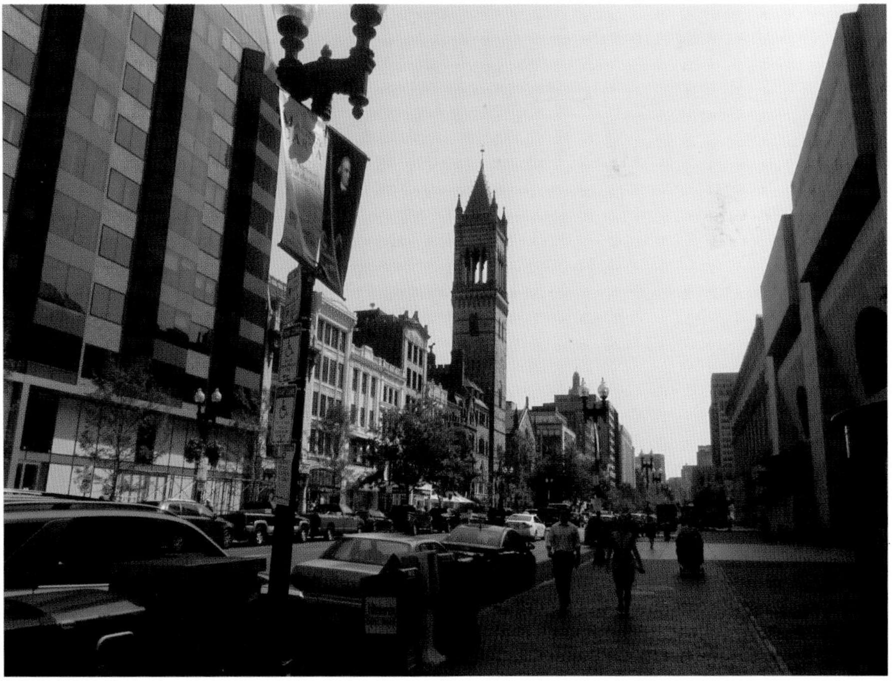

FINISH LINE TOWARD COPLEY SQUARE
COURTESY AUTHOR

The race ends on Boylston Street, where the bombings took place, just outside Copley Square. A memorial service was held there six days before the running of the race, one that had religious overtones as well as a spirit of perseverance denoted by that phrase "Boston Strong." The area had become hallowed ground.

Just up Boylston Street from the finish line is Copley Square, one of the best-known intersections in the city. Here is where Boylston Street, Dartmouth Street, and Huntington Avenue once formed a triangle. It is the notable open space known first as "Art Square."

It earned that name since it was once, and still is, the focal point for Boston as a

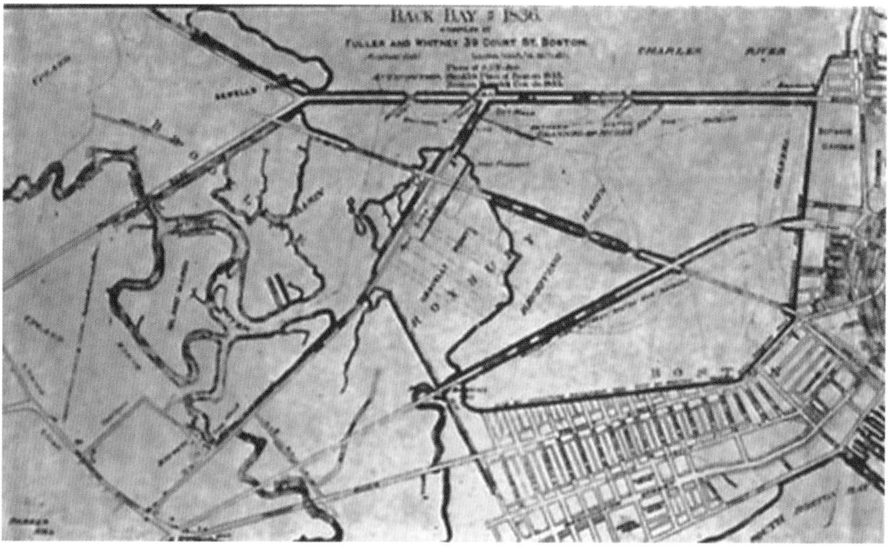

MAP, ART SQUARE

center for the fine arts. The square was framed during the late 1800s by the Museum of Fine Arts, the Boston Public Library, Old South Church, and Trinity Church. The outstanding architecture of the square makes sense of the term "frozen music."

Not music, but noise has been and ever will be associated with the finish line of the Boston Marathon and the tragic, heroic, and even spiritual events that happened there. Those events exemplify the best and the worst of human nature within that few blocks of urban cityscape, and it reminds visitors of the uniqueness that embodies the city of Boston.

The day and the event are associated not only with sports, but with the best of the medical profession—for which Boston had already been well-known—and for the courage and determination of its people, including a civic spirit that it showed in overcoming tragedy, coming back from disaster, and displaying to the world the face of courage. All of these qualities centered about Copley Square which, itself, has many qualities that override the urban ordinary.

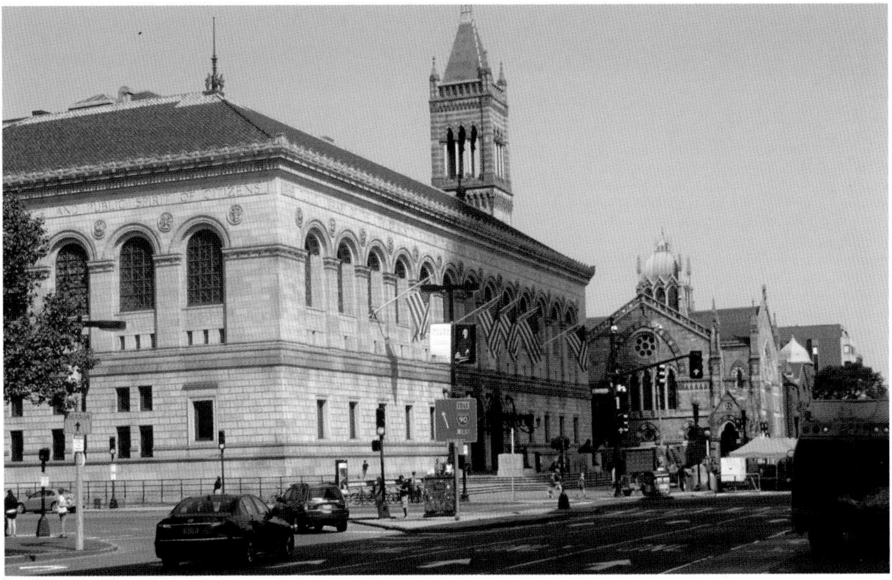

COPLEY BOSTON PUBLIC LIBRARY, OLD SOUTH
COURTESY AUTHOR

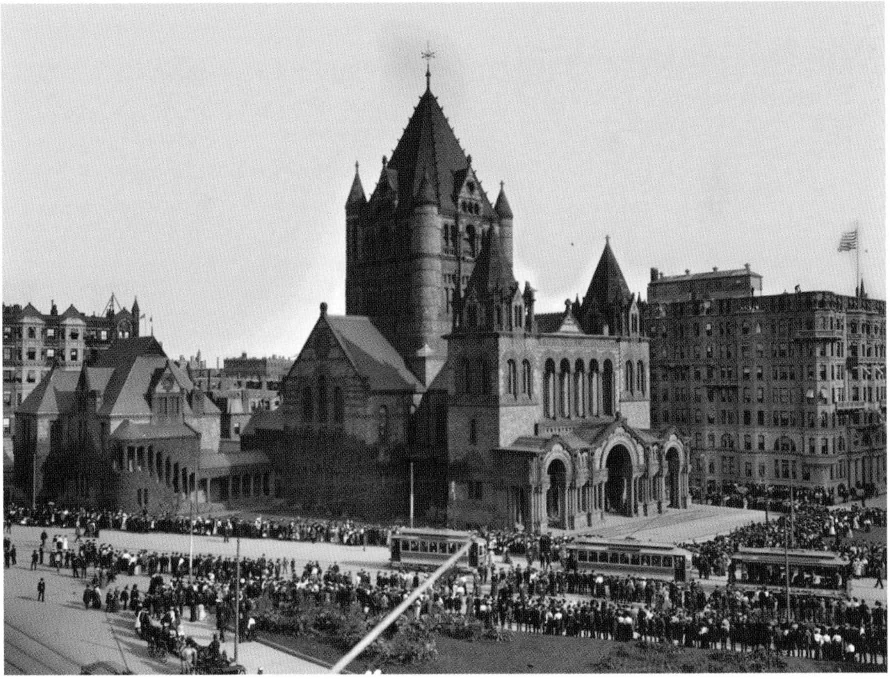

TRINITY, TROLLEYS, HOTEL WESTMINSTER, 1903

Even its shape is irregular and it has not often been a square. The odd shapes of Copley Square are due to the railroads that once entered Boston at different angles from Providence and Worcester, creating adjacent street grids that met near Copley and were cut through by Boylston Street and Huntington Avenue. Many attempts were made over many years to get Art Square, or later Copley Square, to behave like an ordinary urban center. But that's not what it was, and it couldn't behave in an ordinary fashion. Though recently made symmetrical, it remains distinct.

Art Square was renamed Copley Square for famed artist John Singleton Copley, who was raised mostly by his Irish-immigrant mother on Long Wharf. He became noted for his singular portraits of colonial Americans, patriots like John Hancock, Sam Adams, and Paul Revere. These works now hang in a museum just up Huntington Avenue.

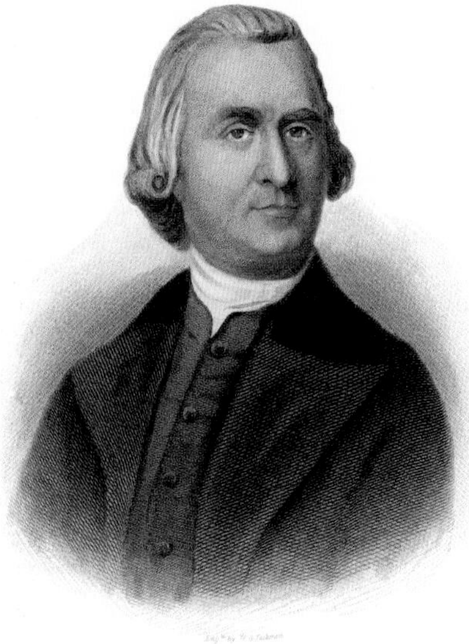

SAM ADAMS SKETCH

These links lie languidly in line, but not perhaps by chance. The whole area is tied together in that way, and we'll show you how that came to be.

Back Bay was built, of course, before Art Square was built upon it. Within the square, at the intersection of Boylston and Dartmouth, was an oval section to be known as Elysian Fields. The choice of a name was a happy one considering the events that would come to pass there. In Greek mythology, according to Homer, the Elysian Fields were the final resting place of the noble and heroic. It was a pleasant paradise for warriors like Achilles, and in *The Aeneid* those heroes spent their time doing artistic things like creating poetry and music.

In Paris, the avenue of the Elysian Fields is known as the Champs Elysees. In America, the first baseball game was held on the Elysian Fields located, jarringly, in Hoboken, New Jersey. Notably, Commonwealth Avenue in the Back Bay was modeled after the broad boulevards of Paris, and leads to the Fenway where baseball is yet proudly played in the nation's most notable ballpark.

Whether the Back Bay would become a paradise or not, it was far from that when Bostonians discussed filling its wide expanse during the second decade of the nineteenth century. At that time, it was a broad part of the Charles River, behind or back of the peninsula of Shawmut, and thus called "The Back Bay." The small peninsula that then constituted Boston Proper was connected to the hinterland of Roxbury via a narrow neck of land along today's Washington Street near the present Dover Street.

The bulk of Boston's citizenry was crowded into this pear-shaped peninsula. Later, during the Great Fire of 1872, it lost many of its buildings. Some of the wealthiest people lived in or near the burned area and would at that time be seeking new residences.

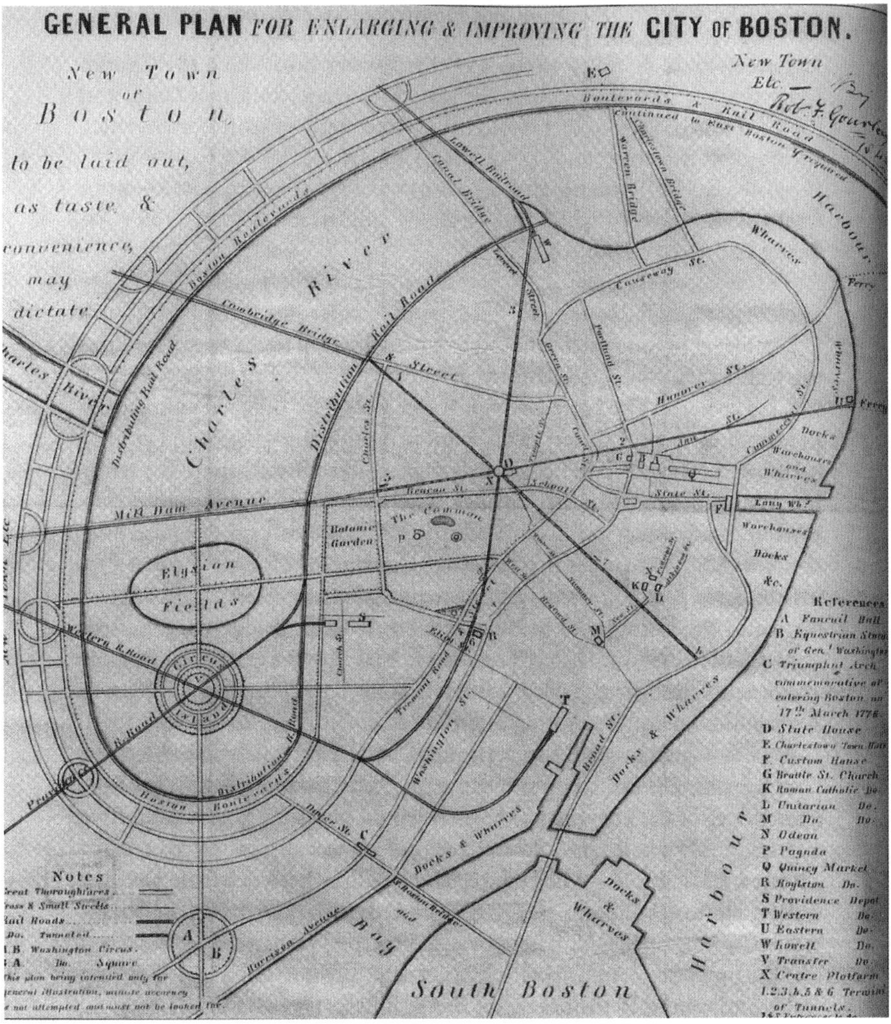

GENERAL PLAN FOR CITY OF BOSTON, 1844.
COURTESY ROBERT GOURLAY

The downtown would, at mid-century, also become the dwelling place of hordes of immigrants, mostly Irish, from whom the upper classes would seek separation.

"Rome wasn't built in a day," they say; nor were Copley Square or the Back Bay. But the construction of both made Roman progress look downright sluggish. The earliest attempts in the second decade of the nineteenth century to improve the Back Bay had been poorly planned and were doomed to failure, as we shall see. The Back Bay, whose currents washed against the foot of the Boston Common at Charles Street, also brought noxious odors, especially at low tide. But in 1814, when the first plans for improving Back Bay were put forward, it wasn't just the bad smells that drove the project; it was

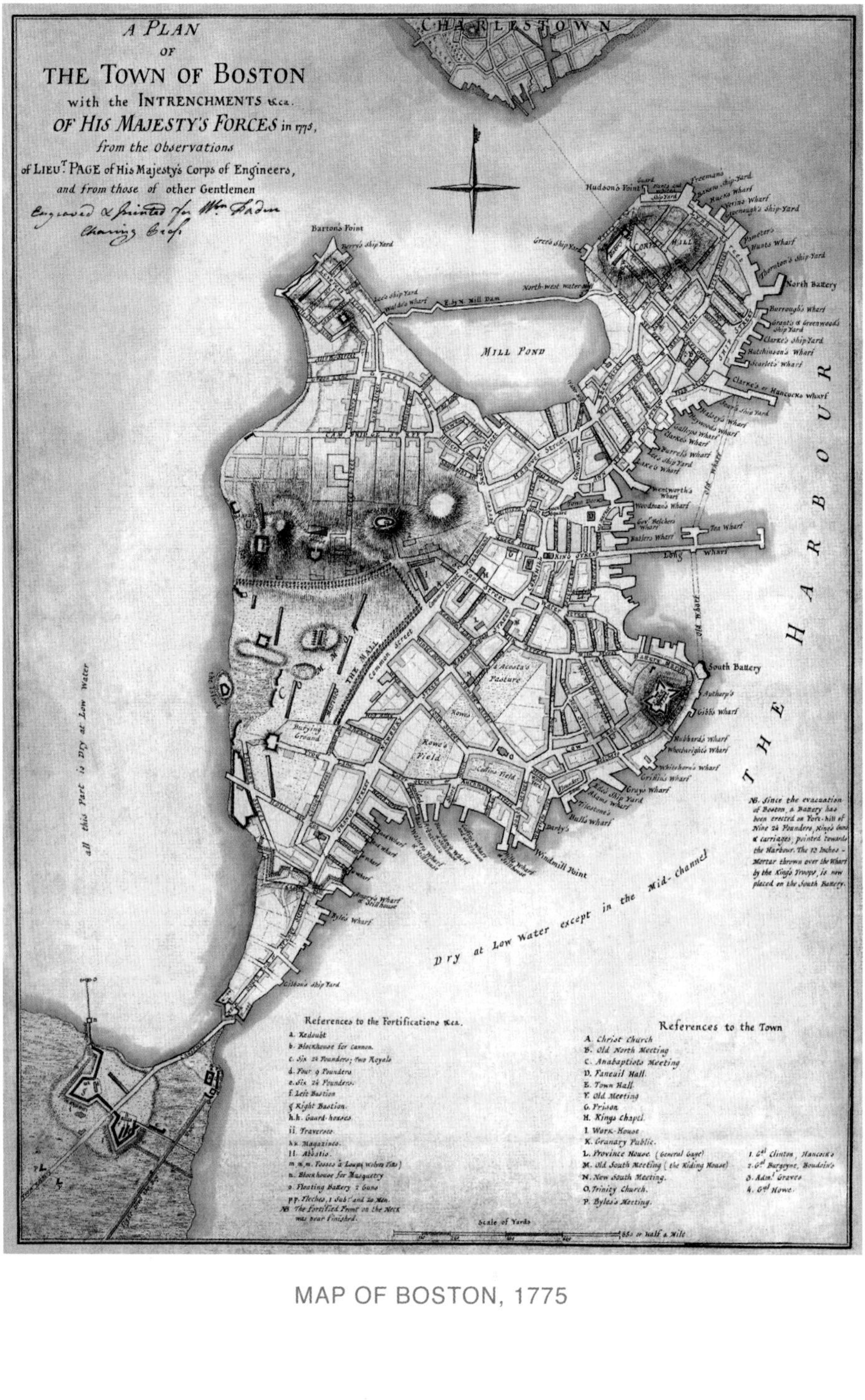

MAP OF BOSTON, 1775

power and money. Progress would be defined by building a dam parallel to the shore, and that dam, plus a cross dam, would provide power for industry and therefore profit. Or so it was supposed.

The Charles River at this point was an estuary, meaning that the tides from the ocean flowed in and out twice a day. A dam would be built to harness the power generated by tidal flow as the water ran through sluiceways in the dam and turned turbines those two times.

The dam, built by the Roxbury Mill Dam Company, followed a geographic line from the junction of Beacon Street and Charles Street west to about where Kenmore Square is now. Atop the dam would be a road that would shorten the trip to Brighton, Brookline, Watertown, and points west.

A cross dam was added that divided the Charles at Back Bay into two basins. No land was made, but the major east-west dam was fifty feet wide and a mile and a half in length, so the look of the Back Bay was decidedly altered, as was the flow of its water.

It did make the trip west shorter. What it didn't do was provide power for factories and make money for its promoters. Few factories or companies were interested. They wanted to make money from the power of the Charles River, but they found it easier to do that where the water fell fast and naturally, at Waltham some eleven miles northwest.

Boston's first families made much of their wealth in trade, though they sometimes used nefarious means—engaging in rum-running and the opium trade, for example.

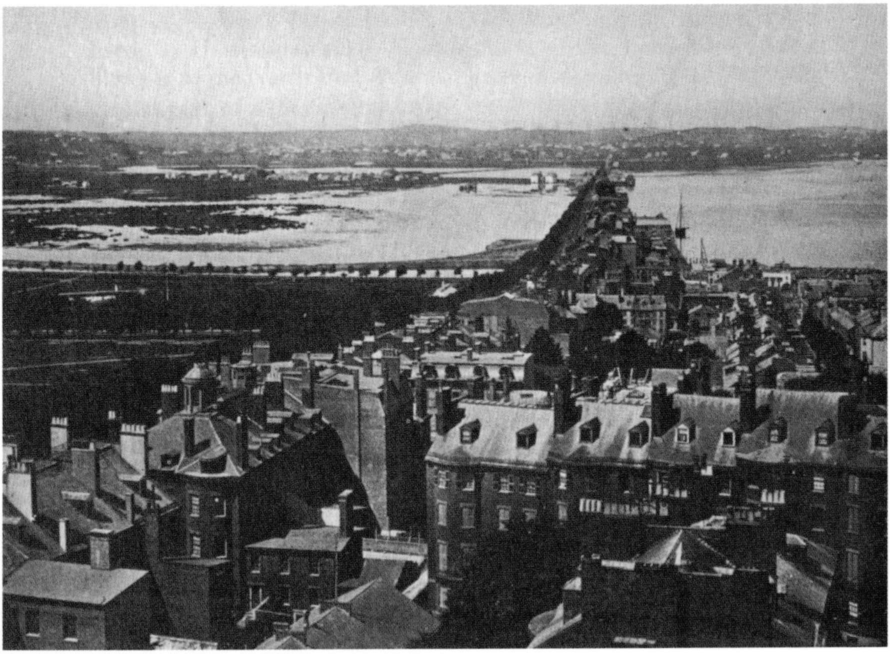

MILL POND FROM BEACON STREET TOWARD WEST

When that era ran out, they turned to making textiles in Waltham and Lowell and then to canals and railroads. Many of them lived on Beacon Hill during that era and would later populate the Back Bay. But for now, the stench from Back Bay endured. The mill dam at Back Bay failed miserably. It was terribly expensive and brought little return. Only three manufacturing companies used the power provided by the dam.

But the city would persevere and snatch triumph from this dismal morass. Boston would turn Back Bay into a pricey residential area of Victorian homes—homes that stand even now. The tidewater would be fully filled and Back Bay and the Elysian Fields would come to pass a few decades later.

Some people thought that the idea of filling in the Back Bay was a pipe dream. They were only half right. It was a dream.

If a person were to lie awake night after night, month after month, hardly sleeping at all, he might be able to use that silent time to think, to plan, perchance to dream big dreams. Such a man did exist in Boston in the 1840s. Robert Fleming Gourlay had come to Boston seeking help with his insomnia. His case was written up in the *Boston Medical and Surgical Journal.* In 1845, he claimed to have slept only rarely during the prior five years and eight months.

A Scot who had lived in Canada but who had been banished for sedition—he tried to suggest changes in the provincial government and had ruffled feathers by criticizing authorities. He had reason to lie awake. And then he came to Boston in 1843. Years earlier he had proposed a new kind of government in Britain that actually passed the House of Commons, but not the House of Lords.

This was our Robert Gourlay, an educated man, who was also a thinker. And, as he lay awake in the Marlborough Hotel on Washington Street in Boston, he had time to think and plan—and he did both. He said he had been trying to "...beguile the watches of the night..." This is rather a nice thought. And while he was at it, he did a bit more, too: He came up with a visionary idea. A new town could be built on the marshes and mud flats that separated Boston from Cambridge, along with a dam to create a fresh-water river basin surrounded by park land. "On this waste," he wrote of the stinking mud flats, "may form a city surpassing all others, either in ancient or modern times." John Winthrop had, just earlier, envisioned and proposed a "City on a Hill." Gourlay saw more details than that and had utilitarian ideas of how to accomplish what he envisioned.

He published his ideas in an 1844 pamphlet entitled, "Plans for Enlarging and Improving the City of Boston, Being Studies to Illustrate the Science of City Building." He sent it to the governor and city officials, but they paid it little heed, apparently thinking he was a crackpot.

He wrote, "During the last twenty years, Boston has doubled in population; but now, the ratio of increase must be greater far. Fifty years hence it will contain 500,000 souls; and within a century a million at least. The peninsula is already crowded; and here, want of forethought has caused confusion beyond remedy, but there is a field beyond which may be planned out and built on, with every advantage."

"A field beyond." That was something! But our Gourlay was drawing on experience, not on imagination alone. He knew something about such things and told of how Edinburgh, Scotland, faced with similar overcrowding, had solved it by connecting

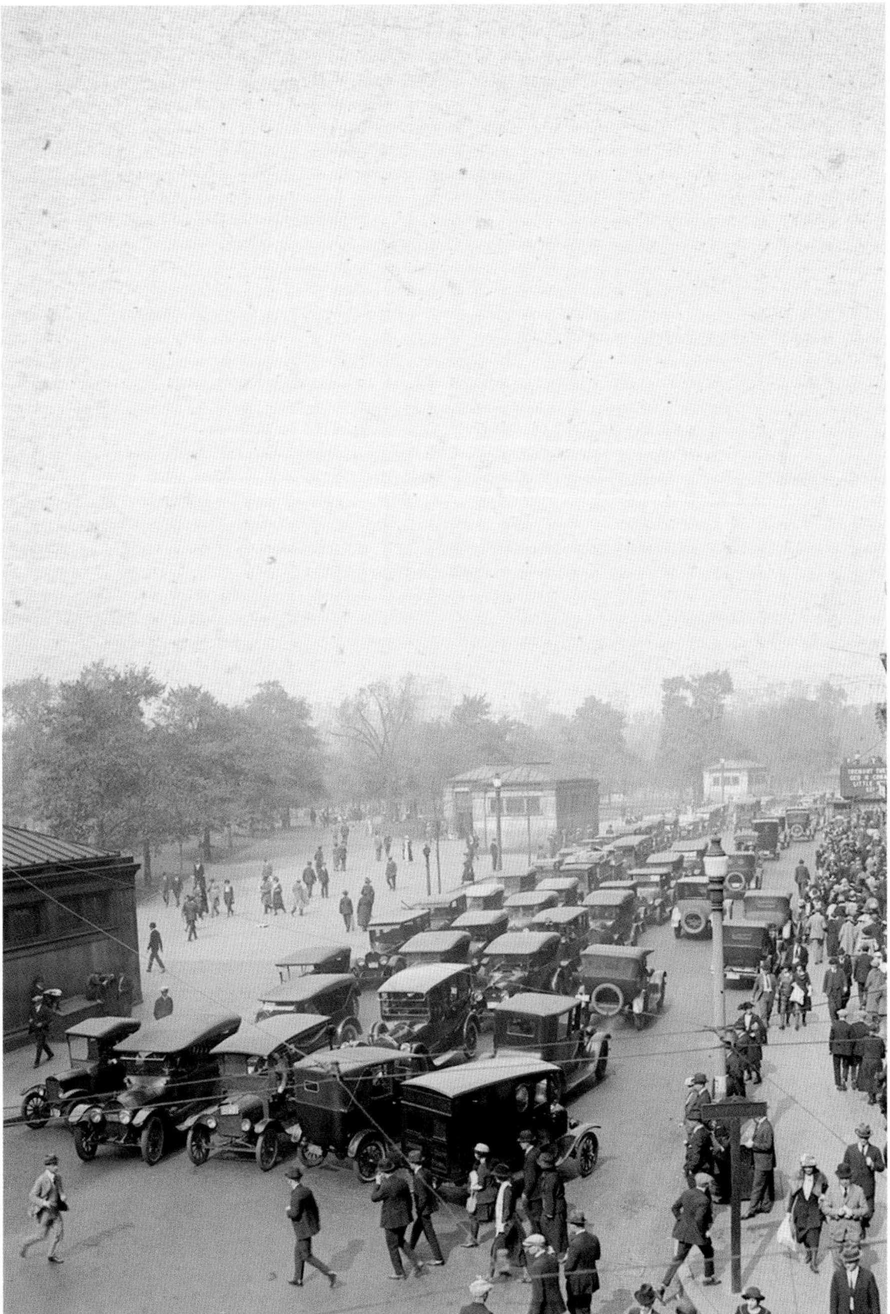

TREMONT AT BOYLSTON, CA 1921

a large plain to the city via a bridge, and had laid out a plan to develop it. His "field beyond" probably meant the outlying areas (today's suburbs) and his plan spoke of how to get there. In the middle of Back Bay, where the railroad lines met, Gourlay proposed a "Circus Island." Being from Britain, he no doubt envisioned a place where streets intersect like Piccadilly Circus.

"Circus Island" would have a railroad transfer depot sunken in the center. Two rings of houses would be built around it, and from there, "sub-urban" railroads would sweep around both banks of the Charles River and also into the city. There they would dive into subways that connected with the various railroad terminals. He proposed a "Centre Platform" at the State House playing the role of today's Park Street Station, which was not yet a gleam in anyone's eye. Gourlay's platform would allow travelers from out of town to bypass downtown Boston, a city already jammed with traffic long before even the notion of motor vehicles had sprung to mind.

He wrote cogently, "Already, Washington Street is crowded to excess, and every day, we witness inconvenience from the noise and collision of carriages. What would it be if there were a million of residents, and tens of thousands of visitors?"

Gourlay envisioned boulevards on both sides of the Charles with railways along the river, a park 200 feet wide and a forty-foot street with houses, as well as other streets. This plan, served by railroads, would create a greater Boston. "How agreeable would it be," he asked, "to have public carriages, hourly, to carry us to each place, in turn, ... to have a steamboat, in connection, running from Squantum Point: touching at certain promontories, islands &tc; and landing at Winthrop's Head!"

Back Bay would be dredged and kept filled with three or four feet of clear water, while the mud dredged up would be used for the construction of an oval island known as the Elysian Fields centered at today's Copley Square. Boylston Street would run across the Bay parallel to the Mill Dam, while Dartmouth Street would cross from the Mill Dam to Circus Island.

Nothing came of this sleepless planning—at least not at that time. In years to come, many of the features would become reality in one form or another, but people then, as now, often brushed aside the views of visionaries, often to their own later dismay. As for Gourlay, hardly anyone in Boston has heard of him today.

Meanwhile, the mud flats and their stench, along with environmental problems not yet understood, continued. It even got worse because all this work, as you might realize, restricted the circulation of water, and the stillness of the mudflats only added to the stench. Two railroad causeways had been built across the water, and that made it worse. The Boston & Worcester Railroad ran from Allston to the South Cove, while the Boston and Providence ran along the path of today's MBTA Orange line, crossed the water of the bay near today's Back Bay Station to end at a terminal near the present Park Square.

That was the situation at mid-century, by which time Beacon Hill, long the enclave of the wealthy, had no more land to accommodate the newly wealthy. Some rich people had moved to the suburbs where railroads and streetcars allowed them to commute to Boston—20,000 a day by 1850. Those with vision could see that a new upper-class neighborhood near downtown, such as a filled-in Back Bay, would sell well and make a fortune for developers. Boston needed people with vision to make improvements.

This time the planning was far better. The land would be filled with gravel—three and a half feet of it—and this would then be covered with soil. The gravel would be brought nine miles from East Needham Upper Falls on a single track of the Charles River Railroad that ran parallel to that of the Boston and Worcester over the existing causeway. A single train of thirty-five cars would shuttle back and forth around the clock, twenty-five trips a day.

It was an amazing engineering accomplishment, made possible by the railroad being able to use gondola cars that turned and tipped and were easy to fill and empty. At the Needham end, Globe Locomotive Works of South Boston provided newly invented steam shovels that took only two scoops to fill the cars in about ten minutes. So it was scoop-scoop-fill, travel nine miles and turn-tip-empty. Using this state-of-the-art technology, fifty-foot cliffs of gravel were flattened to an area of twelve acres.

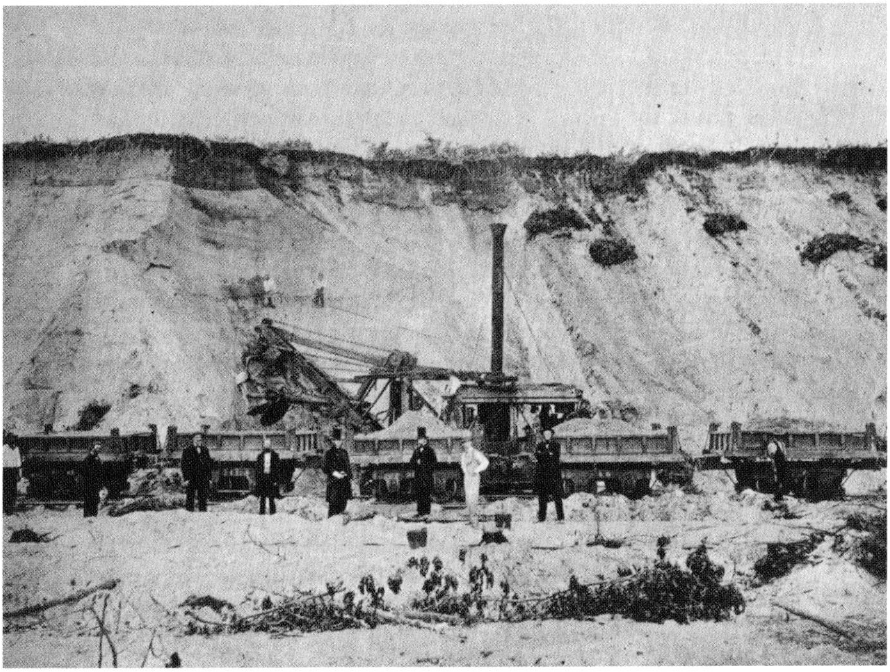

NEEDHAM GRAVEL CLIFFS, CA 1860

At the Back Bay end, short, dead-end (spur) tracks were used to pull horse-drawn cars, now filled with gravel, out to building sites where gravel and then soil were deposited before moving on to the next lot. The whole operation, begun in 1858, was completed in the Back Bay by 1882, though it continued west to Kenmore Square and the Back Bay Fens in ensuing years. It would be a public-private partnership. The Commonwealth of Massachusetts paid for the work and then sold the land to real estate developers who marketed the house lots.

The legislature had not approved any funding for the work, however. So those in charge were in a position something like that of the early settlers, who had to build their colonies, houses and all, on empty land, using only their own ingenuity. Those building the Back Bay (the "Commissioners") harkened back to their ancestors in true New England tradition. They changed nothing into something using the old Yankee technique of trading.

They traded land for labor, making a compact with the contractors Munson and Goss who would fill the Commonweatlh's lands from the Public Garden west to Clarendon Street in exchange for four blocks of land (260,000 square feet). It was Munson and Goss who brought the gravel from Needham. This was in 1858, and they also made other contracts to get other work without cash outlay.

Why gravel, you may wonder. The gravel would provide stability and heft to the new land, but there was still a problem. In order to place buildings on the lots, pilings had to be sunk deeply into the ground to support them. The land itself would be too spongy to support them. They used tree trunks that remained moist since they reached the water table below ground and therefore didn't dry out and rot with time.

In the case of the huge Trinity Church (an edifice weighing 10,000 tons) 4,500 pilings were needed to keep it from sinking into the earth.

Later, when skyscrapers were built on what was called Back Bay's "High Spine," where buildings were allowed to exceed previous height limits, the Prudential Tower and the John Hancock Building used shafts of steel driven deep into the bedrock to support them.

House lots were the right choice, however, for this new part of the city. Perhaps as you think of it, you may imagine new ground being made, house lots drawn up and sold, and houses built one right after the other. But that's not exactly right. During the period of building there were dead points caused by economic downturns. Generally, the lots on the four corners of an intersection sold first, then there might be a sparse area in the next block until finally everything was sold. For a while, lots close to Arlington Street were forming up, but as one gazed westward, things still looked much like a desert. But as house lots sold, churches and institutions followed—or sometimes led.

As mentioned, there was a perceived need for more high-end housing, and this would be a building boom for the developers and for the state. In fact, developers made sure the land would be so expensive that only the wealthy need apply. But those in charge did more than that. They realized that this area would have to wear the appeal of elegance. So building codes were set that required a high standard as well as a uniform height—usually four to five stories. These brownstones were to be some of the city's best architecture for years to come. (The sturdiness of these buildings was demonstrated in the spring of 2014 when a huge fire in one of the brownstones left adjacent buildings essentially untouched except for smoke damage.)

The wealthy people from Boston or the suburbs who would buy these lots and build homes on them were Protestants, and so the churches built there were of Protestant denominations, including Trinity, Old South, the First Baptist, and Arlington Street Church. The nearest Catholic church was off Boylston Street and west of Massachusetts Avenue. It was there that servants in the new homes would attend.

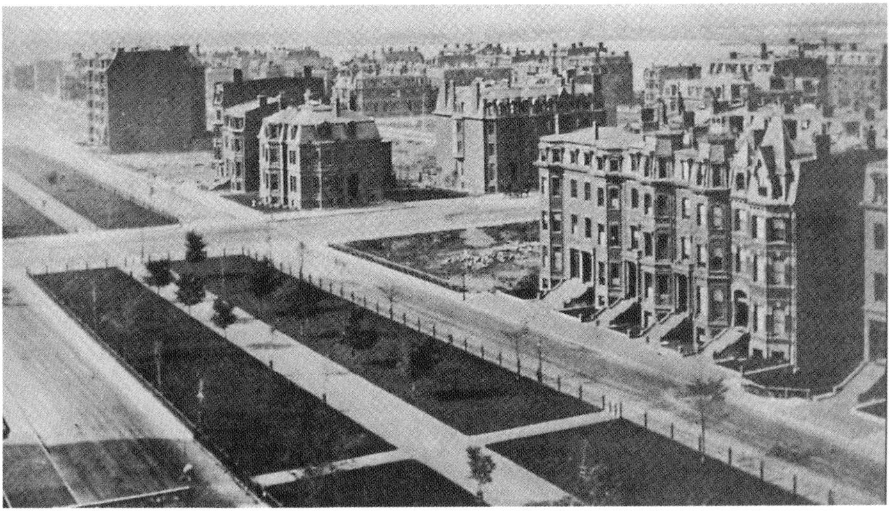

LOTS ON COMMONWEALTH AVENUE, 1880s

The planners of these streets were greatly influenced by nineteenth-century Paris where wide boulevards were being planned; and, visiting the French capital, they may have heard the conversations about great avenues and splendid monuments. London, too, had its great boulevards like those in South Kensington, which were studded with museums and other public buildings, built on land purchased by the commissioners of the Great Exhibition of 1851 according to a plan that called for placing these institutes together. In London they saw how these stately institutes had added value to the area.

Those or similar structures were what the architects were after. Why couldn't Boston be a cultural center, too, like those other cities? That was part of their early thinking, but even without it, they realized that an attractive area like the streets near the Public Garden and Boston Common would surely attract wealthy buyers. How could you beat such greenery just outside your windows along with the chance for a morning stroll that brought you to a duck pond, heroic statuary, and rows and banks of flowers in season?

So, the notion of Boston as a cultural center, and that special feeling tourists had about visiting a Boston that is a comfortable and fascinating place, took hold. Even the exceptionalism mentioned in connection with the Marathon and Patriot's Day arose from things that were conceptualized many years ago. "Boston Strong" may be a new slogan, but its foundations were built on Back Bay beginnings.

Probably the best fulfillment of those visions was created with the laying out of Commonwealth Avenue. This broad boulevard began at the Public Garden and ran west, eventually through Kenmore Square to Brighton and on into Newton. Modeled on a Parisian boulevard or perhaps a stately section of London, Commonwealth Avenue (or "Comm Ave" as it's locally known) was far wider than most Boston Streets, or most streets anywhere—nearly 200 yards just for the roadway, and wider than that in parts of Allston and Brighton. The Back Bay section had twenty-foot setbacks of buildings from the (wide) sidewalks, as well as a pedestrian mall down the center with trees and statues upon it, Parisian in manner if not in provenance. This was the centerpiece, but Boylston and Beacon Streets were also wide, and Newbury and Marlboro, which ran between them, had similar buildings and heights. Intersected at regular intervals with the north-south, streets were alphabetically named westward from the Public Garden: Arlington, Berkeley, Clarendon, Dartmouth, Exeter, Fairfield, Gloucester, and Hereford, followed by Massachusetts Avenue. These streets were also cut through by service alleys, still in use, and were part of the standards being set. Deliveries would be hidden, not visible as in many urban areas.

As land was made, starting at the eastern end, plots were sold and soon homes began to be built on the plots. Not everyone was eager to buy these plots, though. One young man, about to be married, planned to build a new home for himself and his bride in the Back Bay, but the father of the bride would have none of it, telling him that he wouldn't allow his daughter to live on "filled land."

However, plenty of people would, and in time, the houses were built and most of them still exist. If you were to start at the Public Garden and walk in a westerly direction, you would find it like parading through a history of architecture, beginning with old buildings, which give way to newer ones that differ in style, although they are mostly made of the same materials. This was different in the South End, filled in and developed

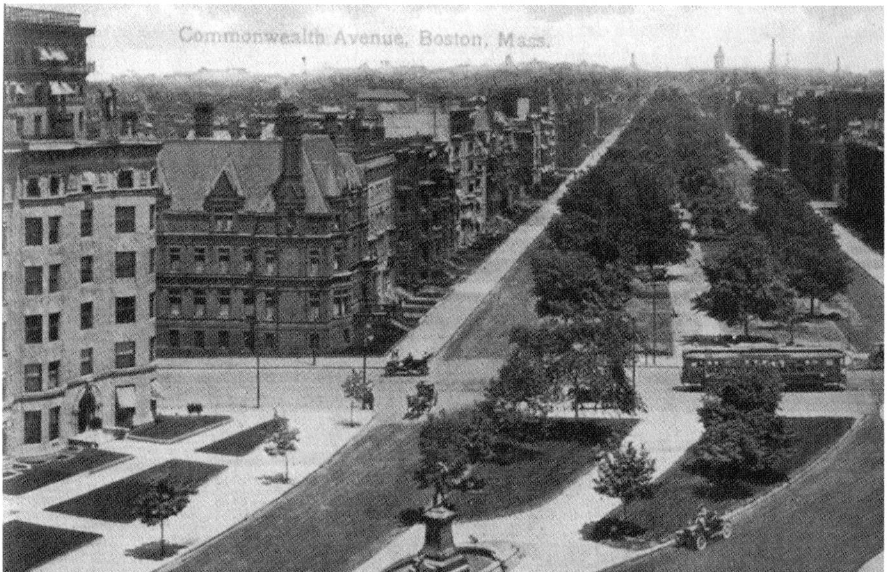

COMMONWEALTH AVENUE

at nearly the same time, where most buildings were brick and similar in style and not built to the same standards as those in the Back Bay.

Beacon Street, connected to the Mill Dam that had run westward toward the future Kenmore Square, developed more quickly than the other streets, so the architecture was fairly similar throughout its length. Arlington Street, with the Public Garden on one side had a number of Victorian-style buildings close together that looked as though they made up a whole block, whereas Boylston had little housing at all.

When Back Bay filling had been completed in the late 1880s, commercial development took hold. Services had to be provided for the new neighborhoods, and, being a capitalistic society, private enterprises filled the bill. The land along Boylston was relatively cheap and available, so that was used for mercantile purposes. Newbury Street, while residential, became a buffer zone between Boylston Street and the residential neighborhoods by providing upscale shopping of the kinds that would be appreciated by Back Bay patrons.

In effect, Newbury Street became an area of mixed use with retail shops on the ground floor and residential on upper floors, so that they had a gradual transition from the residential areas to the commercial ones to the south.

It isn't necessary for you to be schooled in architecture to enjoy walking through the Back Bay. Knowing the names and features of architectural style is enjoyable and useful, but not necessary. If you look at the buildings and pay attention to some of their details, you may easily become a fan and become immersed in the realization that the buildings that surround you are something different and memorable.

When lots in the Back Bay were sold and developed, some brought higher prices than others. A rule of thumb was that the closer you were to Commonwealth Avenue and the Public Garden, the more valuable the land was. The north side of Commonwealth was especially coveted. In the early morning, the sun, rising above Boston Harbor and spreading its yellow glow, peered into the windows of those new homes on the north side of Commonwealth and flooded the rooms of all four or five stories with glorious beams of morning. Beacon Street, being near the Charles River and Beacon Hill, was also attractive. It had, after all, a river view and the panorama of Cambridge and the north of Boston. Art Square, on the other hand, the land on the south side, owned by the railroad and by the Boston Water Company, was less valuable, so properties in the square itself were depressed. In real estate, whether in the early Back Bay years or later, the views from the windows were of great import. If your vista stretched your imagination, then you owned something of moment and value. Our Brahmin ancestors and forebears began at points like this and built Back Bay into a ground that would become not only treasured but hallowed.

CHAPTER TWO

Art Square

Early on there had been a proposal to build a large Coliseum of Art and Science and Historical Relics like the one in London's South Kensington. They actually had diagrams and written plans for a huge building that would have been placed on the Public Garden, but the legislature quashed that. However, the idea for buildings of art and science was not quashed, and many of them were indeed built around Art Square. At the same time, a proposal was made to set aside public land where the square would be built—but not for two decades. The notion of an Art Square and cultural institutions was an early one, and it did come to fruition.

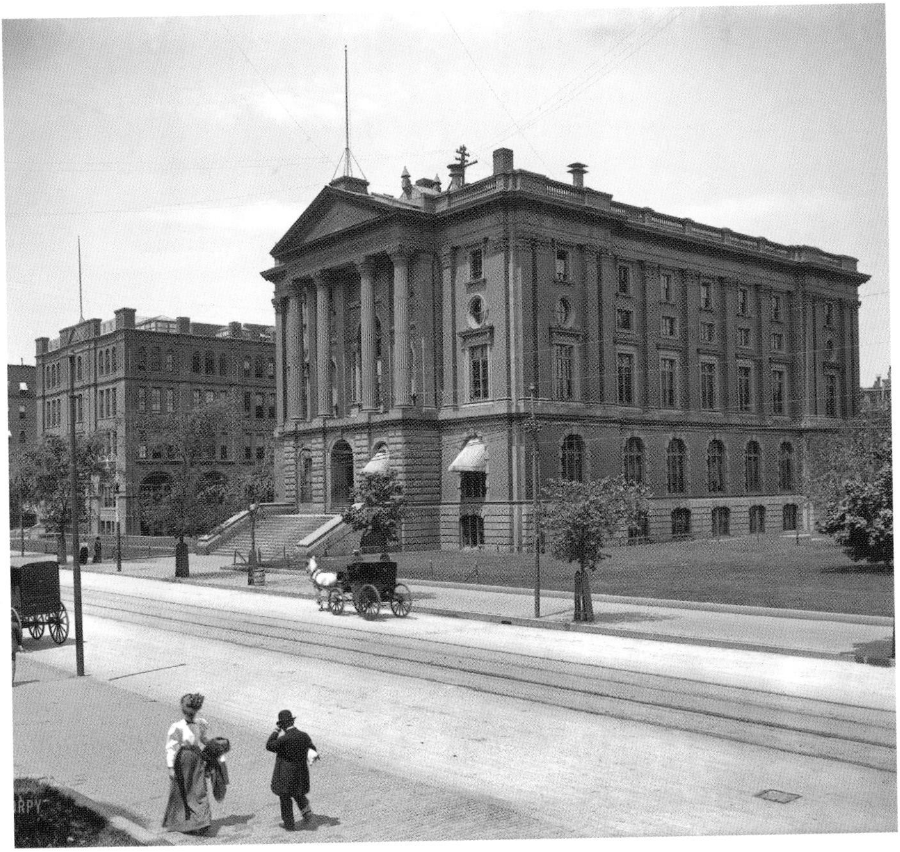

MIT, BACK BAY LOCATION

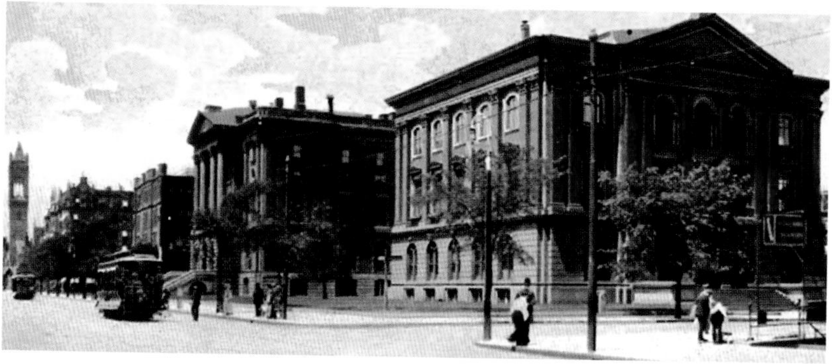

MUSEUM OF NATURAL HISTORY

In the 1860s, land was set aside for the future MIT and a Museum of Natural History between Boylston, Newbury, Berkeley, and Clarendon Streets, at the eastern corner of what would become Art Square. So the nose of the cultural camel was under the tent, so to speak. Other institutions, some cultural, others religious, began to move in, especially after the great fire had leveled much of the downtown in 1872.

So we had a "perfect storm" of things happening that brought us the Copley Square we know today. The Great Boston fire, the press of immigration, the creation of a new, first-class residential area and cultural nexus focused at Boylston Street and Huntington Avenue all took seed at about the same time. That took a little time to flower into what we have today.

Old South Church moved from the edge of the fire zone downtown to the northwest corner of the square, while, diagonally across from it, Trinity Church occupied the eastern edge. The Boston Public Library was also relocated from downtown, and the Museum of Fine Arts was built on the southern side on land that had been designated for it. Each was an outstanding building and I will go into more detail about them later.

I mentioned the two railroads from Worcester and Providence that crossed the waters of the Back Bay, in the early 1830s. The existence of these railroads affected two street grids: the Back Bay and the South End. To give you an idea of where the tracks were located, let's look at their present-day configurations: the Boston and Worcester RR ran about where the Massachusetts Turnpike Extension is now. Where the Prudential Building stands and the turnpike runs in a tunnel, stood the railyards of the Boston and Worcester, filling acres between Boylston Street and Huntington Avenue west of Exeter Street and reaching to Allston.

The Boston and Providence RR ran about on the course of today's Orange line (which runs into Back Bay Station near Copley Square). Its railyards covered an area that centered on Park Square.

In those days, you didn't just tear up tracks to build your neighborhoods—railroads were too important for that.

The street grids of the Back Bay and South End had to accommodate the tracks and railyards, and so they formed around them. The two grids are laid out in different orientations, and they collide at Copley Square like two diesel engines hell-bent for downtown.

An atlas from 1874 shows a school and four lots on the triangle where Huntington Avenue intersected Boylston Street. Even today a look at a street map will show the converging grids that collide in Copley Square and account for its previous triangular shape created where Huntington Avenue and Boylston Street met at a forty-five-degree angle. When the area was "Art Square," there were seven different parcels of land owned by different people, and for twenty-five years, until 1883, there was no plan to develop the area in a sensible or logical way.

Then, in 1883, the city renamed the space called Copley Square and, over a few years, acquired all the parcels that make up today's square. One can speculate that they preserved this as open space, though that was not the stated intent. However, if that land had not been publicly acquired, things would look quite different today. Instead of the sunny place for a farmer's market and a greensward that we have now, the space would likely be cast over by the shadows of large buildings that would have created wind tunnels like the one found on Clarendon Street just east of the square. The wide perspective of the Boston Public Library on one end and Trinity Church on the other would have been occluded, the vista probably ugly-urban and non-inspiring. So history can be thankful for folks with vision who were willing to press their points.

Even with city ownership, the space was, for years, less than satisfying, and periodically someone would call for a new and renewed Copley Square. But things moved slowly and inevitably came up against one stark impediment. The greatest difficulty was the way Huntington Avenue (a main thoroughfare of the grid to the southwest and the South End) bisected the square once it emerged from beyond the library. No master visionary saw a way to overcome that obstacle.

More than eighty years had passed before a master plan of the city of Boston was put in place, in 1965, under the leadership of Mayor John Collins who promised to build a "New Boston." He and Edward Logue, who headed the Boston Redevelopment Authority, were able to build Government Center and to get the Prudential Center for Boston as their major projects. These were people with vision, though their approach was often more like a buzz saw then a pruning tool.

Collins/Logue's plan also addressed Copley Square. Part of the proposal was to close Huntington Avenue. They also held a competition to create a new design for Copley Square, won by Sasaki, Dawson, DeMay of Watertown. Suddenly the square was sunk below street level as the winning design lowered the square's surface twelve feet below the surrounding streets and separated it from them by walls. The new square was not covered with pedestrian-friendly grass either. It was mostly hard surface, not grass, and a fountain was added at its lowest point. Ed Logue predicted that Copley Square would become as well-known internationally as Plaza San Marco in Venice or St. Peter's in Rome.

It would; but not with this design that was meant to separate the public from traffic and the hustle-bustle of the city. It was like a plaza, but people did not flock to it, didn't like its isolation. There were no people feeding pigeons as in Venice or faithful followers gathering beneath the windows of the Pope as there were in Rome. In Boston, at least before the marathon brought so many, people had to provide their own amusements, and the new square fell short.

It made the buildings around the square more distinct from one another. When the John Hancock Tower was built on the southeast corner, the space was closed in, but it didn't knit together the theme of a public square as part of outstanding architecture. Citizens wanted something more.

Noted *Boston Globe* architecture critic Robert Campbell wrote in 1983:

> What's wrong with Copley Square is that it contains no life of its own—no activities like shopping, eating, performance or recreation—while, at the same time, it is walled off from the city activity around it by being sunk behind big, fortress-like concrete mounds. This was all deliberate. Copley Square was planned as an "oasis" from the busy city. The trouble is that people don't like dead, isolated places and don't go there.

Fortress Copley was an invitation with few takers.

That very year, Mayor Kevin White appointed the Copley Square Centennial Committee (CSCC), which met to gather ideas for a new design and came up with plans for a second competition and ways to raise funds. The winning design by Clarke and Rapuano was in place by June of 1989. The old plan was swept aside by the concept of inclusion.

The concrete was replaced by wide swaths of grass and brick sidewalks.

Grassy areas with benches and trees were located so that the views of the outstanding buildings around the square were not obstructed. It was very popular, but maintenance, especially of the plant life has been a problem. Private groups have taken a hand in upkeep and support of the square, and the design is far less formal than the previous one. The many seating locations and open views have discouraged the kind of petty crime and drug use that plague similar squares that are often deserted.

There is also a fitting sculpture of the Tortoise and the Hare (a fable told by the ancient Greek, Aesop) It's sponsored by the Friends of Copley Square who like the idea of coupling the fable about a race with the Marathon. It also appeals to children. Its sculptor, Nancy Schon, is from nearby Newton where, as a child, she watched the race on Heartbreak Hill. She said:

> After watching the 1991 Marathon, I started thinking about what a sculpture might be like for the Boston Marathon, the oldest foot race in the United States. I wanted to create a sculpture that would be attractive to children, yet be a meaningful metaphor for the race. I knew the marathon was based on a Greek warrior who, in 490 B.C., ran approximately twenty-five miles to announce the news of a great military victory. The Greek connection of using another kind of race, that of the fable of the Tortoise and the Hare created by Aesop, came to mind.

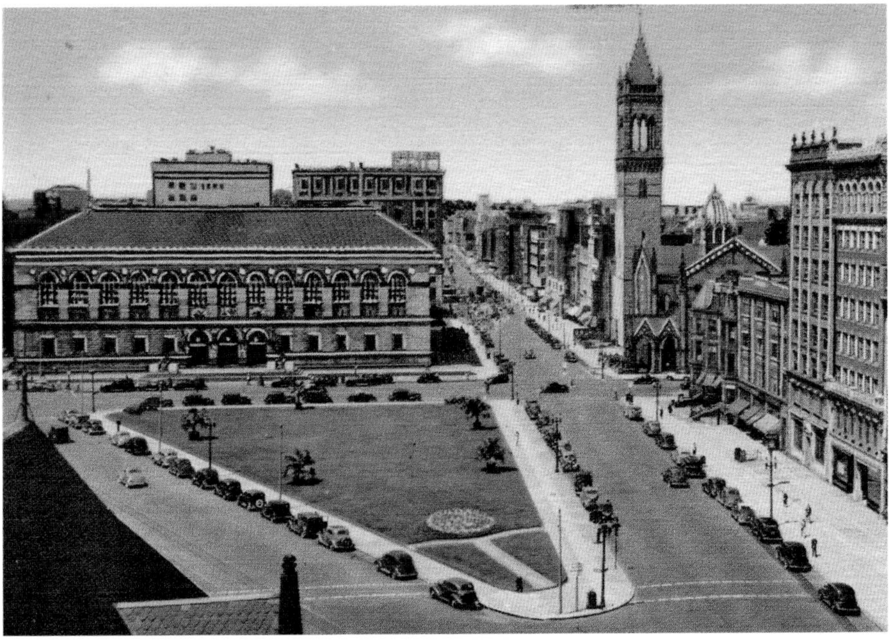

COPLEY SQUARE, PREVIOUS CONFIGURATION

COURTESY BOSTON PUBLIC LIBRARY

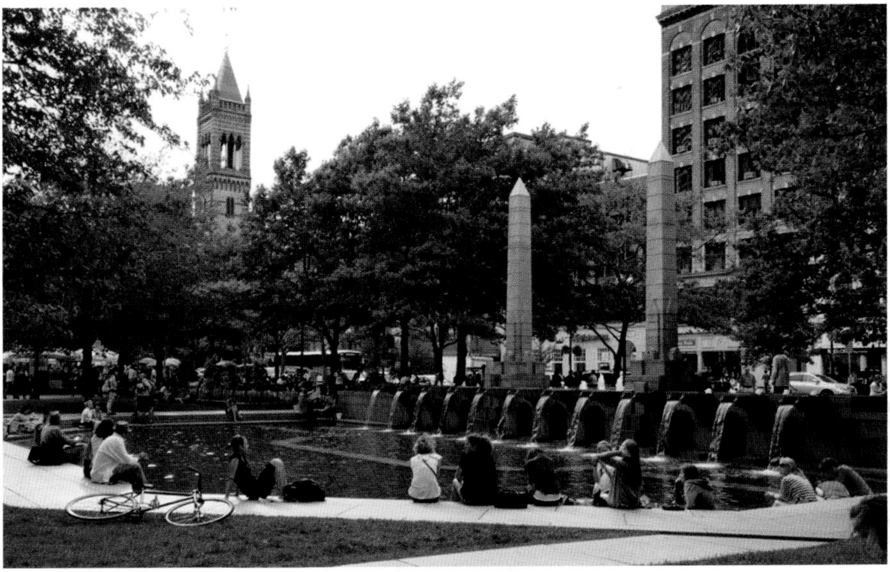

COPLEY SQUARE—EARLIER DESIGN WITH FOUNTAIN

COURTESY AUTHOR

Copley Square is a lively place most of the time. Rather than formal events, it holds special ones, like a farmer's market, food vendors, and ticket sales (it has an original-design ticket kiosk reminiscent of those used by European vendors). The square offers an array of city activities. At New Year's (First Night) it is a place for ice sculptures, on race day it is filled with athletes and supporters, and at noontimes it becomes peopled by office workers or readers from the library. It has become an important place for those who live or work nearby, as well as for out-of-towners, for whom it is a target destination, the largest number on Marathon Monday.

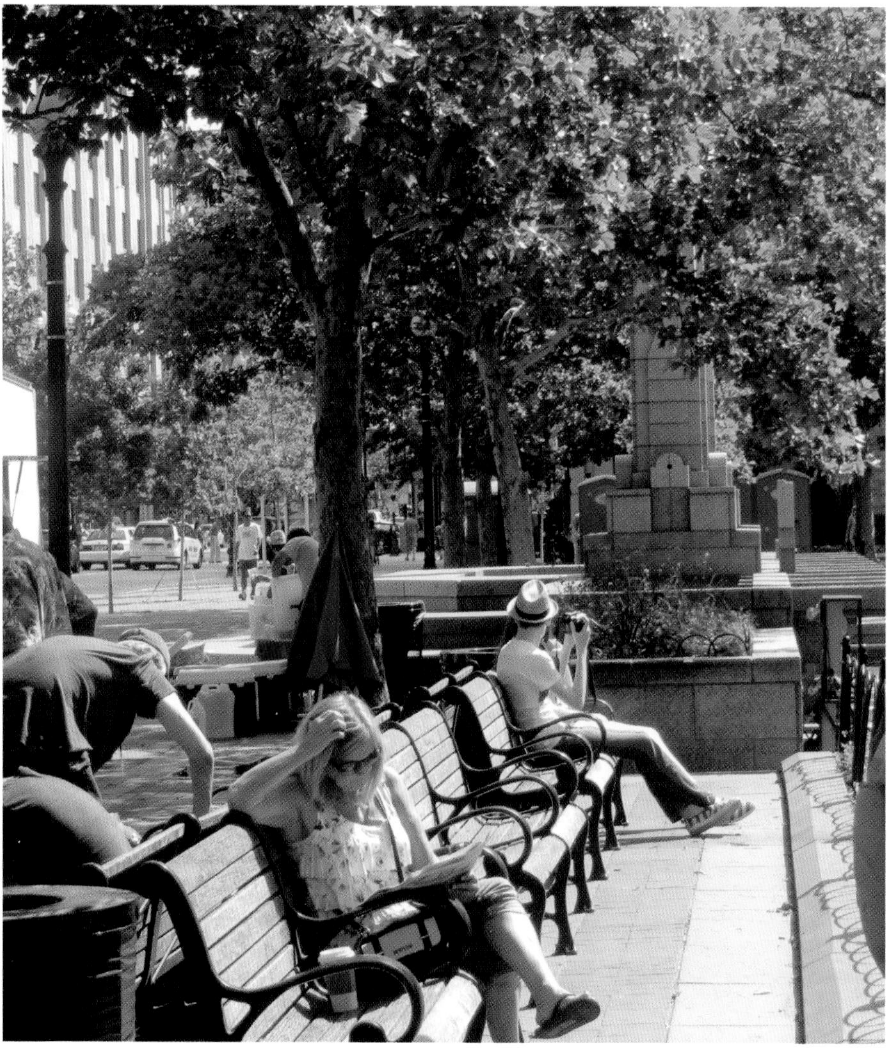

BENCHES, COPLEY SQUARE
COURTESY AUTHOR

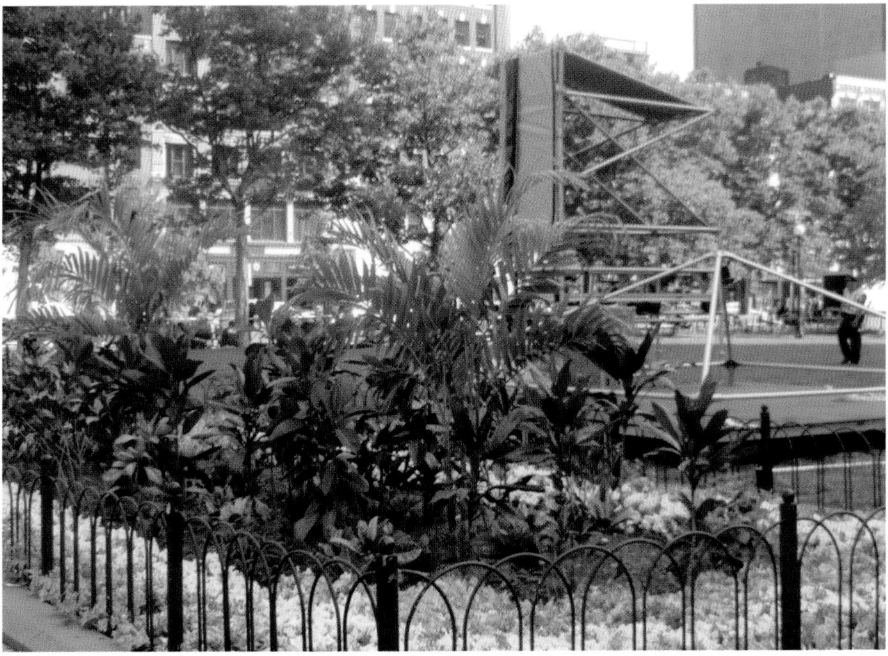

GARDEN AT COPLEY
COURTESY AUTHOR

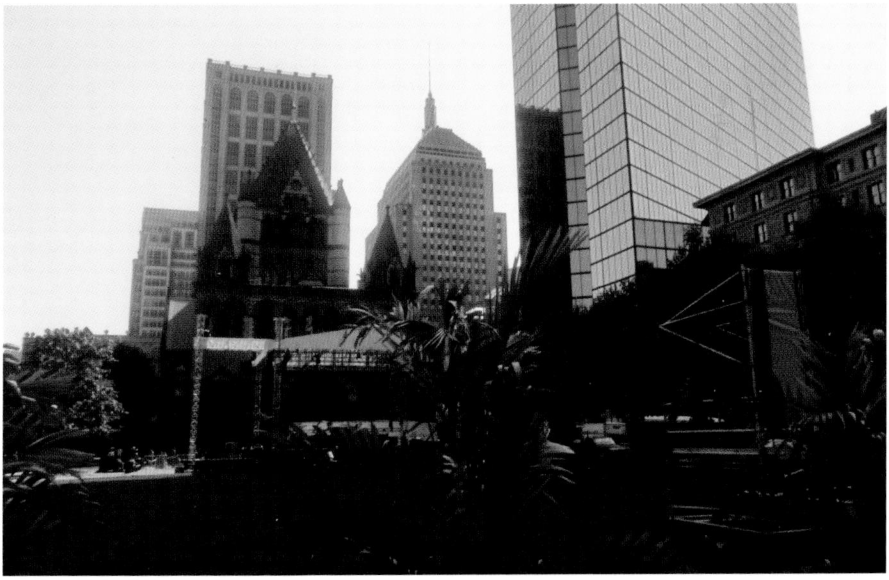

CURRENT SQUARE
COURTESY AUTHOR

CHAPTER THREE

Copley
Not Just a Place—a Presence

Copley Square isn't just a place in the Back Bay. It's a green presence that announces itself with significant architectural gems that surround the quadrangle where people gather on sunny days throughout the year. Any square in any city would be proud to have any of these buildings grace its open space, and Copley has at least three that land on architectural best lists and have done so for over a hundred years. There are and have also been others that are at least notable.

The square was anchored in the last part of the nineteenth century by three major architectural gems that are still there. Trinity, the church that would locate at the east end of Copley Square opened there in 1877, after it had been gathered at Summer and Hawley Streets in the downtown (where Filene's once stood). That building was destroyed in the Great Fire. However, plans had already been made to move, the land was purchased in Copley Square and the fire only accelerated events.

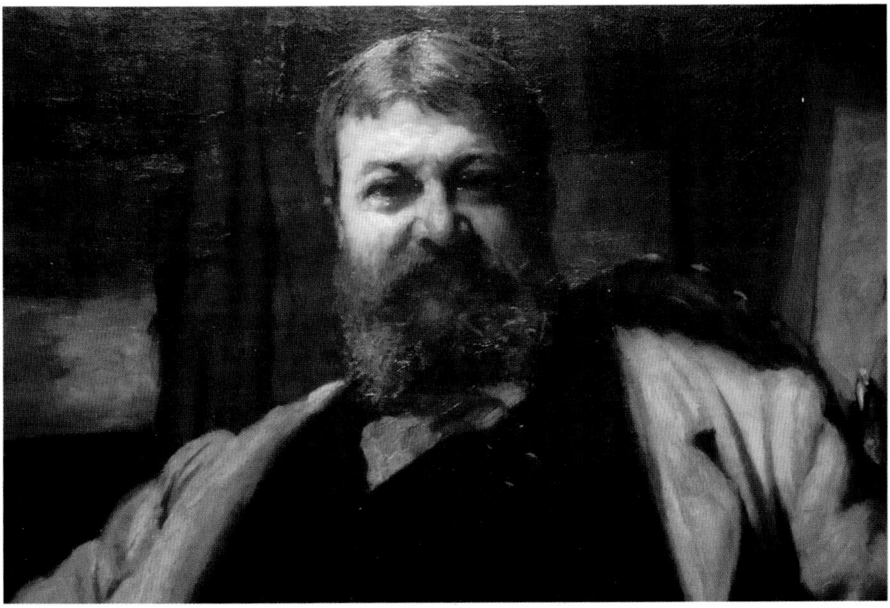

HENRY HOBSON RICHARDSON, ARCHITECT
NATIONAL PORTRAIT GALLERY

When the church began to plan for a new building, they held a competition among six architectural firms who were asked to submit designs. The winner was Henry Hobson Richardson, a large (six-foot-four, 300+ pound) man, who had graduated from Harvard and had been a member of the Porcellian Society along with some of those who selected his design. It is assumed that his Harvard connections helped him, as the competition was steep.

When Henry Hobson Richardson heard that his design had been selected, he ran next door to his neighbors' where they were having breakfast. Waving rolled-up drawings over his head, he shouted, "I've got it! I've got it!" Alarmed but puzzled, one of them replied. "I see that you have, but what is it that you have?" "The church," Richardson answered. "Trinity Church . . . in Boston . . . and I've got it!" Without a further word of explanation, he dashed out again, no doubt to further wave the drawings and spread the word.

The word would spread well enough, but it would be his work that would carry the message. Trinity was to be Richardson's crowning achievement (although he liked others of his buildings better). He was right to wave the drawings excitedly and to shout in triumph—it was indeed a momentous moment, not just for him, but for Copley Square and for Boston.

Henry was not a Bostonian by birth. He had been born and raised in Louisiana, went to Harvard as noted, and then had trained at the Ecoles des Beaux-Arts in Paris. Richardson was influenced by European styles, especially by the medieval Romanesque buildings of France, Spain, and Italy. He used these in a new way in designing Trinity. His time in Paris had also led, no doubt to an appreciation for fine cuisine and wines, as evidenced by his massive size.

Richardson had been working in New York, but, following his selection, moved his practice to Brookline, moving in with his family, his library, and many apprentices whom he treated as family, and for whom he was a great teacher. It was said that he could—amazingly—follow the work on the Trinity Church in Copley Square from his home on Cottage Street in Brookline, not far from Jamaica Pond. This serves as an indicator of the rural nature of the countryside at that time and the lack of intervening buildings. This, though, was probably the least amazing thing about Richardson's career.

For example, Henry Hobson Richardson is the only American architect to have a style named for him. "Richardsonian Romanesque" is best exemplified in Trinity Church, a new style of church architecture, a departure from the Gothic style used in Europe and also from the simple white churches that were and are so prevalent in New England. Richardson was far from your typical Yankee. He forged his imprint on things architectural and brought new and significant buildings to Boston—Trinity only the first of them.

Trinity's design, based on a Greek cross, fit the style of Trinity's famous minister Phillips Brooks, known for his eloquence. Rev. Brooks was glad to have a style that departed from that of European cathedrals, which recalled for him Roman Catholicism. He felt, and people agreed, that in America, people should be willing to try new ideas. But Richardson's design was also made to order for Brooks's popular style of preaching.

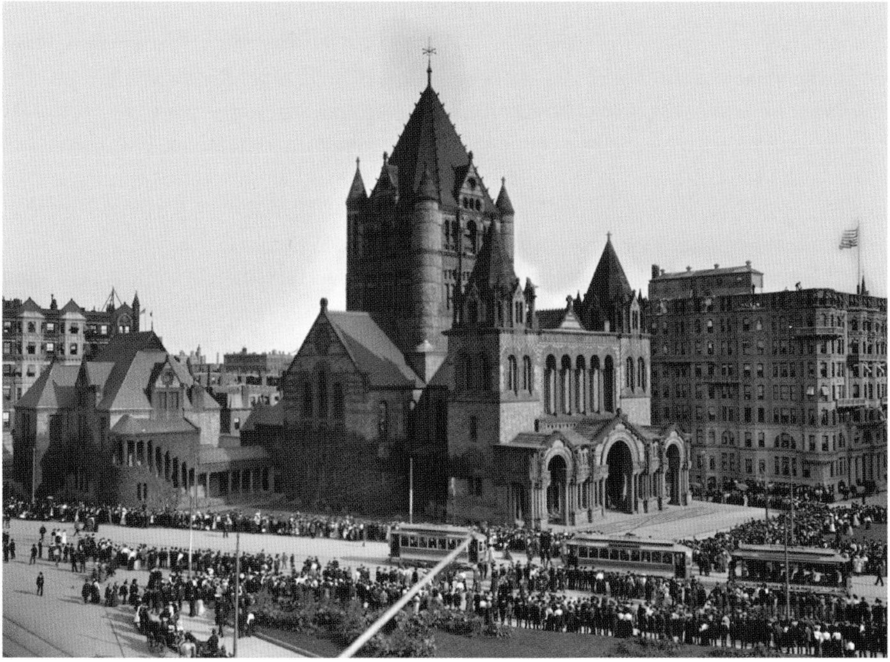

TRINITY, 1903
COURTESY LIBRARY OF CONGRESS

Trinity Church

Rather than long rows of pews with stone columns blocking views, Hobson's plan centered around the minister. (Until 1888, Trinity had no pulpit and Brooks spoke from a lectern.) The rows were short enough to fit within a limited space and close enough that everyone could hear the preacher. And that preacher was no ordinary one. The celebrated rector of the church, Phillips Brooks, was a man similar in heft to Richardson. Brooks was also six feet, four inches and over 300 pounds, and he, too, had an interest and knowledge of European architecture, having traveled widely in Germany and Italy, where he was greatly influenced by liturgy, music, and events like Holy Week in Rome. He didn't like Catholic rituals, but he was a supporter of the singing of the liturgy, and during eucharistic services, he would come down from the pulpit to preach in the white supplice and stole of a priest.

Think of the convergence of these men and their ideas. Ask yourself how often in history do two strong men with original ideas come together and work together to produce a significant change in the way a church should be built, an architecture created. No wonder, then, that Richardson and Brooks created this significant structure, different from what had gone before. Perhaps it takes this "perfect storm" of a meeting of minds and a willingness of a populace to embrace their creation.

So Brooks had strong ideas of his own, but he approved of Richardson's revolutionary design for Trinity and involved himself in the details. Picture then, these two huge men hovering over rolls of drawings and details, probably by candlelight, and deciding the fate of this major architectural work in the making.

Brooks would have a strong input on what the new church should be like, but he and Richardson were able to work well together, along with other artists. The windows were one thing. At first, they were of plain glass, but that would not do at all. Richardson and Brooks realized that the interior must be richly colored. They hired John Lafarge, who had already revolutionized window glass, to design four of them, and another four were designed by Edward Burne-Jones and executed by William Morris. These stained glass windows were and are a main feature of the building. Brooks wanted them because he wanted to look at something inspirational while he preached, and he said so. There are also more than 20,000 square feet of murals done by American artists, and sculptures rendered by Daniel Chester French and Augustus Saint-Gaudens, two of Boston's and America's greatest sculptors.

Many visitors comment on the three-dimensional effect of the church's massive open, indoor space, a design that has no historical precedent. This space seems to rise from the modified cross-shaped perimeter straight into the tower, like a single cross reaching to heaven in a quiet shaft of space and light.

Richardson accented this open space with flecks of color and detail reflected in the murals and stained glass windows. Phillips Brooks, preaching from the pulpit near the chancel entrance, often looked for inspiration to Lafarge's stunning Christ in Majesty windows. So there was a lot of thinking that went into the design and details.

Richardson was also aware of the small triangular plot on which he had to build, and its position as a focal point in Copley Square. He had it built so that the tower stood at the center of the plot. His design of a rather short building took advantage of the view of the church from so many streets, where the tower could be viewed equally from all directions. Richardson said this:

> The struggle for precedence, which often takes place between a church and its spire, was disposed of by at once and completely subordinating nave, transepts and apse, and grouping them about the tower as the central mass.

Its walls of rough stone with its rounded arches and massive tower, brought a new look to America, a style soon to be copied around the world. Copley Square, too, was a beneficiary of this new style. When both the church and the public library had been built, we had the view from one to the other, two of America's most significant buildings looking at each other over the expanse of Copley or Art Square and establishing this as one of Boston's most hallowed grounds. It took no bombs to make this space significant. These two men had tended to that. Trinity Church was consecrated in 1877.

Brooks was known for his eloquent preaching. He preached at Westminster Abbey and at the Royal Chapel at Windsor Castle for Queen Elizabeth I. Phillips Brooks preached every week to large congregations, and in 1891 was made Bishop of Massachusetts. However, he is best known to many Americans for having written the

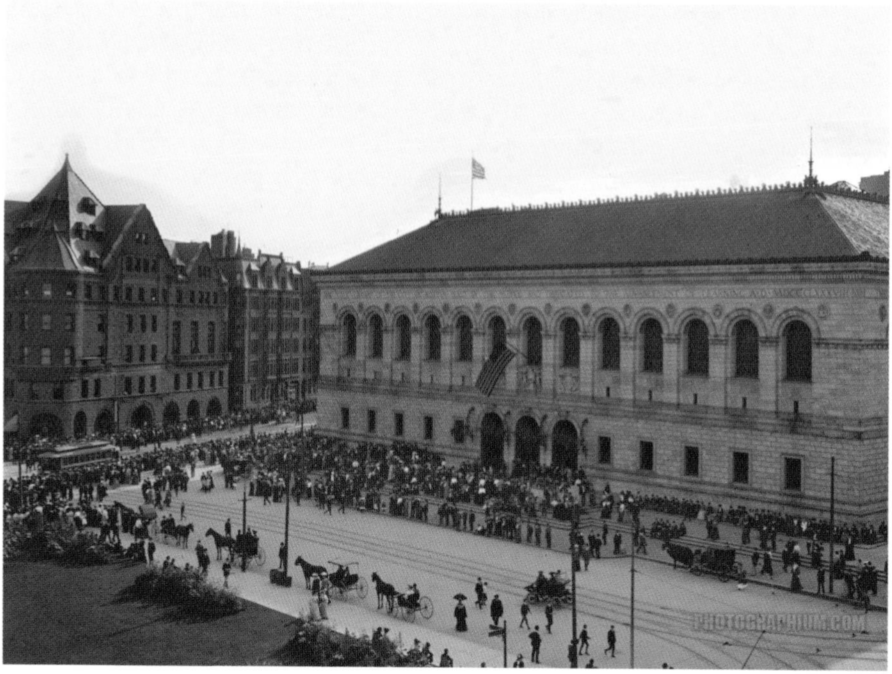

BOSTON PUBLIC LIBRARY, 1903

lyrics to "O Little Town of Bethlehem." It was he who introduced Helen Keller (one of his parishioners) to her teacher and friend, Annie Sullivan. Brooks never married. He died in 1893, his funeral a major event and attended by people of all faiths. His body was carried on the shoulders of Harvard students.

At the western end of Copley Square, on Dartmouth Street, between Boylston and Huntington Avenue, stands the impressive granite block of the Boston Public library (BPL), the first public library in a large municipality in the US, and one of its best even today. It makes an excellent anchor for that end of the square and, with its light granite pattern of blocks, makes a good counterpoint to the darker stone of Trinity Church mixed with lighter stone, a massive building holding sway at the opposite end of the square. Trinity and BPL look across at each other, but viewers of both most likely reflect upon what a special space they're in.

BPL didn't just happen, even when the land was granted. Several false starts were made in designing the building before the architectural firm of Meade, McKim, and White were called upon to make it happen. And happen it did, and in no ordinary way. It was a Boston happening then, and it still is.

The architects were faced with a problem similar to those of the early colonists of Massachusetts who were in many cases pioneers each time they chose to do something. Charles Follen McKim would be following that tradition since no public library of any size had yet been designed. So as an architect with a major project, he had little to guide him. He had to erect a building that would hold 700,000 volumes for lending, but it would be far more than just a lending library. Like George Washington or even Sam Adams, he would be doing things that set a precedent and would be copied far and wide.

His creation, the Boston Public Library is as much a museum as it is a library. A widely studied, cosmopolitan man, educated at the Ecole de Beaux Arts in Paris (as was Henry Hobson Richardson), McKim drew inspiration from the Bibliothèque Sainte-Geneviève in Paris, but there are certainly elements of the Italian Renaissance both inside and outside of his library. The wide building stands upon a terrace of shallow steps, and its symmetrical granite block façade offers an Italian face to the viewer standing on Dartmouth Street. Such a viewer will have much detail to absorb.

McKim brought together fine sculptors and artists to construct what is a masterpiece of fine arts combined in a single place. In fact, that was the idea. The exterior, in particular, was meant to present an appreciation for the fine arts, and this bringing together of painters, sculptors, and architects, working in concert, made this a civic monument —a "palace of the people dedicated to the advancement of learning" as is inscribed upon the building.

The eyes of that viewer in Copley Square are likely to take in the sloping roof of red tile, crested in copper (now green) above the arched windows and the arches of the three main entrances. Instantly eye-catching as well, are the wrought-iron lanterns with their stretching branches and the tablets beneath each window, etched with the names of great artists, scientists, men of religion and statesmen. There are also the sculpted head of Minerva, the goddess of wisdom, in the central keystone and two large statues on platforms representing art and science, and many other details.

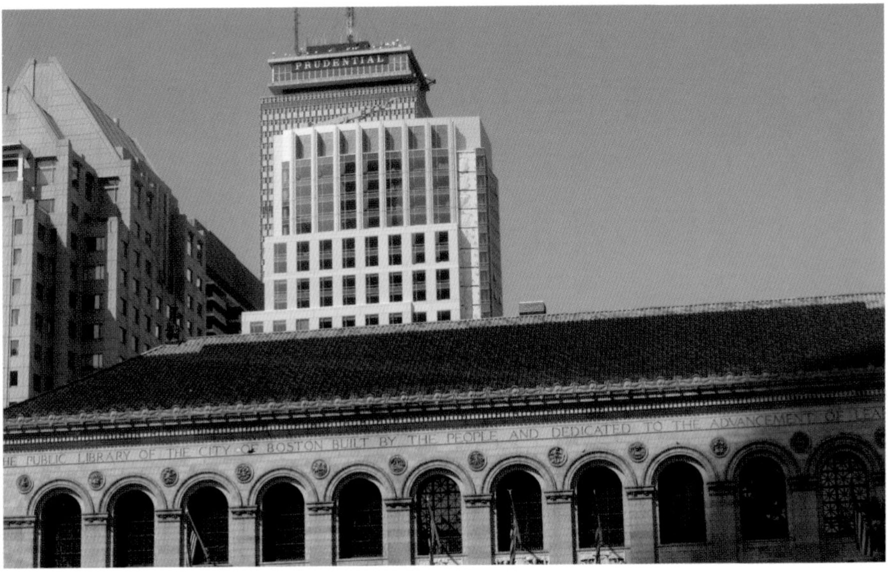

BOSTON PUBLIC LIBRARY, ROOF
COURTESY AUTHOR

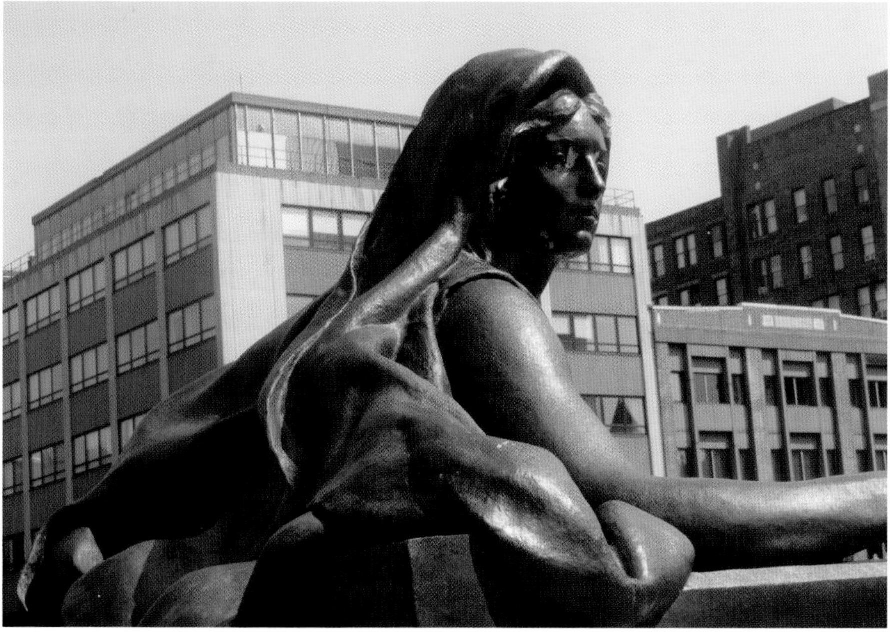

SCULPTURE OUTSIDE BOSTON PUBLIC LIBRARY
COURTESY AUTHOR

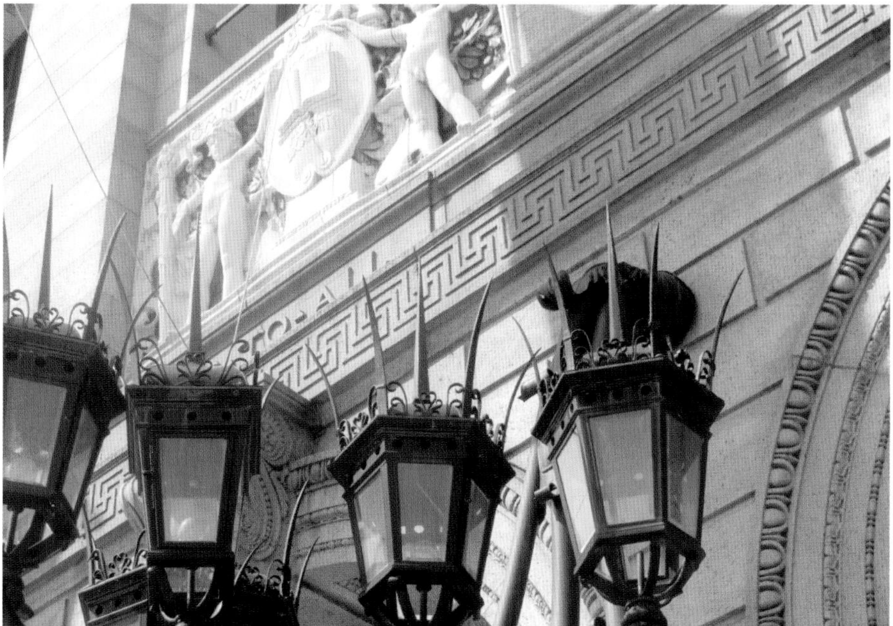

LANTERNS AT BOSTON PUBLIC LIBRARY ENTRANCE
COURTESY AUTHOR

If that viewer were to step into the vestibule, he or she would become part of a unique artistic experience, from the marble of the floors, walls, and ceilings to the exceptional sculptures, including the three 1,500-pound bronze doors carved by Daniel Chester French and representing Music and Poetry, Knowledge and Wisdom, and Truth and Romance. There is also the statue of Gov. Sir Henry Vane.

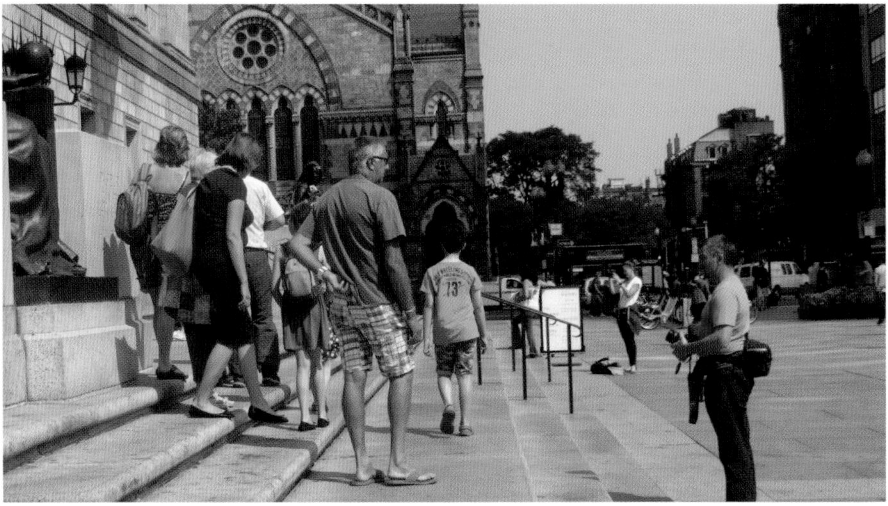

STEPS AT ENTRANCE OF BOSTON PUBLIC LIBRARY WITH VISITORS
COURTESY AUTHOR

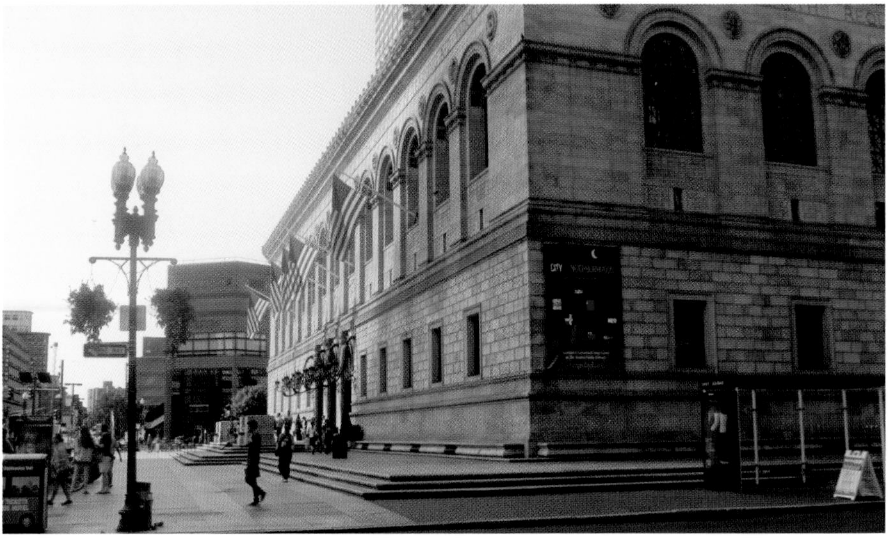

BOSTON PUBLIC LIBRARY, DARTMOUTH AND BOYLSTON
COURTESY AUTHOR

Next, our visitor would come into the wide entrance hall of three aisles with its piers of sandstone and its vaulted ceiling covered with a magnificent marble mosaic and names of famous Bostonians. The marble floor has a brass inlay in the center depicting the signs of the Zodiac.

Ahead is the main staircase, entered through a triumphal arch. The stairs and sides of the staircase are also marble, and at the top of the first flight wait two crouching lions of Siena marble resting on pedestals, all of it carved by Louis Saint-Gaudens. They are memorials to Massachusetts's two Civil War infantry divisions. Above is a coffered ceiling of plaster. In the staircase and second and third floor galleries are murals by Sargent, deChavannes, and Abbey.

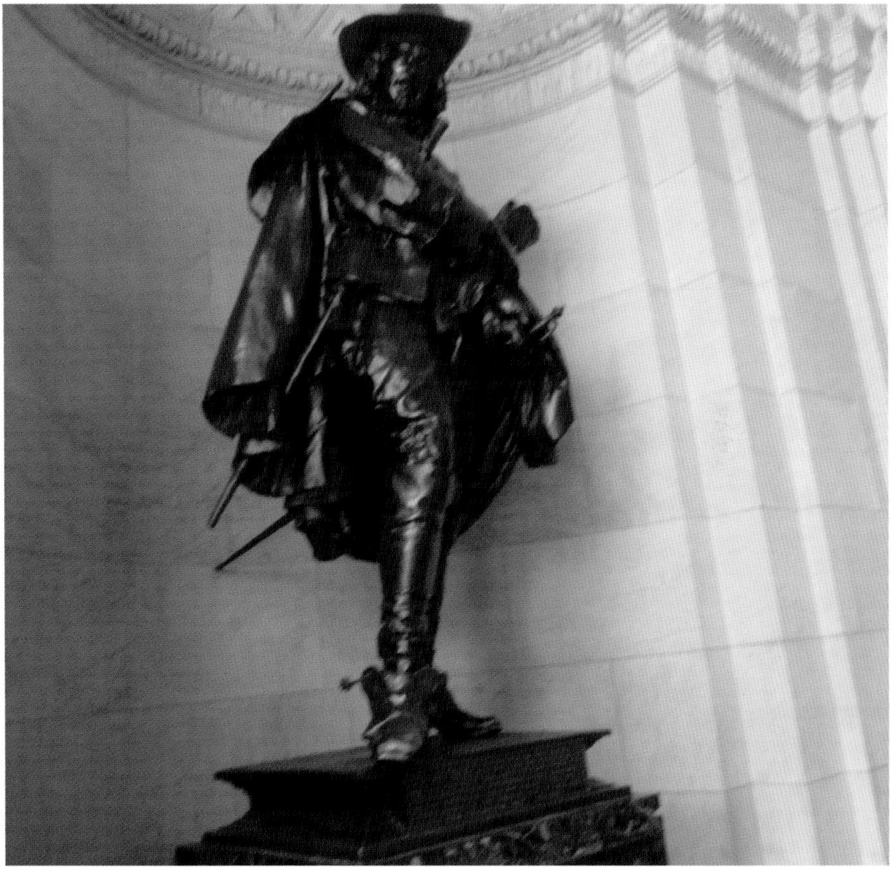

GOV. HENRY VANE, INTERIOR OF BOSTON PUBLIC LIBRARY
COURTESY AUTHOR

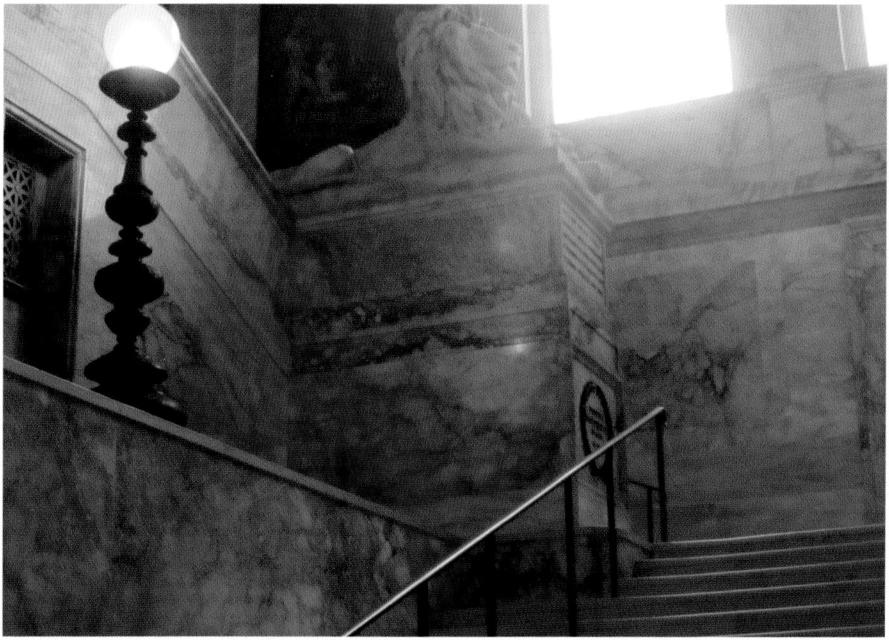

LIONS ON STAIRWAY, BOSTON PUBLIC LIBRARY INTERIOR
COURTESY AUTHOR

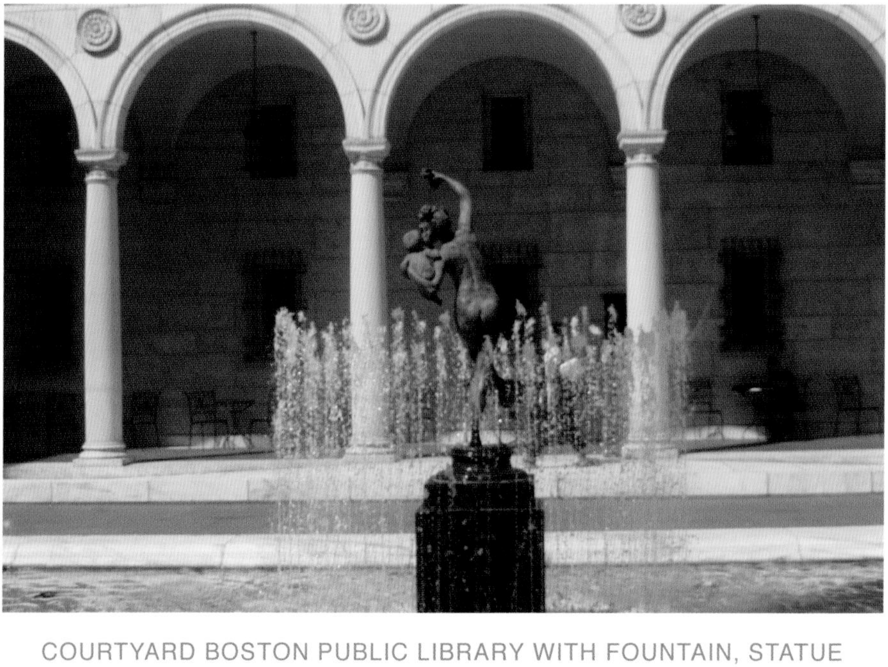

COURTYARD BOSTON PUBLIC LIBRARY WITH FOUNTAIN, STATUE
COURTESY AUTHOR

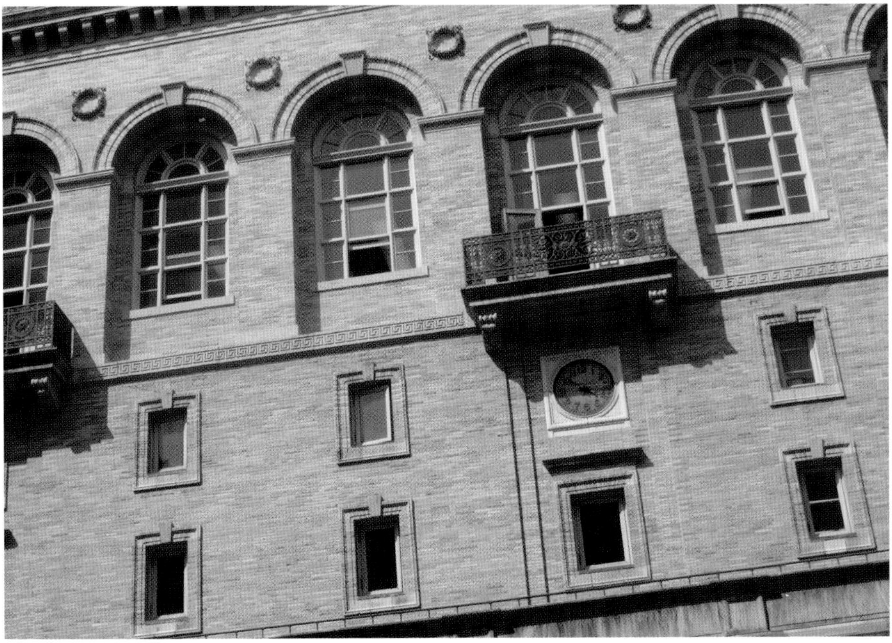

COURTYARD, WINDOWS
COURTESY BOSTON PUBLIC LIBRARY

A unique feature is the interior courtyard, a quiet, restful place on sunny days with its arcaded promenade on three sides, a near-copy of one found in a Roman palace.

Upstairs, on the Copley Square side, the second floor is dominated by Bates Hall, a vast, barrel-vaulted space with arched windows on one side, rows of tables with green-shaded lamps, and an apse at both ends of what looks much like a cathedral. The room was recently restored with the help of a grant of two million dollars from the US Department of the Interior. The room is 218 feet long by 42.5 feet wide and 50 feet high and is a National Landmark. It is named for an original donor to the library.

Boston's civic pride and generosity are involved in the library as they are in other buildings on nearby Huntington Avenue. Two individuals, in particular, did much to make the library what it became: Joshua Bates and John Deferrari, two men from quite different backgrounds, but each successful in the world of finance.

Bates, a Weymouth native, lived most of his life in London where he rose to become a major partner in Barings, the famed financial house. Joshua was largely self-educated. As a boy he used to hang out in Boston bookstores since there was no library. He would read a lot and buy nothing. After he had made his money, he read that Boston planned to open a public library and he offered $50,000 to get it started, to which he later gave a like amount in books. He attached a caveat, however. Part of the money had to be used for a reading room where 100-150 people could sit at any time.

The first public library was a small one on Mason Street, followed by another on Boylston, about where the Colonial Theatre stood, beginning in 1900. This library had a large reading room, but when the McKim building was placed on Copley Square, the whole second floor on the Dartmouth Street side was made into a reading room known as Bates Hall.

The story of John Deferrari has some strands that run through the Bates tale, too. John was the oldest of eight children born to an immigrant family of Italians in the North End when the area was mostly Irish. His father was successful in the fruit business, but demanded the same drive from his children. When John was still a lad, his father thrust a basket of fruit at him and told him to cross Atlantic Avenue into the business district and sell the fruit. Implied, though not stated, was the command to not come home before it was all sold. So that day and for every business day, John sold all his fruit. By age thirteen, he had done so well that he could buy a horse and wagon and sell more widely. And he had something else, too. He observed the men to whom he was selling fruit—the way they carried themselves and their bearing of self-confidence. He also became a little envious of their wealth and well-being.

When some people become envious they resent the objects of their envy, or just give up trying, but not John. He had seen what effort and perseverance could do for him, and he became determined to do well himself. Before long, he was able to buy a store at Dock Square near Faneuil Hall, and then to buy the whole building and became a wholesaler in the fruit business. Then he moved uptown to Boylston Street where he found a good location where people walked by on their way to or from the railroad station at Park Square. His store prospered, so much so that he could now let others work in his store while he invested its profits, and by age twenty-eight, he sold the business and spent full-time investing. He bought stocks and real estate and tended them instead of a fruit counter.

The store was next door to the Boston Public Library, and he began to use it to read about business law and real estate, anything to help him invest wisely. He never relied upon bankers or lawyers, but he felt he owed a debt to the library, which had by then moved to Copley Square where 900 people could sit in Bates Hall and other reading rooms, using the 600,000 volumes that made it the second largest collection in the US after the Library of Congress. The building was by 1947 filled to overflowing.

John Deferrari decided to fund a new wing for the institution that had helped him so much. In 1947, at age eighty-four, he left his shuttered old homestead in the North End and visited the McKim building to make a gift to the trustees. He was received in a room where he stood under the photograph of John Benton, a trustee who had given a million dollars to the BPL thirty years before. The image in the portrait looked familiar to John because Benton used to stop in his fruit store on Boylston Street on the way to his office.

Benton wouldn't have known John, though. John was sort of an invisible man despite his eventual wealth. He was rather nondescript, dressed plainly, had no car, not even a telephone. His name wasn't known, either. He paid for everything in cash, lived like a hermit, had no friends or companions. The fence around his shabby house was kept padlocked.

The trustees of the BPL were absolutely stunned when this man they'd never heard of offered to set up a trust fund for more than a million dollars. He hadn't come to Copley Square looking for anything for himself, but when he saw Benton's portrait, he said he might like one of himself in the new John Deferrari wing.

The fund for a "wing" evolved into a new building, with a room dedicated to John Deferrari and a bust of him in its Boston Room. Three years later, at his death, another half million came to the library via his will.

In 1972, Philip Johnson and John Burgee designed the addition to the library in a square block directly behind the original building, which is as ornate as the new one is sparse. Other than their size, the two buildings are quite different in look and in use. The new one handles borrowing and the old one is now used for research. The new building stands on Boylston Street at the finish line of the Boston Marathon. It has become a familiar sight on national television. Those who follow Marathon history will perhaps find it ironic that the Johnson Building is composed partly from pink Milford marble, stone that was quarried in Hopkinton, where the Marathon starts.

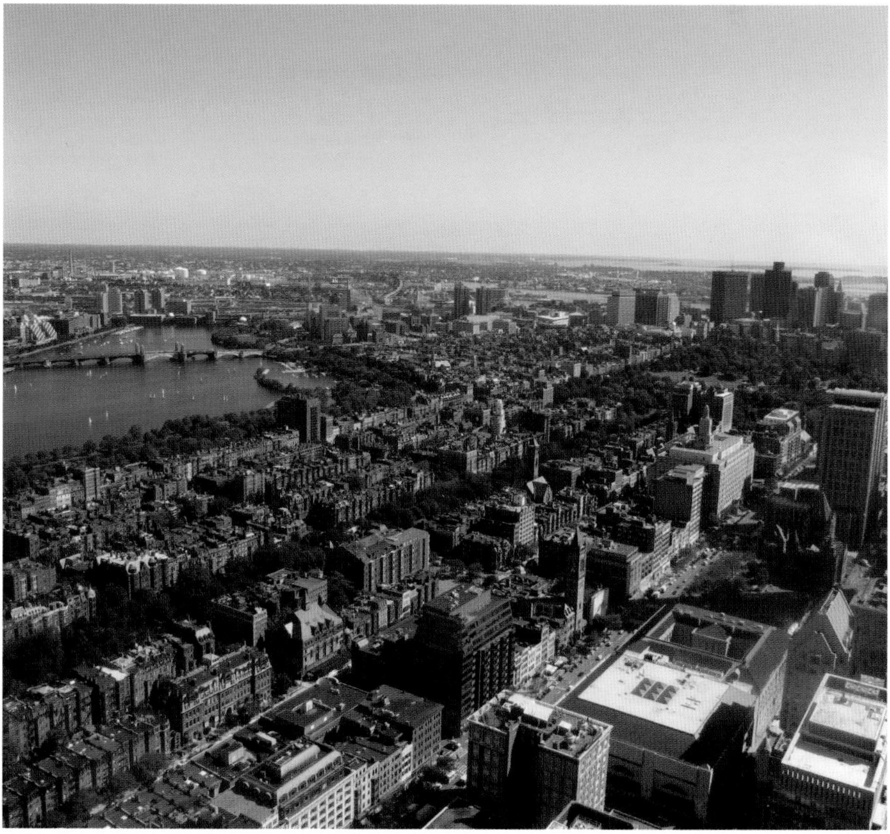

BACK BAY, COMMON
COURTESY AUTHOR

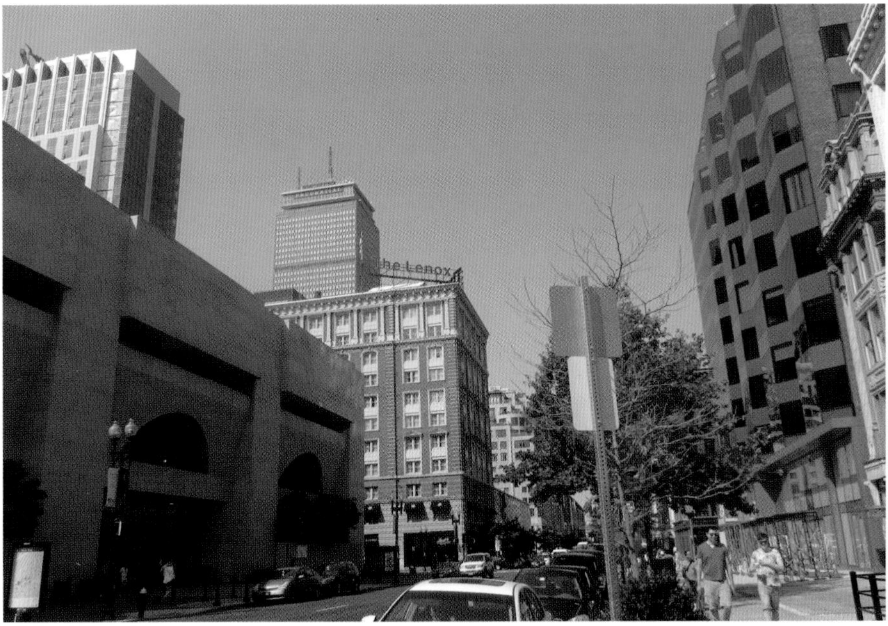

JOHNSON BUILDING
COURTESY AUTHOR

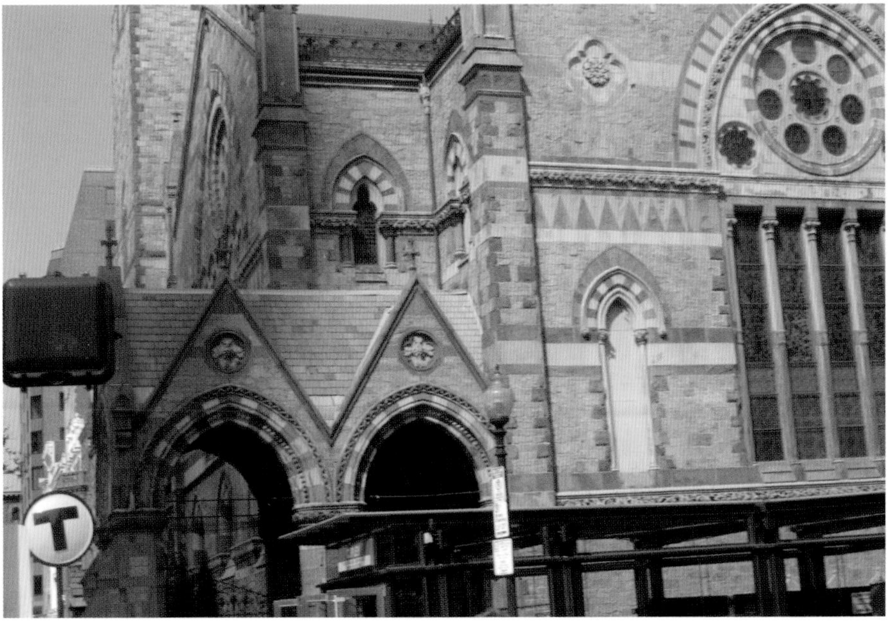

OLD SOUTH AND T ENTRANCE
COURTESY AUTHOR

The BPL has several notable firsts: the first municipal library to lend books, first system with branch libraries, and first children's room. Another donor has a statue across the street from the Dartmouth Street entrance, the Lebanese poet/philosopher Kahlil Gibran, who educated himself there as a young immigrant. Its inscription reads, "It is in my heart to help a little because I was helped much." His bequest was helpful, too.

"The Church of the Finish Line of the Boston Marathon" —Old South Church is the third of the buildings that graced Copley Square at the end of the nineteenth century all of which are still there. At the end of 2013, Old South Church, north across Boylston Street from the Boston Public Library and, dating from 1875, had major structural problems requiring millions of dollars in repairs. The Italian Gothic National Landmark is also a landmark for marathon runners who can see its tall campanile long before they reach the finish line.

South has a long history involving famous people and events, and the year of the marathon bombings, 2013, proved to be a time when the past rescued the future. The history of Old South (this is its third building) included a minister named Thomas Prince who served during the colonial period (1718-1758).

Prince collected books—practically everything available during that time—and also wrote them, beginning with his *History of New England*. He left his large library to the church, and it is now deposited in the rare book room in the McKim building of the BPL in Copley Square.

At least, all but one of the books is there. The one that isn't is called *The Bay Psalm Book*. It was the first book printed in North America, and he had it in his collection. It was printed in Cambridge in 1640 in many copies, but only eleven are known to exist, two of them owned by Old South until the congregation voted to sell one of them at auction to raise money for the needed repairs. It was sold by Sothebys on November 26, 2013, for $14.2 million, the highest sum ever brought by a book in an open sale. (The previous high-selling price was $11.5 million for Audubon's *Birds of America* three years earlier.)

So, Old South and the causes it stands for will continue for times to come as the poet John Greenleaf Whittier predicted when he wrote: "In Old South" in the latter part of the nineteenth century. One of its stanzas read:

> So long as Boston shall Boston be,
> And her bay tides rise and fall,
> Shall freedom stand in the Old South Church,
> And plead for the rights of all.

Whittier was an abolitionist, and the Old South was a center of anti-slavery sentiment. In fact, during the Civil War, 1,012 men enlisted there in one day to fight for the Union. Another preacher on the question of conscience was Samuel Sewall, who had served as a judge during the 1692 Salem witchcraft trials, but had repented his sins, and then became a witness against slavery in his writing, *The Selling of Joseph*. He was also, perhaps, one of the first abolitionists in colonial times. Sewall was later appointed chief justice in Massachusetts.

But he was only one among an array of fighters for freedom among Old South members. The Sons of Liberty gathered in large numbers and began the Boston Tea Party at the previous home of the church called the Old South Meeting House, located then and now at Washington and Milk Streets. When Sam Adams gave the signal, activists in the audience responded with war whoops. Sam's signal began a silent procession to the harbor, a march culminating in the breaking open of tea storage bins on three ships and the dumping of the tea into Boston Harbor in order to protest the tax on it, levied without representation from the colonists who were expected to pay the tax.

If that hadn't been enough history, we must quickly add that Old South was also the church where Ben Franklin was baptized in 1706. Phyllis Wheatley, poet and African-American, was a member, as were William Dawes and Samuel Adams, both involved in the action at Lexington.

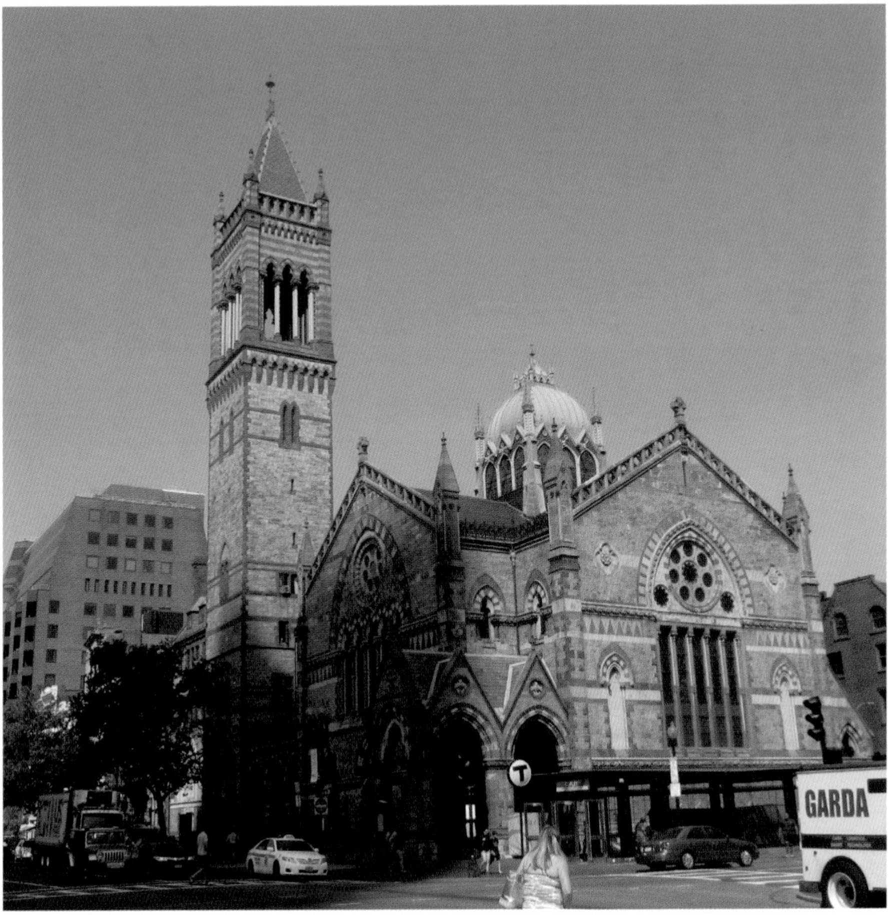

OLD SOUTH
COURTESY AUTHOR

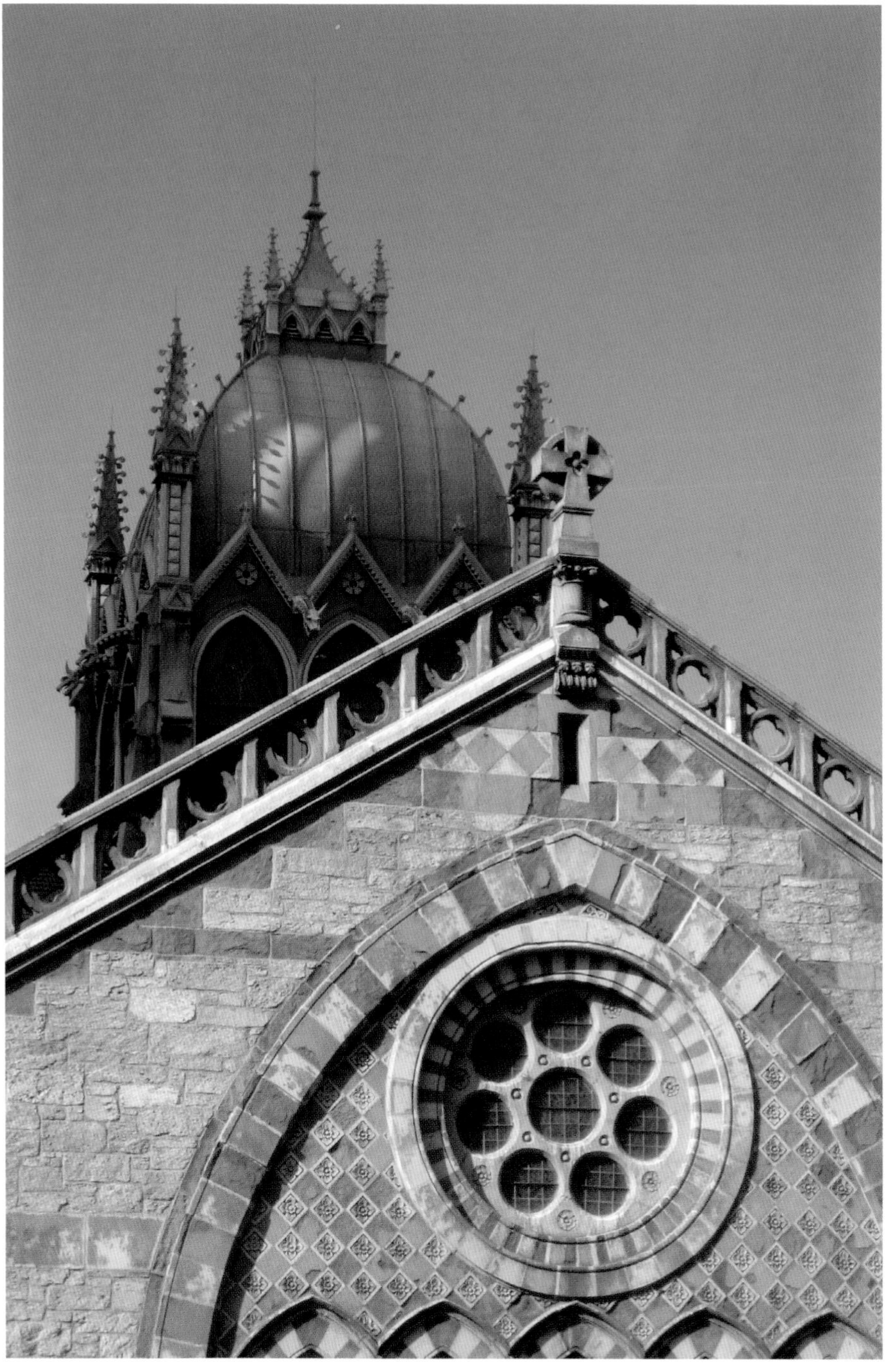

OLD SOUTH LANTERN
COURTESY AUTHOR

These things happened mostly at the second building, which was barely spared by the heroic action of fire companies during the Great Boston Fire of 1872. At that point, the church moved to Copley Square and, fittingly, chose a building design that was also radical for its time. John Ruskin is not one of the famous names usually associated with the church, but he well might be. His design for a Congregational Church in New England (1875) is more reflective of the Industrial Revolution than of colonial Boston. Its prominent bell tower, polychromatic roof and copper cupola must have astounded citizens of that day to whom the new church looked more like Venice than Boston.

These visuals were no more revolutionary though than the actions of the church over time. Its congregation espoused freedom of religion, free speech, public education, and civil rights, as well as many causes for economic and social justice. Old South Church moved into its Copley Square location in 1875, and since the first marathon, in 1897, has often been called "The Church of the Finish Line of the Boston Marathon."

It looks anything but Boston, though Copley Square has certainly been receptive to all sorts of architectural forays. Ruskin's design looks much like medieval Venice while using local stone—Roxbury puddingstone—on the outside. Its architects (Cummings and Sears of Boston) used Venetian mosaics and fifteenth century stained glass on the interior, prompting the long-defunct Boston Transcript to call it the "most beautiful basilica in North America."

In fact, Old South's lantern was inspired by the Basilica of Saint Mark's in Venice. It is a cupola covered in copper and surrounded by Gothic-style arched windows like the one in Venice. It also has mechanically operated louvers, which were able to cool the church's interior in the days before air conditioning—or even electric fans.

The bell tower or campanile with its Moorish arches, may be seen from a great distance as it soars to 246 feet above the square. Its bell weighs more than a ton, and this mass caused problems because the footings and piles on which it rested were not strong enough to keep it erect above the soft, filled-in land, and by 1920, it began to lean to one side (something like another Italian landmark). A replacement was built (1922-1937) using steel pilings. Since that time, annual testing has shown that the new tower has maintained the proper altitude. The bell, too, had to be replaced in the year 2006.

The interior of Old South is and has been artistically exceptional, with its stained glass windows, carved woodwork, and mosaics, but this was enhanced in a 1905 renovation by Louis Tiffany, changes that were, themselves modified during the 1950s when another renovation took place.

The church's organ, built in 1921, has 115 ranks and 7,625 pipes ranging from 0.25 inches to thirty-two feet in length. It is on a hydraulic platform that allows it to be raised for concerts and hidden otherwise. In 2008, the MBTA's Copley Square Green line station underwent renovation during which the church was damaged. In order to protect the organ from damage, it was not used for several months.

The exteriors of the three principal buildings of Copley Square—Trinity Church, the Boston Public Library and Old South Church—are architectural treasures, but their interiors are exceptional as well, and deserving of a visit.

CHAPTER FOUR

The Underground and the Unicorn

The clay-like sub-strata of filled-in land in the Back Bay and Copley Square presented an immediate need to shore up buildings, especially big ones like Trinity and the Old South. But the land could not yet be left restful. Another big piece of digging was for the Boylston Street Subway. This was an extension of the Tremont Street Subway, the oldest in the nation, built in 1897. That one had a portal on Boylston Street near the Public Garden, with stops at Boylston, Park Street, and later at Scollay Square and Adams Square.

Subways were built in order to get some of the many, many trolleys off the streets where they were clogging things up. Strings of clanging trolleys came in from the suburbs and from outlying parts of Boston and all came together in the downtown, creating a deadlock that couldn't last. These trolleys got their power from overhead electric lines from which the current ran to the engines from trolleys atop the cars.

From the Public Garden, trolleys ran along Boylston Street and Huntington Avenue, and Copley Square was a beehive of trolley activity. It soon became clear that the subway ought to be extended, and it was, the newer part connecting with the older subway and running to Copley Square and Massachusetts Avenue stations before ascending east of Kenmore Square on Commonwealth Avenue.

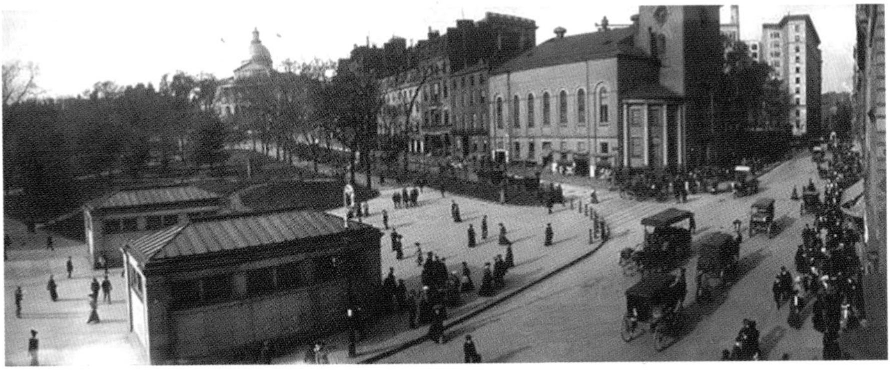

TREMONT AND PARK STREETS
COURTESY BOSTON PUBLIC LIBRARY

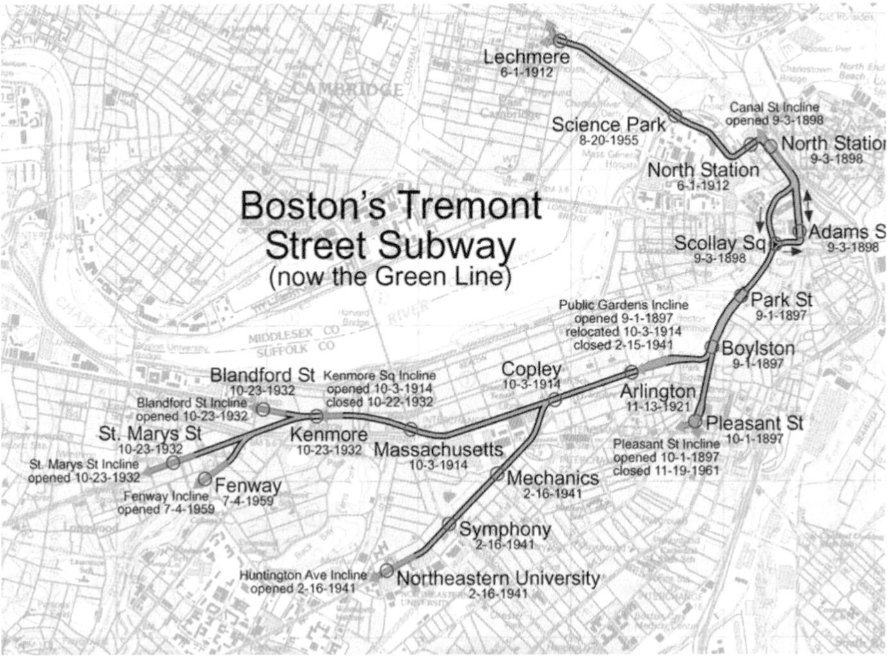

TREMONT STREET SUBWAY
COURTESY BOSTON PUBLIC LIBRARY

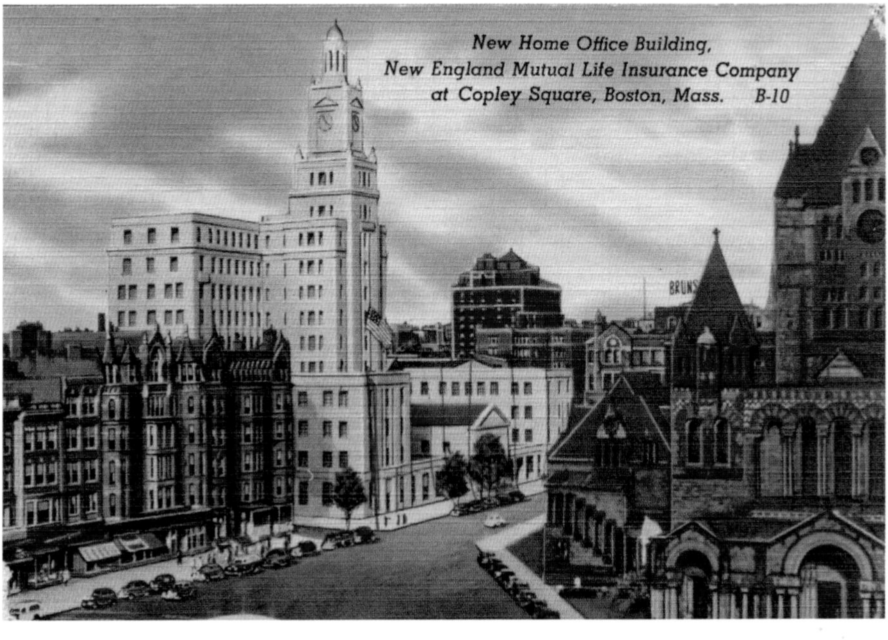

NE MUTUAL LIFE POSTCARD, CA. 1940

During all this disturbing of earth, historical artifacts were uncovered. Digging for the subway along Boylston Street unearthed something quite unexpected: fish weirs. Long before the Puritans settled in Boston, the native population had built fish weirs across the tidal flats so that fish coming in on the high tides would be caught in their nets. Then when the tides receded, they would wade out and gather their catch.

Subway diggers had reached thirty-two feet below Boylston Street when they found many stakes used in the fish weirs. Researchers believed that the weirs were at least 2,000 years old and were part of a single large weir. But the unearthing was not at an end. Twenty-six years later, excavation for the New England Mutual Life Building, just east of Copley Square, uncovered further stakes, and maps were drawn that showed, in theory, an extensive fish weir covering more than two acres of Back Bay. The find garnered considerable publicity and further theories about the large size of the tribe that had used it. More stakes were uncovered in 1946 when the earlier John Hancock Building was constructed.

Historical accounts are often built on evidence that comes to light in drips rather than torrents and over a period of time. It may be archeological information, as it was in this case. However, the pieces don't always fit together neatly and there may be a tendency to want to make them fit a promising theory. Oftentimes, a second find will contradict the first one and a later one may disagree with both. It's wise to remain open to new evidence, though some become fixed on an idea and are loath to part from it. On Boylston Street, the case was not closed.

Additional excavations came, in 1985, for a building at 500 Boylston Street, but this time radiocarbon dating was used to establish the date of the fish weir stakes, showing them to have been built over a 1,500-year period as part of many smaller weirs, not one big one. The theory emerging from this study said the weirs were probably made by clans of thirty-five to fifty people migrating from inland areas for summer fishing, who also used the fish to nourish the soil for farming. A more recent study showed that the weirs were built near the shoreline and had moved periodically to higher locations, indicating a rise in sea level (thought to be due to climate change).Meanwhile, the subway rumbled on. Copley Station opened in 1914, and like most things about the square, the station was different—even from its inception—from most of the Green line. With its entrances on Dartmouth and Boylston Street, it offered access to either inbound or outbound trolleys, but never both. Once you paid your fare at Copley, you could not cross over and head the other way without paying again. If you wanted to change direction, you had to travel to the next stop where you could go upstairs and down again to access the other-direction tracks.

The Boylston Street subway was extended west of Kenmore Square in time, with a new incline and portal on Commonwealth Avenue west of the square.

Later portals offered ascent onto Beacon Street near St. Mary's Street, and much later into the Fenway area (1959) for the Riverside line. In 1941, there was further digging along Boylston Street when the Huntington Avenue Subway conjoined the one beneath Boylston Street, veering to the left at Exeter Street with stops at Mechanics (Hall) and Symphony (Hall), and an exit at Northeastern University. When this branch opened and you entered it for the first time, you noticed the glaring whiteness and clean

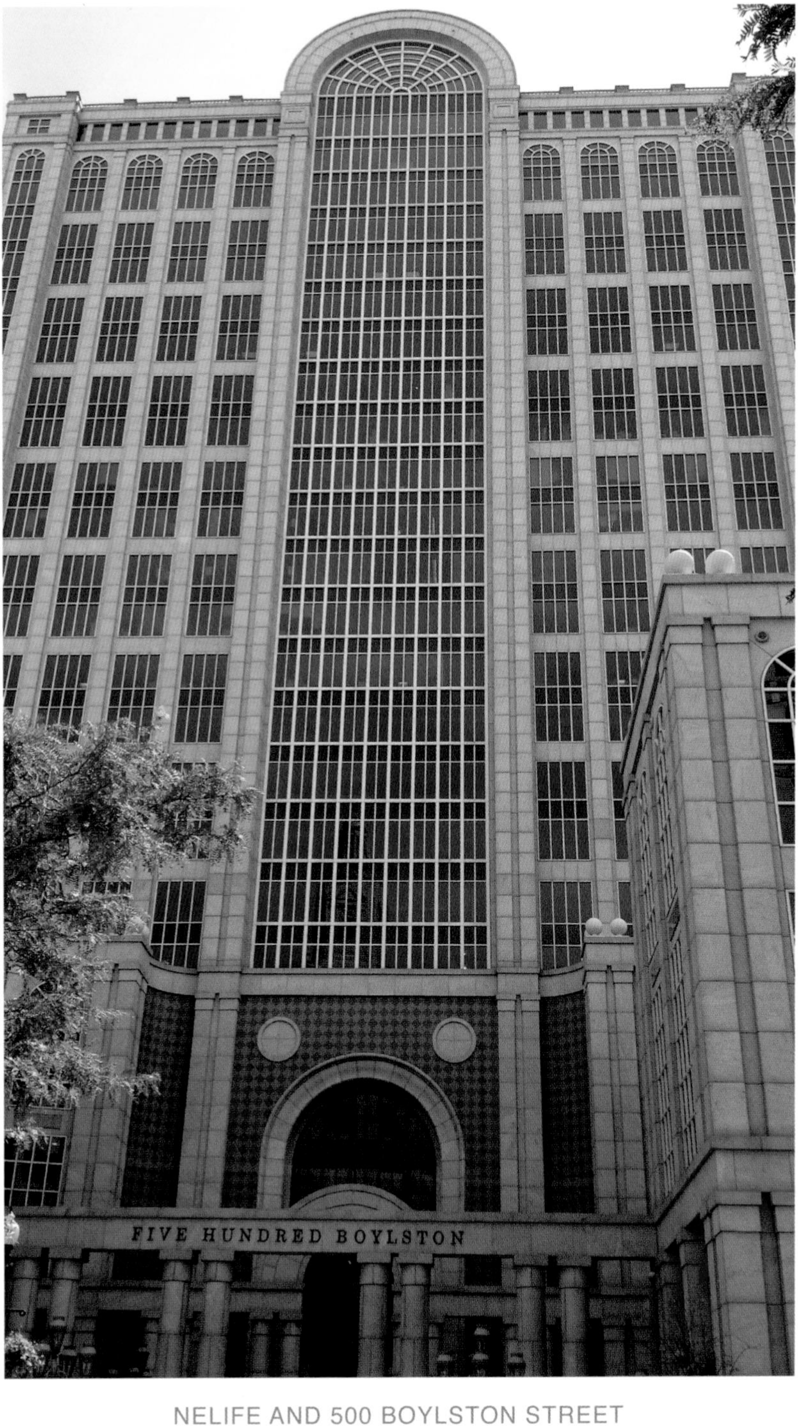

NELIFE AND 500 BOYLSTON STREET
COURTESY AUTHOR

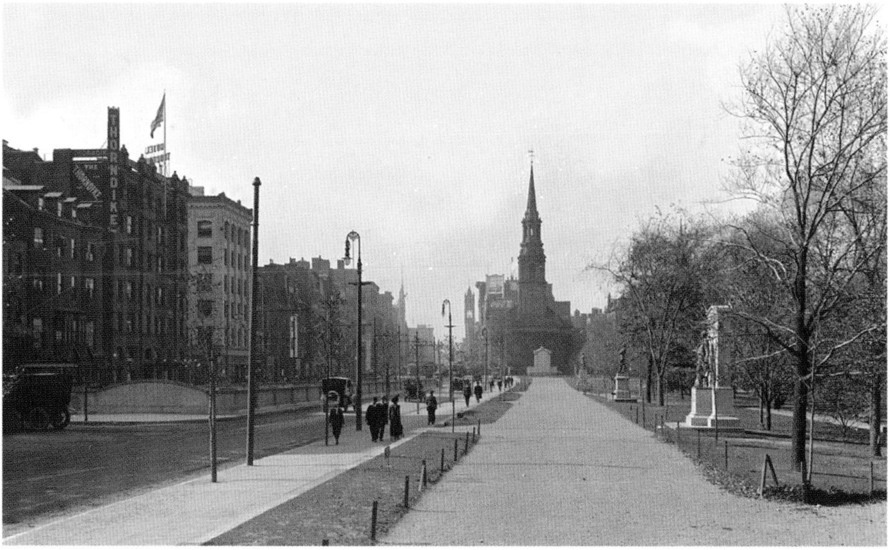

BOYLSTON STREET NEAR SUBWAY ENTRANCE, 1904

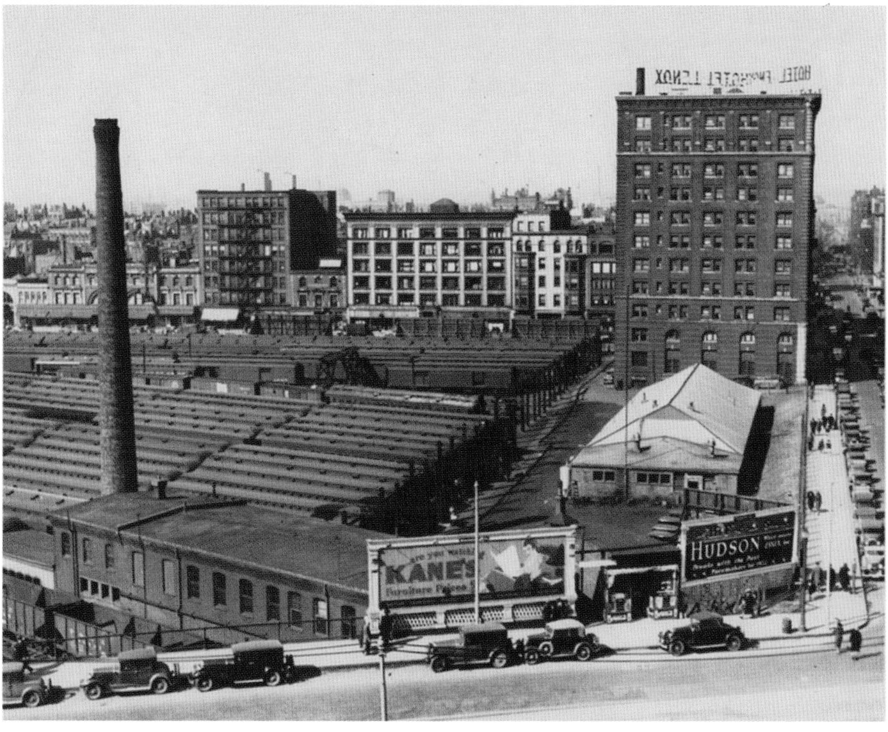

RAILYARDS AT EXETER STREET
COURTESY BOSTON PUBLIC LIBRARY

look of the stations. Like most of the Back Bay stations, they were close together and the ride beneath Huntington Avenue was a quick one.

If you are traveling west from Copley Station, after just a few yards, you would and will notice a jarring and rattling as you cross over the switch that will bring "E" line passengers to the left and into the Huntington Avenue branch of the subway. At this point, the tunnel veers beneath familiar marathon ground. It begins its left turn near the finish line and under Exeter Street to Huntington.

The former Mechanics Station is now Prudential Station. A second stop is at Symphony (Massachusetts Avenue). The subway then emerges onto a streetcar reservation near Northeastern University.

Some decades ago, the driver of an automobile, heading east on Huntington, mistook the tunnel entrance for the regular roadway and rode down into the subway and on through lighted stations before realizing the error of his ways. Similarly, a riderless horse and wagon ventured down into the subway at Kenmore and clattered along the tracks to Massachusetts station before it was reined in.

Neither of those things has happened at Copley. The Boylston Street entrance at Copley Square could and can be at once recognized by its ornate wrought iron head house from which a passenger could descend steep stairs into the station below with the name of the station spelled out in mosaic blue and white tiles—an artistic flourish that has perished with the passage of time. The two Dartmouth Street head houses, however, have been replaced in the 2008-2009 renovations when new tiles appeared, along with better lighting and an easier descent.

One would not notice those changes on a Marathon Monday for the simple reason that the station is closed on that day because the entire Copley Square area is nearly wall-to-wall with spectators, race volunteers, and others, making foot traffic the only thing moving—and even that moving more like the tortoise than the hare.

The marathon ends, just up Boylston Street from Old South, in front of the Johnson Building of the Boston Public Library, once the site of the Boston Athletic Association (BAA) clubhouse, a building large enough for a gym in which a track meet could be held as well as many other athletic activities. This clubhouse, built in 1888, on Exeter Street just set back from Boylston, also had a bowling alley, a hall for billiards, Turkish baths, and tennis courts. In addition to that building, the BAA owned a country club and a shooting range. At the main facility, the big sports were boxing, fencing, water polo, and athletics, all of which were Olympic events. The organization first held a track and field competition in 1890, an event that was later held at Boston Garden each spring.

When the modern Olympics were held for the first time in 1896 in Athens, the American contingent of fourteen men was led by nine members of the BAA, and the US won eleven gold medals—the most of any nation at those games. The following year, 1897, the BAA organized the first Boston Marathon, which ran 24.5 miles from Ashland to Boston. Fifteen runners participated; ten finished. The race would be held annually thereafter.

The first race ended with the runners passing the BAA clubhouse on Exeter Street, then right on Huntington Avenue, left on Irvington, and finishing with a lap of the Irvington Oval, which took forty seconds to complete. Subsequently, the race finished for many years on Exeter Street at the Hotel Lenox, but would be moved west up Boylston Street to the Prudential Center in modern times, and then to its present location opposite the Johnson Building of the Boston Public Library.

The starting line was moved from Ashland to Hopkinton and also had to be adjusted to match the official distance. In the centennial year (1996) a record of over 38,000 runners started. What began as a lonely race became world famous with crowds higher than half a million plus large numbers of viewers, many via electronic media. "Boston" is a highly prestigious event as well as being the world's oldest.

Unicorns, symbol of BAA and found on the marathon medal, are representative of speed and strength. They are noble and hard to catch. They are also healers—which fit well with the 2013 event.

As you review the earlier years of the marathon and the various races, you may be struck by the general politeness of the viewing audiences, the almost pastoral nature of the race through rural areas and suburbs, and the genteel behavior of people at the time.

Things have changed. The world is a less friendly place. Within sport and competition, sportsmanlike behavior has often become lost in the mists of time. However, the Boston spirit was shown at its best in 2013 when so many on the crime scene ran *toward* rather than away from the bomb blasts, indicating an ability to quickly adjust to changes, drastic as they have become. The marathon is no longer symbolized by the tortoise and hare. It has become, when necessary, the unicorn vs. the forces of evil.

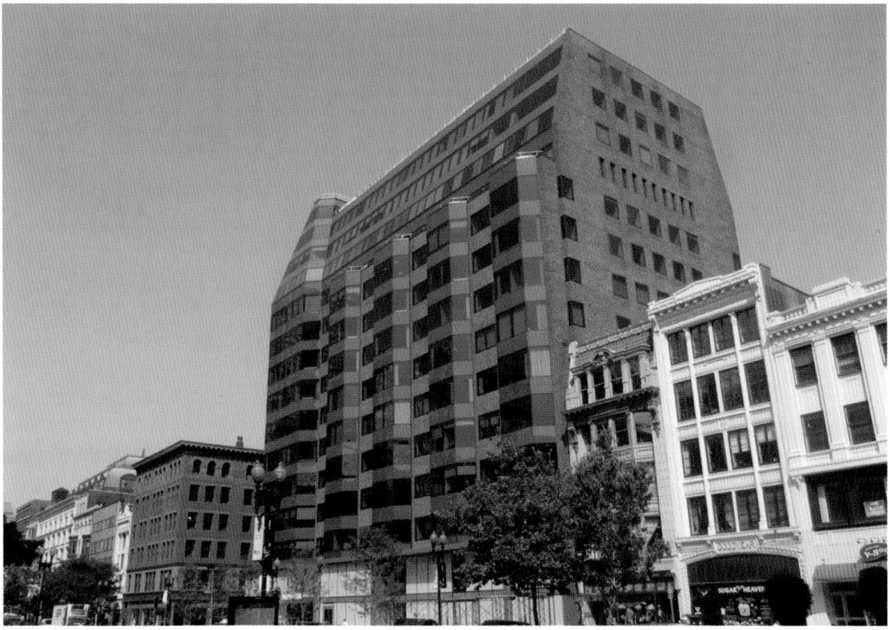

BOYLSTON STREET OPPOSITE MARATHON FINISH LINE
COURTESY AUTHOR

CHAPTER FIVE

The Copley Area

In addition to Trinity, Old South, and the Boson Public Library, Copley Square had a number of significant nineteenth-century buildings, plus others that came later. Some were replaced by cultural development as Art Square gave way to the Avenue of the Arts (Huntington Avenue), where citadels of art, music, and education sprouted up during the first decade of the twentieth century and beyond. These magnificent structures stood like sprinkled grace notes or even palaces of the arts on the separate sides of the square along the empty streets that would one day teem with activity.

We have earlier mentioned MIT and the Museum of Natural History between Berkeley and Clarendon Streets, along Boylston east of Copley. These were the bedrock bastions that set in motion the presence of the influential educational centers, plus the library that made the area attractive to other institutions who would also move in near the square or along its offshoots, Huntington or Boylston. The names of some of these will be familiar even now: they were the future Massachusetts College of Art, Horace Mann School, American Academy of Arts and Sciences, Boston University, Northeastern University, and Harvard Medical School. Probably now forgotten, was also the Chauncey Hall School, located on Boylston Street between Dartmouth and Clarendon, directly across from Trinity Church, a building with three spires, made of stone and covered with ivy. It was made to be architecturally memorable, but surviving the centuries takes, perhaps, more than that.

Also among the forgotten we presume were splendidly elegant hotels, notably the Westminster (often called the Westminster Garden), which stood just about where the John Hancock Building is now, a nine-story, widespread building with occasional awnings and balconies that gave it a rather asymmetrical façade. Later, the lot next to this one would be occupied by the Copley Plaza Hotel. Looking at the occupancy of that lot, first by the Westminster, then by the Hancock tower, gives a startling juxtaposition of the past and present that is quite startling.

Another hotel was the Brunswick, which lasted until 1935 and was again renovated in 1946 for students. The Brahmin-appealing Brunswick stood on the southeast corner of Boylston and Clarendon Streets from 1874, where for nearly seventy years it catered to what an 1880 advertisement called "... influential persons of taste," who enjoyed its marble-floored hallways, high-ceilinged bedchambers, and tiny-tubbed bathrooms. Their narrow-vista views gave way onto Copley Square and the avenues beyond, while offering luxury to their occupants.

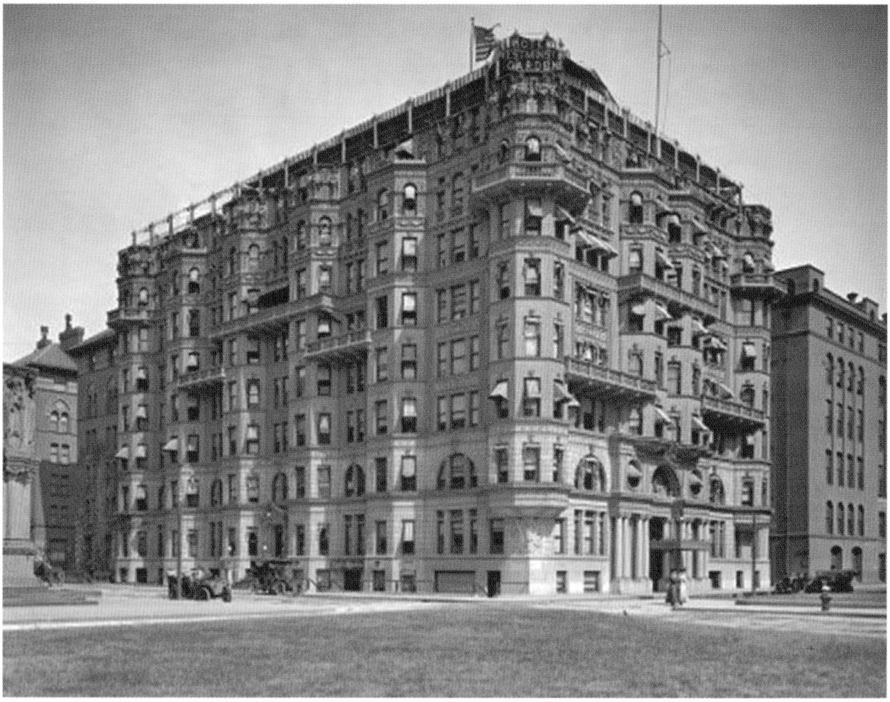

THE WESTMINSTER, 1914
COURTESY CITY OF BOSTON ARCHIVES

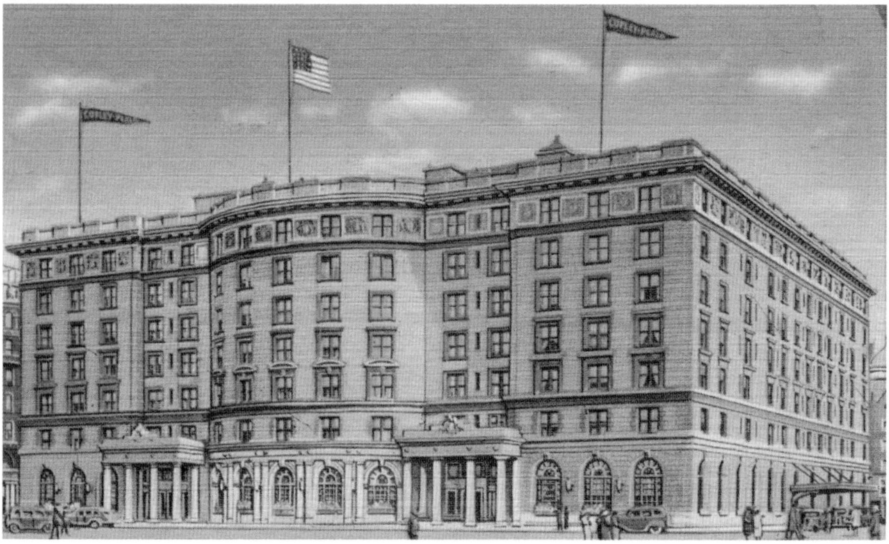

COPLEY PLAZA POSTCARD

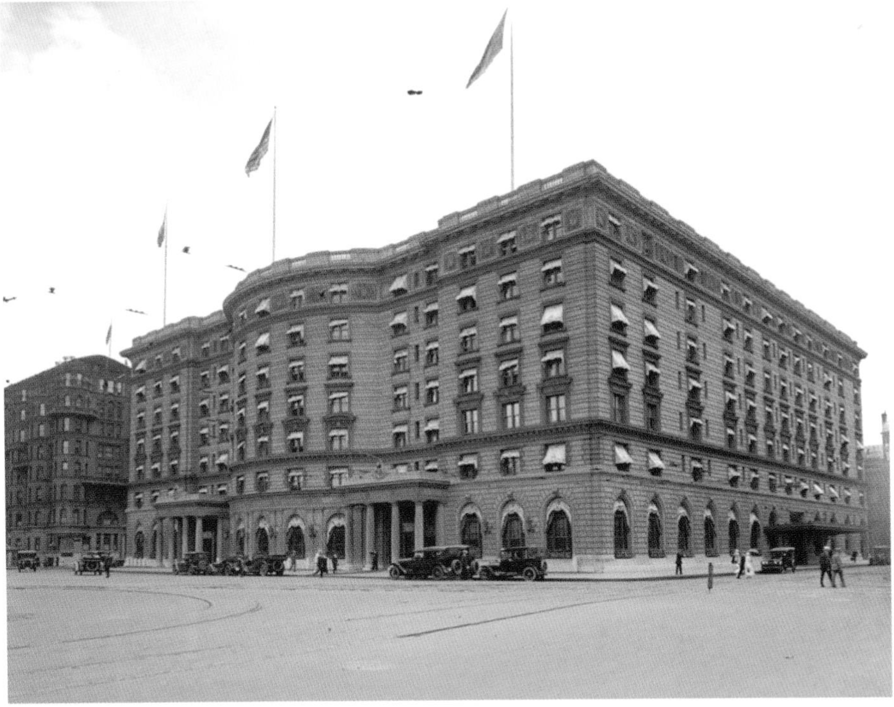

COPLEY PLAZA

The Brunswick was replaced by the post-modern building at 500 Boylston (where fish weirs were found during excavation). Thus the corner went from classical sturdiness to post-modern practical, another startling change from the settled conformity of the early twentieth century.

This award-winning building, designed by Philip Johnson (who also designed the addition to the library) has a lower section used for retail and a top for nineteen floors for office space. It also has a large underground garage.

Boylston had elegance during the last quarter of the nineteenth century, and later it had a strong commercial presence. However, it had only a brief brush with single-family residential buildings, or even apartments, unlike much of Back Bay. This was probably because of the railroad yards south of the street, which were not viewed as favorable neighbors. The clanging noise from coupling cars and the huff-puffing of switch engines clattering over the tracks, the snorting of locomotives with the accompanying smoke and cinders at any hour of day or night had little appeal for homeowners.

On the north side, at the corner of Arlington and Boylston in 1883, the Arlington Street Church stood where it stands today, brownstone sturdy and open for business. But that corner is where Arlington Street ended. This English-style church, still standing and still used, has an exterior that was based on London's notable St. Martin-in-the-Fields Church.

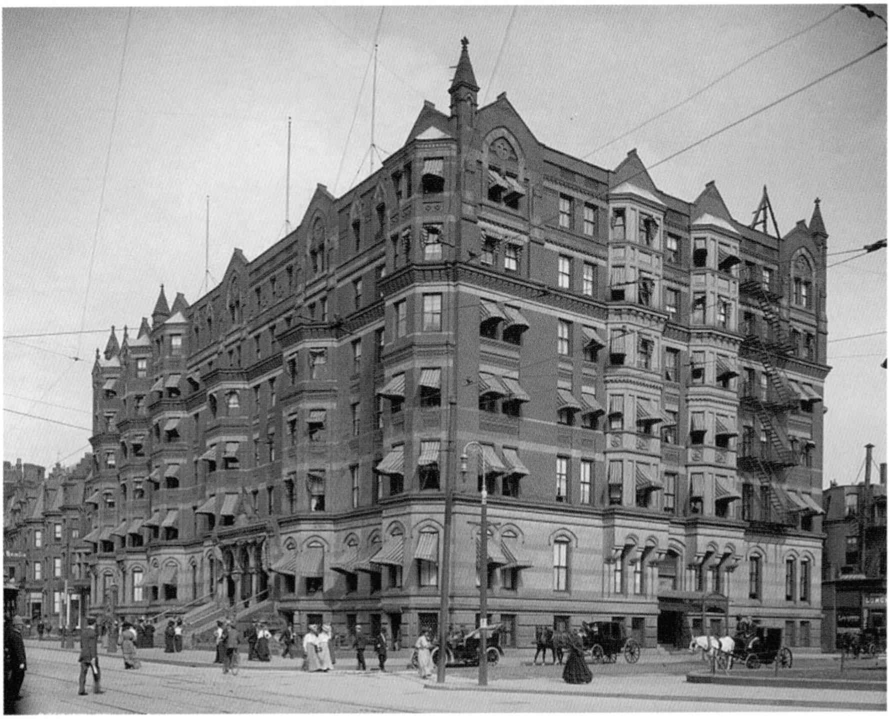

HOTEL BRUNSWICK POSTCARD, CA 1930

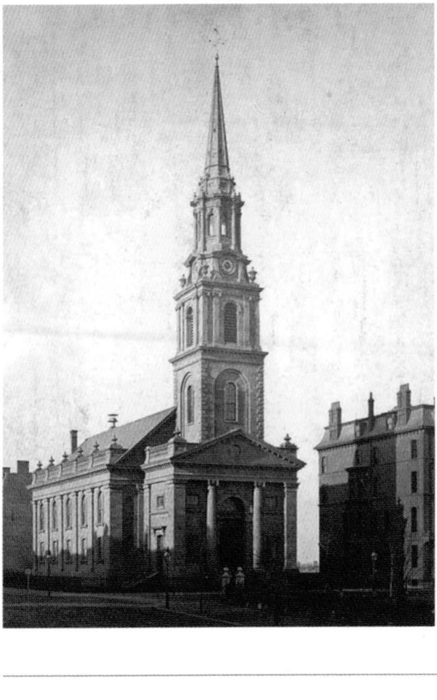

ARLINGTON STREET CHURCH
COURTESY JOHN PHELAN

Like other buildings in the Back Bay, this one, too, is supported by wooden pilings driven deeply into the mud—999 of them. The building has a tower with sixteen bells, each with a passage from the Bible etched into its echoing bronze. They are still rung by hand.

However, if you were to cross Boylston at this point in those days, you would run up against the houses, because Arlington Street ended at Boylston then.

On the other side stood the residences, extending east toward the downtown for about another block, so that some of them stood opposite the Public Garden, and in back of them were the railroad yards of the Boston & Providence Railroad and the towering passenger depot that operated from the 1870s to 1910 to the time when South Station supplanted it. It was this station from which passengers walked downtown, some of them visiting the fruit store of John DeFerrari or people like John Benton, both donors to the library in time to come. When the subway was completed, it saved people that walk because the trolleys emerged not far from the depot. The so-called "Providence Depot" at Park Square was the largest in Boston at a time when there were ten of them. It was the main station for trains to New York.

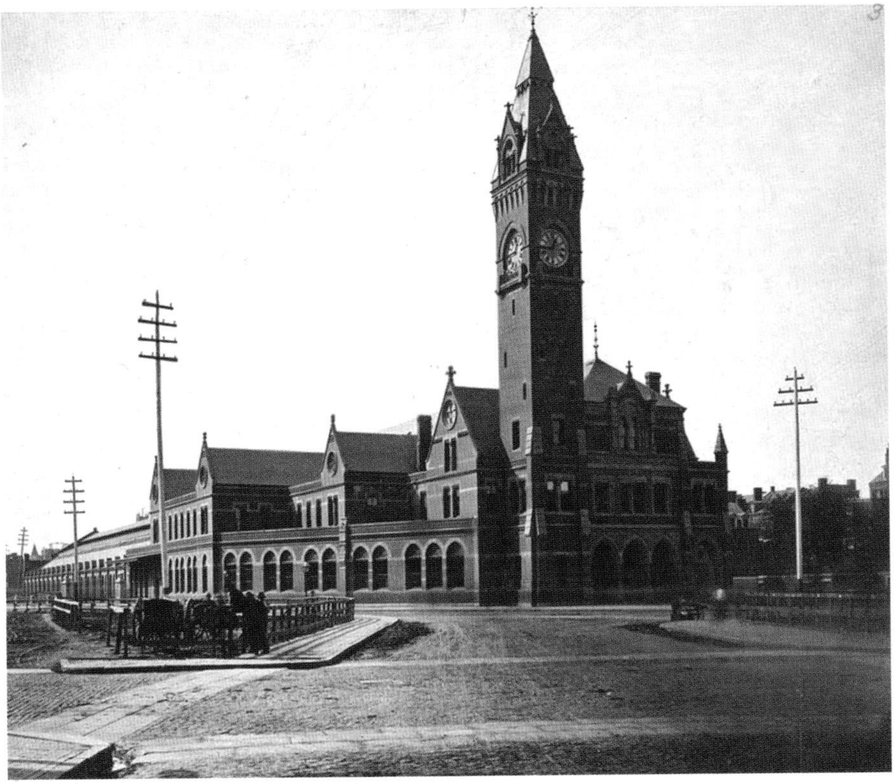

BOSTON-PROVIDENCE TERMINAL
COURTESY BOSTON PUBLIC LIBRARY

Before Back Bay was filled in, the Boston and Providence RR and the Boston and Worcester RR crossed the water on two trestles that met and crossed near today's Dartmouth Street. The Providence Depot was at that time on a pier next to the Common, and Park Square arose at that point.

When the Bay was filled in, the depot was replaced by one with a tower that had a high steeple. When South Station was built in 1900, all the railroads from south of the city used that, and the previously proud Providence Depot was used for a while as a skating rink, then razed.

The railyards for this depot covered sixteen acres between Boylston and Columbus and between Park Square and Clarendon Street. A piece of real estate of that size in the middle of a growing city is just begging to be built upon, and in the first part of the twentieth century, this nearly empty land was developed, most of it by insurance companies like Liberty Mutual and John Hancock.

The Statler Hotel (now Boston Park Plaza) was later built over the place where the station platforms were. To the west of there, Paine Furniture Company was built on Arlington Street (which then ran through Boylston into the South End). The location is now on the National Register of Historic Places and is occupied by Suffolk University. Where the yards were, the original buildings of Liberty Mutual and John Hancock were built.

During the time of the Great Depression in the 1930s, Park Square suffered economically, but was somewhat revived by the coming of the Greyhound Bus Terminal and other bus lines. Greyhound later moved to St. James Avenue, and presently, all bus lines use a new terminal at South Station.

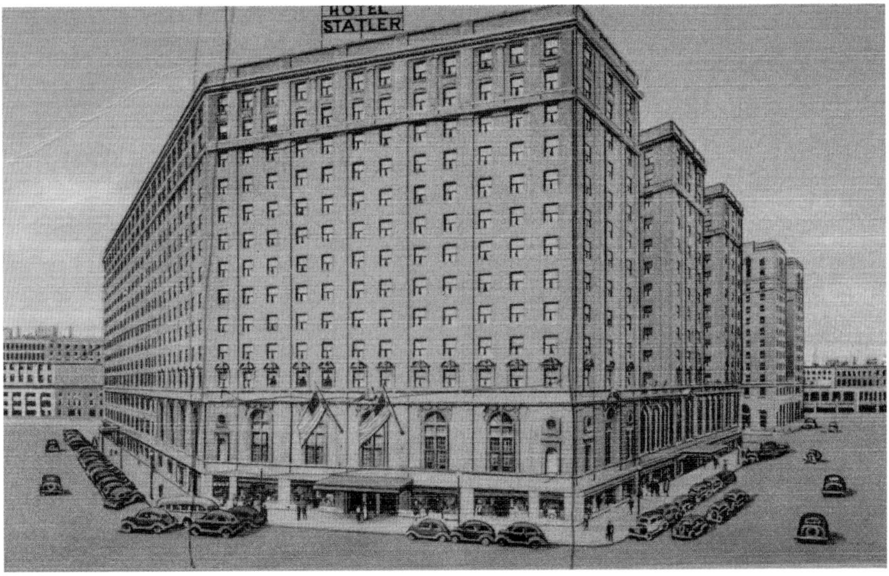

STATLER HOTEL POSTCARD

On the western side of Copley Square, along Boylston Street, were more railroad yards but a totally different set, these belonging to the Boston and Albany Railroad, which was formerly the Boston and Worcester. The yards ran east nearly to Exeter Street between Huntington and Boylston, and to the west they ran to Allston where there were classification yards, a roundhouse, and other railroad buildings. The main line of the rails continued through the yards and the western suburbs to Worcester and beyond.

This part of Boylston Street adjacent to the railyards became commercial quite early on, and by the year 1912, many of the businesses that opened there were connected to automobiles, which were just beginning to become popular with the wealthy. Cars and automotive products could be delivered by the railroads to auto showrooms, and there were also tire companies like B. F. Goodrich and Diamond Rubber.

Those disappeared but were replaced with other businesses, and eventually by the Prudential Center. It has long been a busy stretch of road, and its wide sidewalks have made it conducive to pedestrian traffic. In more recent times, these accommodated large crowds watching the finish of the marathon. It was almost made for this type of activity, allowing huge crowds to stand and watch the most meaningful part of the race over the length of nearly four city blocks. From an aesthetic and sportive point of view, the increasing height of the buildings ahead, such as the Old South and the Hancock, give anticipation and perhaps incentive to the runners as they force their weary bodies toward Copley Square and the finish line.

The runners stop there, but Boylston Street continues. After it passes through the open sward of Copley Square and goes by Trinity Church, other impressive buildings appear. Among them 500 Boylston and the New England Life building, erected in 1941 and recognizable from its gold cupola. This area has become a nucleus for insurance companies and the office buildings that house them.

Prior to all of that development and before 1900, Copley Square boasted two significant buildings that were not, however, architectural gems. These were the original Museum of Fine Arts on the south side of the square and S. S. Pierce on the southwest corner at Dartmouth and Huntington.

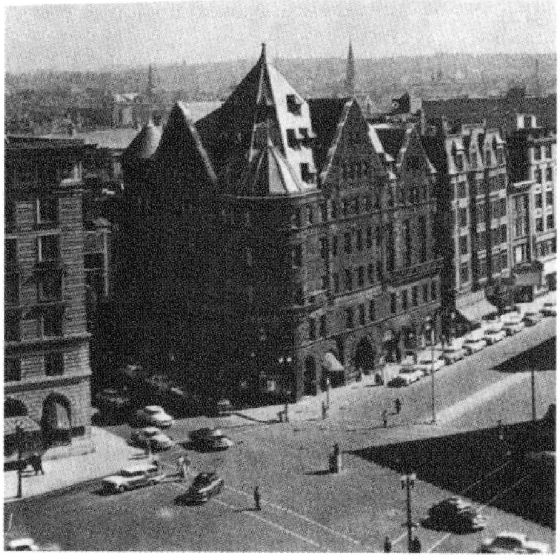

S. S. PIERCE AT COPLEY SQUARE
COURTESY BOSTON PUBLIC LIBRARY

In any discussions of "old Boston companies," S. S. Pierce is likely to be mentioned. Samuel Stillman Pierce and his partner Eldad Worcester began their partnership by furnishing provisions to ships that lay at anchor in the busy Boston Harbor, where Pierce often bartered with ship captains for the delicacies they brought from distant ports. Those items started a trend. The company would specialize thereafter in fine products not usually found in other stores.

Pierce said, "I may not make money, but I shall make a reputation." He made money, too, and boosted his reputation from the quality of his customers—men like John Quincy Adams, Daniel Webster, and Oliver Wendell Holmes who said, in a typically old-Boston way, "I was brought up on S. S. Pierce's groceries and I don't dare change."

S. S. Pierce & Co., Importers and Grocers began on Tremont Street where it meets Court Street (near Scollay Square) but moved in 1887 to Copley Square. The building, designed by S. Edwin Torrey was described by the *Globe's* architectural critic Robert Campbell: "It's no masterpiece of architecture, but it's great urban design. A heap of dark Romanesque masonry, it anchored a corner of Copley Square as solidly as a mountain."

It had offices and retail there, and the building stood at that corner of the square until 1958 when it was demolished. In its retail store and catalog (1886), it offered for sale "Groceries, wine, cigars, perfumes, gelatine, isinglass, chutneys, French vegetables in glass jars, Alghieri's soups, Wiesbaden Russian cigarettes, Egyptian cigarettes, quadruple essences, tooth brushes, soaps assorted, inexhaustible salts, and much more."

The company was known for its customer services as well as its products. A *Time Magazine* article in 1967 recalled:

> The company hired horse-drawn sleighs to deliver groceries when snowstorms closed roads to auto traffic, and maintained a well-drilled corps of salesmen who would phone housewives at appointed hours. They not only suggested menus but answered such arcane questions as how to cook an ostrich egg (boil it) or how to extract the flavor from a 6-in. vanilla bean (bury a 1-in. cutting from the bean for a month in a pound of sugar). Once when a hostess in Poughkeepsie, N. Y., complained that a case of turtle soup had not arrived, a Pierce salesman took an overnight train to deliver it in person—just in time for her party.

A second building, Tudor style, was opened in 1898 at Coolidge Corner in Brookline and still stands, though not as an S. S. Pierce. It also had an establishment at Chestnut Hill and a business office on Brookline Avenue. The Copley Square building was demolished in 1858, leaving an empty space or parking lot for many years.

Copley Place stands there today. It is a large complex with two hotels, an upscale shopping mall, a parking garage, and office space. It opened in 1984 at a time when Boston's downtown shopping area was in decline and shoppers were headed for the suburbs. Copley Place offered an in-town alternative and people flocked to the two-level mall that is connected via walkways to the shops at Prudential Center and Back Bay Station. The entire complex is extensive and allows a hefty walk from one end to the other—if one didn't stop to shop or visit a restaurant.

The Museum of Fine Arts, or the "MFA" as it is often called, was established in 1870 and received a gift of public land on the south side of the square. Most of its collection came from the Boston Atheneum Art Gallery. In 1869, the Atheneum agreed to give part of its art collection, owned mostly by old Boston Brahmin families, to a museum for "… the preservation and exhibition of works of art." Six years later, when the Lowell family gave the artifacts that John Lowell had collected in his travels

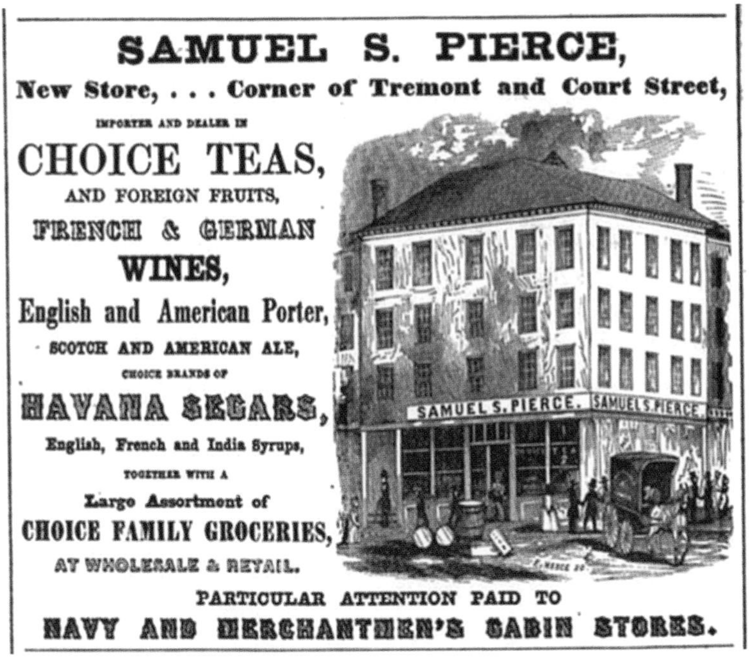

ADVERTISEMENT, S. S. PIERCE HANDBILL

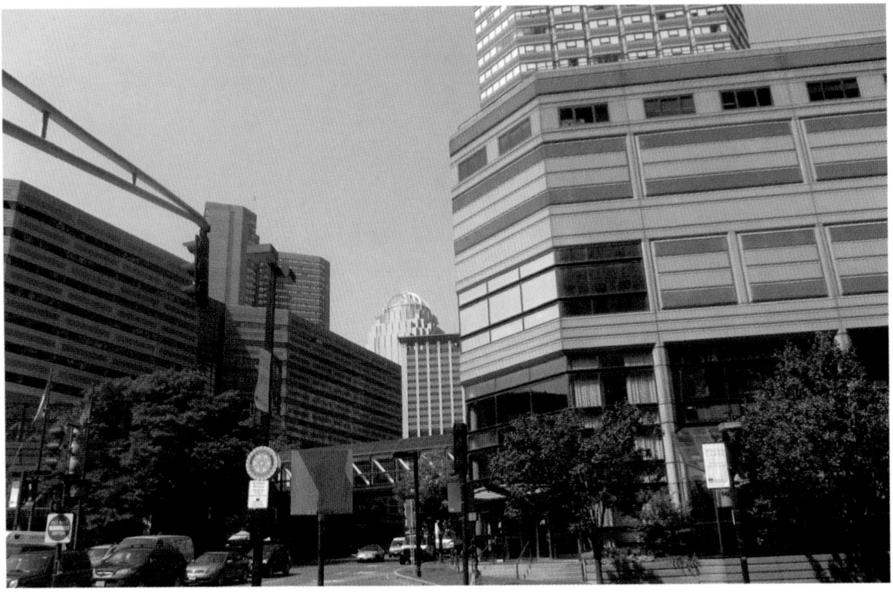

COPLEY PLACE
COURTESY AUTHOR

through the Middle East, they became a nucleus of the Egyptian wing, which remains a prominent MFA collection to this day.

An Art School was attached to the museum. This original museum was built in a highly ornamented brick, a Gothic revival building designed by Sturgis and Brigham, with large amounts of terra cotta. So, the museum had a new home in an excellent location, but as the century drew to a close, space became a premium for the museum's expanding collections, especially display space. Like anyone in cramped quarters, the staff made adjustments, but there were only so many of these, and it became clear that a new building was needed, a place with more room built on land where they could spread out. They would find such a plot. When the museum moved to Huntington Avenue, it was replaced by the Copley Plaza Hotel, which is still a hotel but with a somewhat different name.

The Copley Plaza was made of limestone and buff-colored bricks in Beaux-Arts style. The pilings beneath the seven-floor building descend seventy feet below the surface. It opened in 1912 in a ceremony led by Mayor "Honey" Fitzgerald, grandfather of JFK.

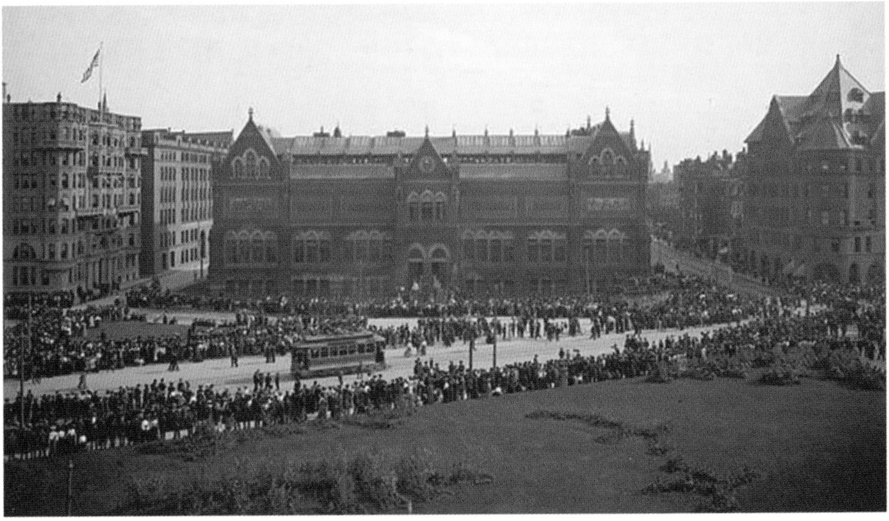

MUSEUM OF FINE ARTS, COPLEY SQUARE
COURTESY LIBRARY OF CONGRESS

For many years, the hotel was the location of post-football-game dances, especially Harvard-Yale. These must have been wild for that era since local women's colleges forbade their students from going. But the hotel catered to the elite, many of whom held events there. John Singer Sargent, the famous painter, kept rooms and painted portraits there. In fact, he used one of the employees as a model for Apollo in his decoration of the Museum of Fine Arts.

Not all news from the Copley Plaza was good. The grandfather of Secretary of State John Kerry committed suicide in the hotel in 1921 with a gunshot to the head. In recent years, a disgruntled employee set fire to the hotel causing one death and numerous injuries. One of the injuries was to business tycoon Sumner Redmond who injured his hand badly while hanging onto a third-floor windowsill to escape the fire. On the other hand, civic leaders held a dinner in 1935 for Babe Ruth as he joined the Boston Braves, returning to Boston after all those (sixteen) years with the Yankees. The dinner did not lift the "Curse of the Bambino," nor did Ruth's return to Boston help the Braves. Such lifting would come sixty-nine years later when Boston won the 2004 World Series.

Since the 1920s, the entrance hallway inside the Copley Plaza has been called "Peacock Alley." The huge lobby with its twenty-one-foot coffered ceiling, its crystal chandeliers, and marble columns made an impressive entrance, just as its mirrored ballroom and Oak Bar do. It was the first air-conditioned hotel in Boston and the first to accept credit cards. In recent years, various chains have owned it, most recently the Fairmont.

It has hosted every US president since Taft, plus royalty from many countries and scores of celebrities including Elizabeth Taylor and Richard Burton, who spent their second honeymoon there.

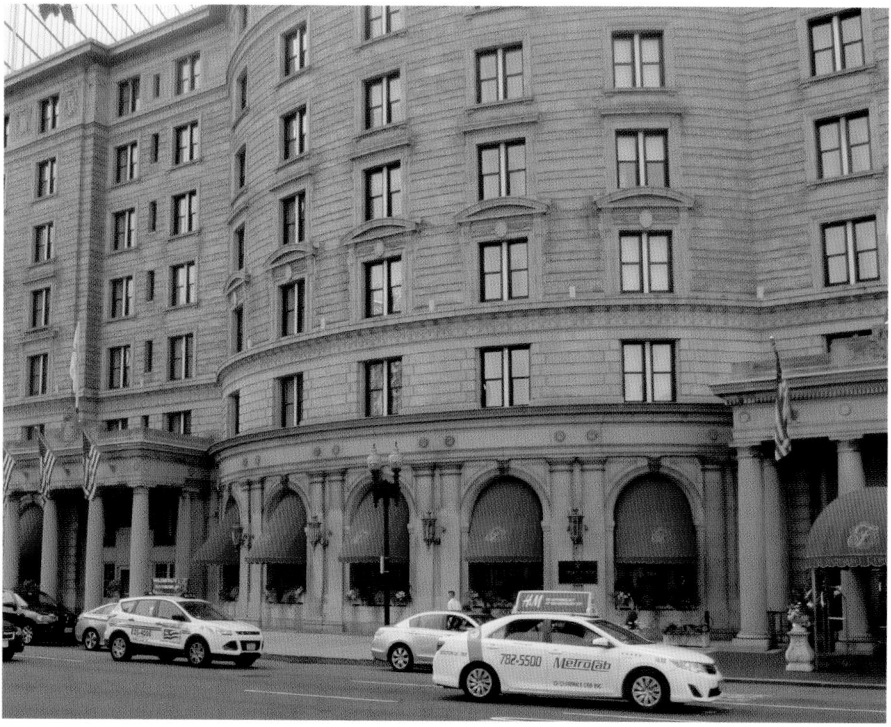

FAIRMONT, DARTMOUTH STREET
COURTESY AUTHOR

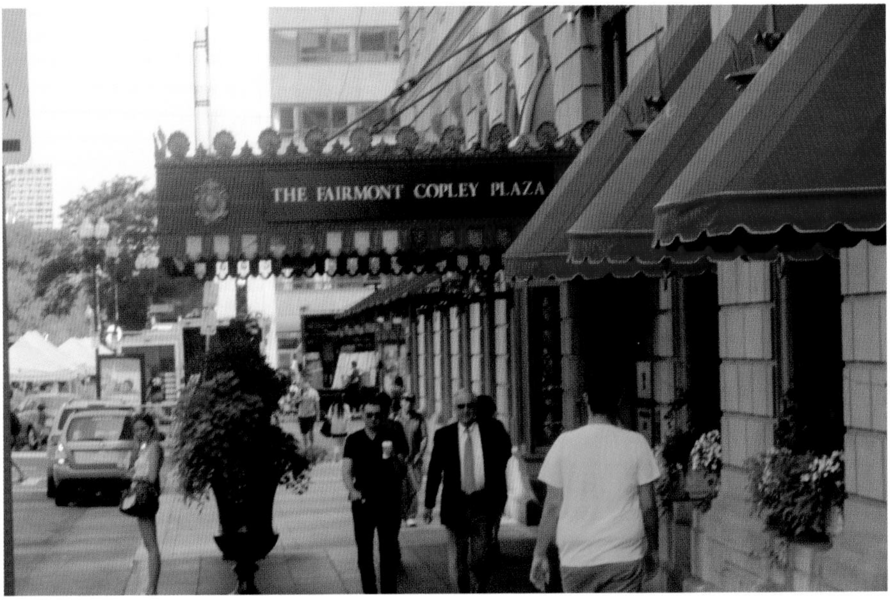

FAIRMONT FROM COPLEY SQUARE
COURTESY AUTHOR

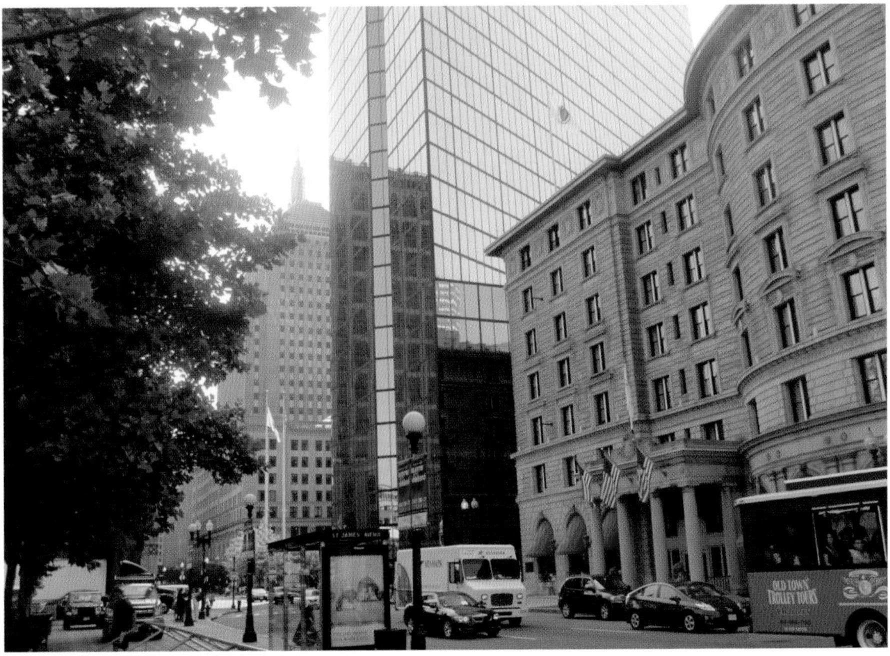

FAIRMONT AND JOHN HANCOCK BUILDING
COURTESY AUTHOR

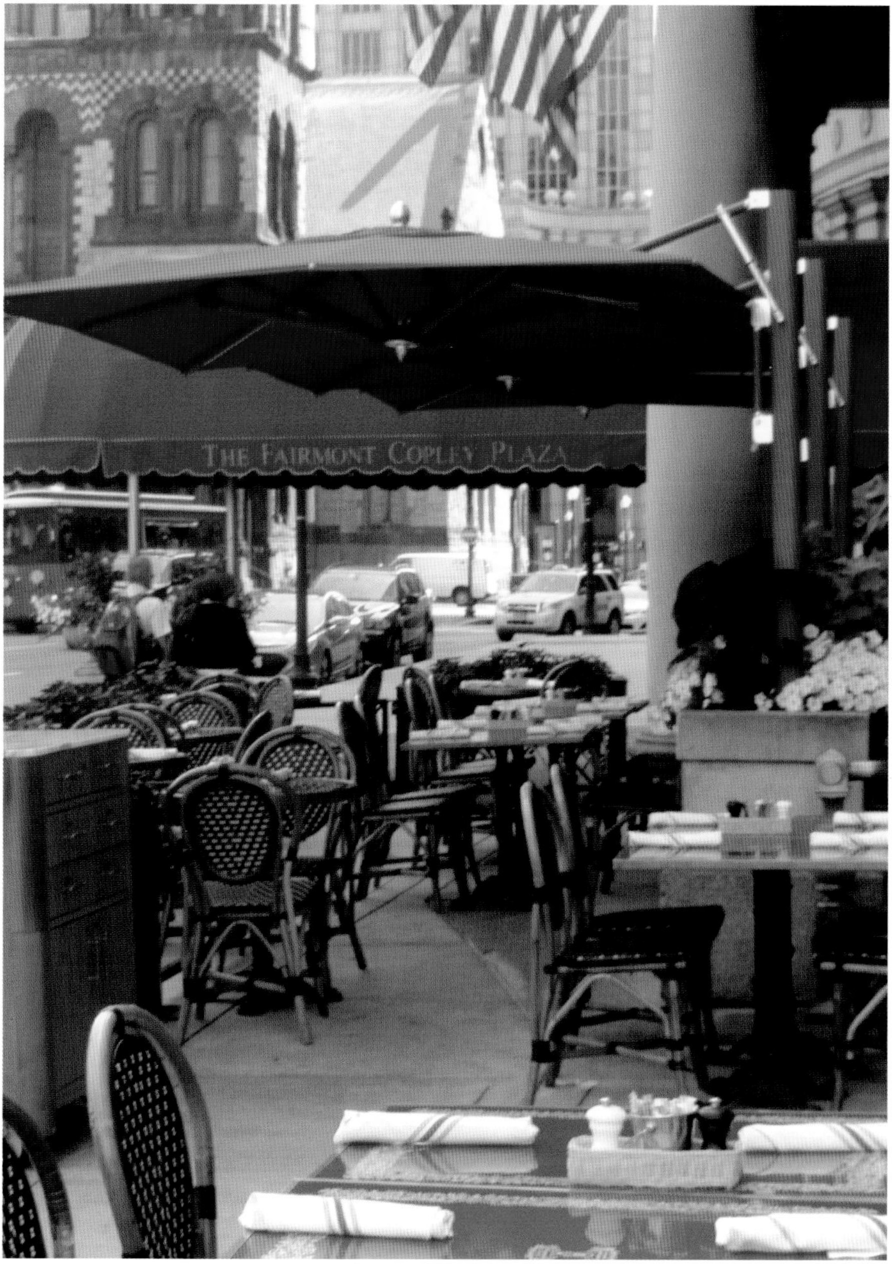

OUTDOOR CAFÉ AT FAIRMONT
COURTESY AUTHOR

CHAPTER SIX

John Hancock

One of those Boston patriots we spoke of at the outset had a name bigger than most, and a signature even bigger than that. John Hancock, an ally of Sam Adams, and rescued at Lexington by Paul Revere on April nineteenth (later Marathon Day) in 1775, was an unlikely person to become a patriot, but his name was a good choice for the name of an insurance company, which has also used his signature in its advertising. Sprawl your signature across an historic document and you've "branded" yourself for ages ever after. Go figure.

The wealthy Hancock had a fortune larger than most in New England and seems at first glance to have been a likely choice as a loyalist to King George III of England, as many wealthy Americans were. His shipping interests and valuable property were at a level that made most such men retain close allegiance to the king during the Revolution and especially before it. Want to protect your property and status? Go with the powers that be. Or at least that seemed like the logic.

But Hancock had been radicalized because the British were threatening his liberty, and that was important to him. We often under-rate the importance of this freedom that we have earned, but Hancock was able to see how restrictions imposed by Parliament and the king's ministers harmed his life and his livelihood. So, he took this to heart and started to think of how best to stand against it. He realized he could best help himself if he helped to bankroll the Revolution. And he was a godsend to the patriot cause. History often turns on small considerations like this one, and here we have our own homespun example.

Many have assumed that Hancock was sort of a puppet of the clever and stern Sam Adams, but it's more likely that each found assets in the other man that he himself did not have. They were an unlikely tandem, Adams fifteen years older, with a somber attitude and plain dress; Hancock something of a dandy, always well turned-out. But, vain or not, Hancock's sympathies were democratic and he used his wealth to help the patriots. Though he had a political ear to the wind, he was passionate about having the freedom to wheel and deal, pursuits that he was so good at, and he sympathized with others who faced the same restrictions. Unlike many, he was in a place to make a difference.

He used his special position and the regard he had brought to himself to serve others as president of the Second Continental Congress, and as first governor of Massachusetts.

Hancock inherited much of his wealth from his uncle. They lived in a home on Beacon Street above the Common near where the State House is now. Curiously, the only neighbor to the west would be John Singleton Copley for whom the square was later named.

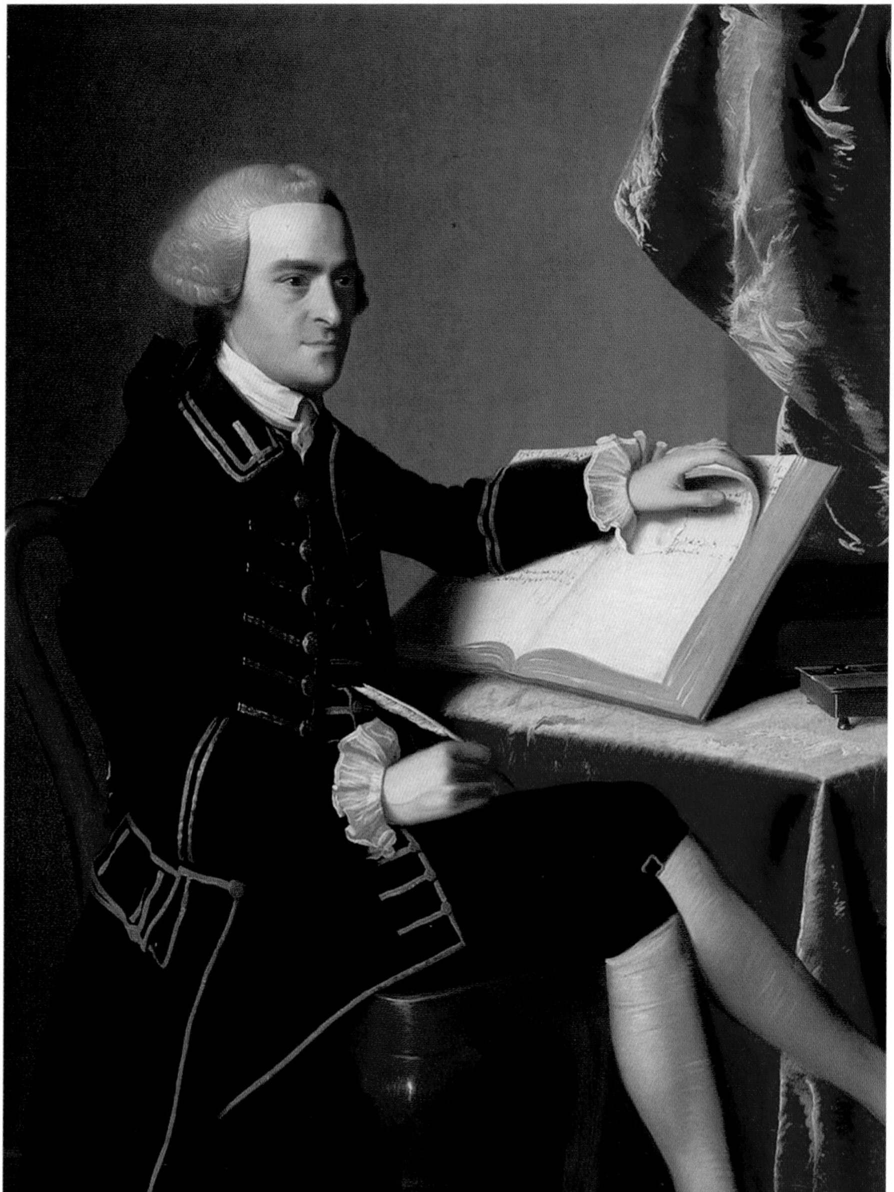

JOHN HANCOCK PORTRAIT BY JOHN SINGLETON COPLEY

Copley, of course, was usually in England, and his dealings with his Beacon Hill neighbors were not on a good footing. Harrison Gray Otis and others learned that Beacon Hill was to become the site for the new State House, and they bought up land it would sit on at a cheap price. The fifteen acres belonged to Copley, who was away, but had an agent who handled the sale. When he got back, Copley felt cheated since the land was worth far more than they had paid his agent for it. He tried to have the contract nullified when he learned about the plans for the state house, but he wasn't able to get satisfaction from the Brahmin families, who were better "Yankee Traders" than he was, and who all stuck together.

Hancock's house, which then stood next door, has not been saved for posterity. One sad thing about Hancock's remembrance is that he was renowned during his lifetime as one who used his position to help the common weal—like many of today's politicians. But he couldn't quite escape the suspicion that his dealings were calculated and politically driven, as perhaps some of them were.

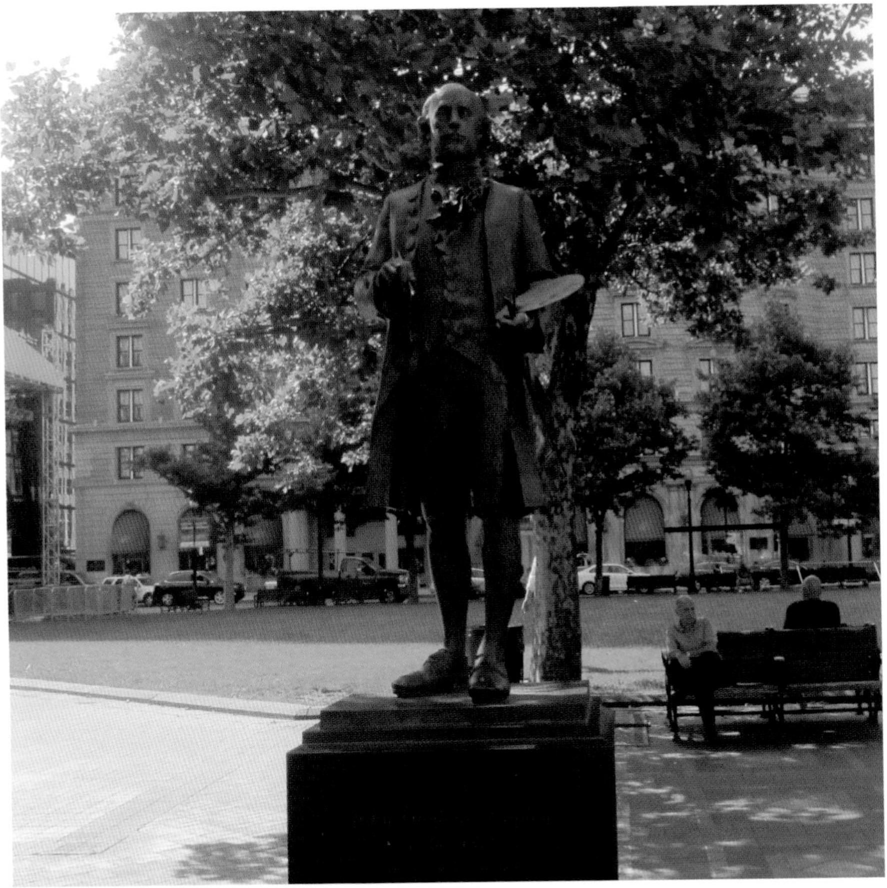

STATUE OF JOHN SINGLETON COPLEY AT SQUARE NAMED FOR HIM
COURTESY AUTHOR

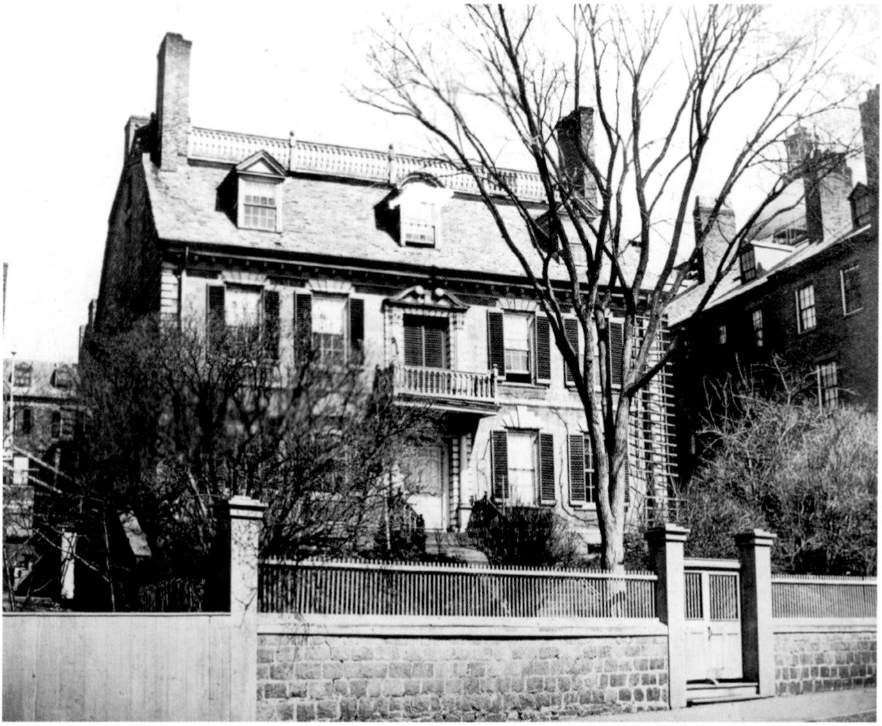

HANCOCK HOUSE ON BEACON STREET

His house should have been spared, however, both as the home of an important Revolutionary and Massachusetts figure, but also as an example of a home of an aristocrat in Boston during the late 1700s. That kind of feeling was sadly missing at the time it was needed. But the loss of the house, when people looked at the empty face and felt the loss of the building, spurred a movement to save other buildings, like the Old South Meeting House, the Paul Revere House and, in time to come, the Old State House.

Perhaps ironically, the name of this patriot with the political skills would not be forgotten because it chanced that his name and his fame as a signatory to the Declaration of Independence outstripped his fame as a patriot.

The John Hancock Insurance company began in 1862 and was named after the man with a big name and big signature. The company has since evolved, and has occupied three different buildings near Copley Square, the most famous, the 1976 skyscraper of gleaming glass, sixty-two stories tall, designed by the I. M. Pei Company on the site once occupied by the Westminster Hotel.

This was not, however, the first John Hancock Building. There are two others that still stand. A 1922 building at 197 Clarendon Street became too small for the offices and a new one (called now the "Old Hancock Building") was built right next to the old headquarters with an entrance at 200 Berkley Street. The two were and are connected at street-floor level. The co-joined building has an 1,100-seat auditorium plus office space.

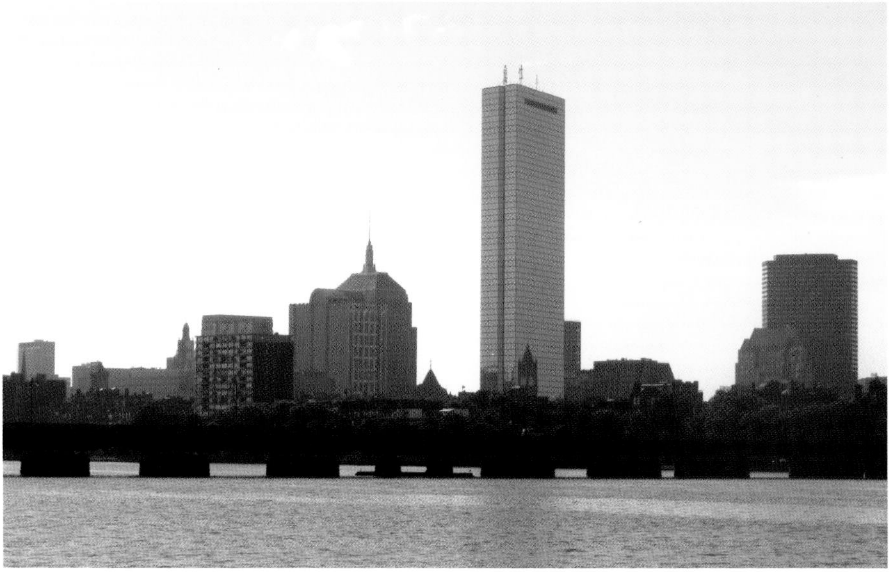

JOHN HANCOCK TOWER FROM THE CHARLES
COURTESY AUTHOR

The "Old Hancock Building" opened in 1947, and, at twenty-six floors, was at once the second-tallest in Boston. When it rose, it gave a boost to Bostonians, whose city had grown dingy and had not seen new tall buildings since 1913 when the Custom House Tower was built. Before this, no tall buildings had been built in the Back Bay. With so few tall buildings in Boston, if you stood on a high hill at a distance, the Hancock, with its lit beacon, stood out as a handsome newcomer among the drab, older buildings.

This was a striking change, and it would set a precedent for others, like the Prudential (1964), the 1976 John Hancock Tower, and more. But we didn't know that then. It just seemed that Boston was getting a new building and was perhaps ready to outgrow its dingy dilapidation. If that was the case, it had an example to follow.

But it was more than a model. Starting in 1950, Bostonians learned to rely on the art deco style Berkeley Street building for things other than insurance. At its top was a spire with lights that gave instant weather forecasts that people could understand by memorizing a short verse:

Steady blue, clear view. Flashing blue, clouds due.
Steady red, rain ahead. Flashing red, snow instead.

However, during baseball season, flashing red means the Boston Red Sox game has been called off on account of weather. During the energy crisis of 1973, it was shut off (as was the Citgo sign in Kenmore Square). Since 1983, it has run continuously.

The importance of sports to the civic consciousness is often reflected in the city's institutions. When the Red Sox won the World Series for the first time in eighty-seven

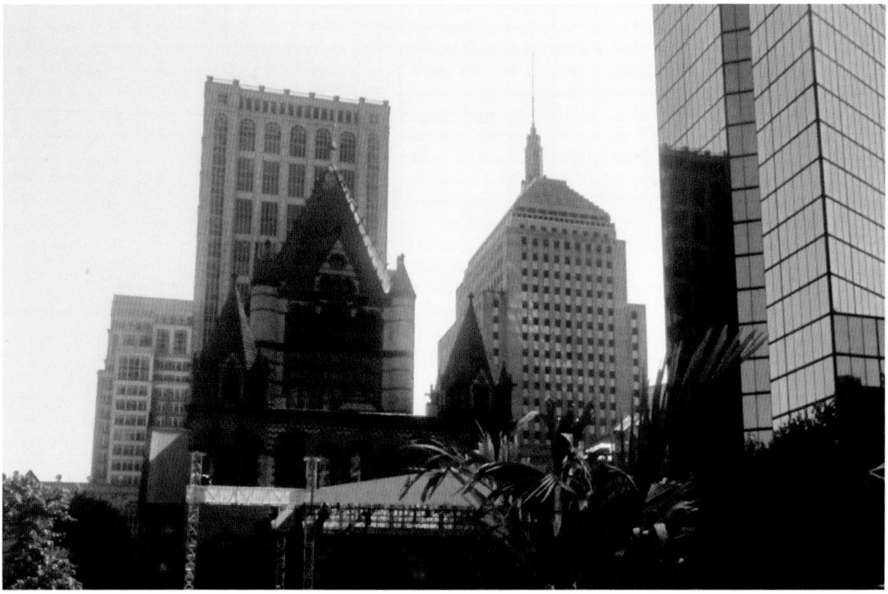

OLD JOHN HANCOCK
COURTESY AUTHOR

years in 2004, the beacon flashed red and blue for the first time. The same happened with the Series wins of 2007 and 2013.

But clearly, this building was ready to draw attention to itself and to become the center attraction in Boston. The spire stands atop a shallow pyramid on top of the otherwise heavy building. When the new, slender, blue-skinned building was later designed by I. M. Pei, it contrasted with the older, heavier building and made the new one seem even lighter. This happened when the company outgrew the old building. The new one was finished in 1976. The two buildings represented a change in eras.

The insurance company made other history through its advertising, for which it produced many collectibles. One of the first company presidents put up tin signs at railroad depots that advertised the company. These are now collector's items as are the many booklets that agents gave out door-to-door, including such items as song books of Christmas carols used for years by school children before that kind of thing was frowned upon.

But these well-used booklets were not the only successful Hancock advertising devices. During the 1940s and 1950s, mini-biographies were presented in Hancock advertising handouts and copied in mainstream magazines. These found readers, not only among average Americans but in the world of advertising, too, where they found many admirers. Today, if you want to find these artifacts, you may sometimes find them in museums and at art auctions.

The Hancock House would no doubt have become a museum had it survived, and, as you'll see in what follows, there was some irony in its demolition, because it raised an outcry that led to a preservationist movement in Boston. The irony came much later. When the city's tallest building, bearing Hancock's name, was to be erected, Boston's latter-day preservationists rose in protest.

Although the razing of Hancock's house had caused great outcry and stirred up preservationists, Boston had shown an interest in preservation before that, going back to the development of Back Bay where, as mentioned, restrictions were put in place to guarantee the integrity of this new neighborhood. Heights, for example, were controlled by restrictions written into the deeds. Boston's regulations of the heights of buildings were the first in the country and set a precedent for zoning, which would follow both there and in other places.

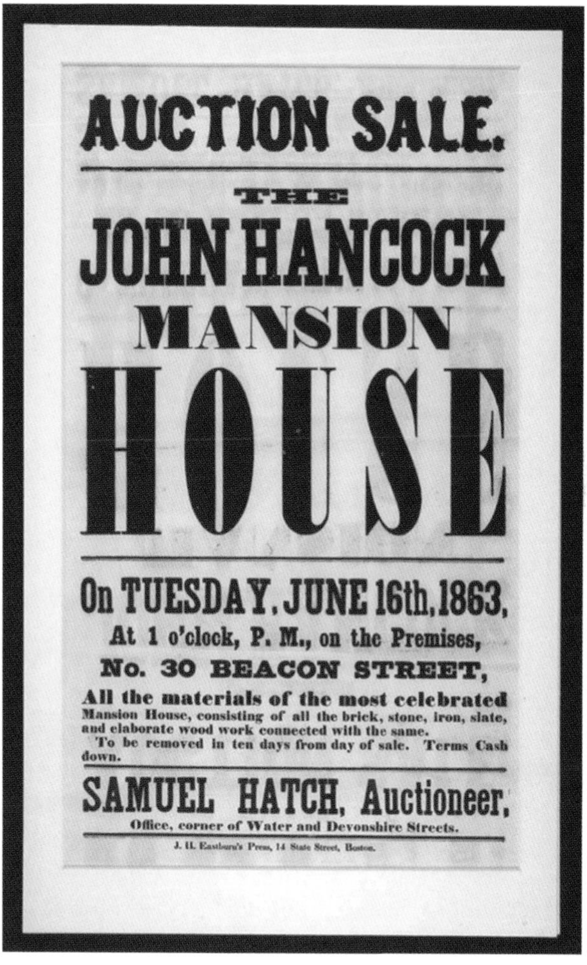

AUCTION POSTER, HANCOCK HOUSE

Another Boston "first" that began at this time was the effort to preserve public open land from the encroachment of urban growth. This is seen in the planning of the Public Garden and the later work of Olmsted. The hiring of landscape architect Frederick Law Olmsted who devised and established an "Emerald Necklace" of parks was the beginning of this new approach. The Common, which had been treated shabbily, was restored by Olmsted's company, and commercial uses were excluded from the green areas as were streets.

Charles Eliot, a disciple of Olmsted, later got the legislature to establish the Metropolitan Parks Commission and to gradually build a park system in and around Greater Boston. Eliot, who had worked with Olmsted on his projects in New York and Boston, published an article in 1890 called, "Waverly Oaks" in favor of preserving an area of oak trees in Belmont and other areas of scenic beauty in the way that the Boston Public Library preserved and held books and the Museum of Fine Arts pictures. His writing led to legislation that created the Trustees of Reservations the following year. This was the first organization in the world created to "...acquire, hold, protect and administer, for the benefit of the public, beautiful and historical places."

After the great fire of 1872 burned 65 acres of downtown, construction boomed, and people also emigrated to Back Bay and the suburbs. There were more calls for city planning and preservation, galvanized by the demolition of the John Hancock house on Beacon Hill. It led directly to a campaign to save the Old South Meetinghouse as a historic landmark (site of the Boston Tea Party gathering). The building had been narrowly saved from the fire, but the congregation had moved to Copley Square and the old church was slated for removal. In 1876, the Old South Meetinghouse was auctioned off for $1,350 for the value of its copper and lead. Removal of the copper had begun when a group of twenty women of Boston were able to stop it (with the help of famous people like Ralph Waldo Emerson, Louisa May Alcott, Henry Wadsworth Longfellow, Wendell Phillips, and Julia Ward Howe) and raise $400,000 to preserve it. This was the first time a public building had been saved in the United States because of its historic significance. It became a museum. The campaign further aroused the interest in Bostonians for preserving history, and it would continue.

There was a desire to protect the prominence of the capitol dome in the Boston skyline, and a law was passed in 1891, limiting the height of buildings, the first in the nation of its type. But there were other such laws in the Back Bay where an apartment building, Haddon Hall (which still stands on the corner of Newbery and Berkeley) rose to 125 feet, making it stand out like an untamed cowlick among its lower neighbors.

It was able to do this because the Back Bay deed restrictions were written before elevators were invented and they had a minimum height limit of three stories, but no maximum limit. Quickly, the community fixed that and in 1896, a height limit of seventy feet was imposed on Commonwealth Avenue, followed by one of ninety feet for buildings on the south and west sides of Copley Square.

These height restrictions would come notably into play in a lawsuit filed by the Commonwealth of Massachusetts over the height of the Westminster Chambers in Copley Square whose ornate cornice exceeded the ninety-foot height restriction then in force. The case, the first in the nation about height restrictions, went to the Supreme

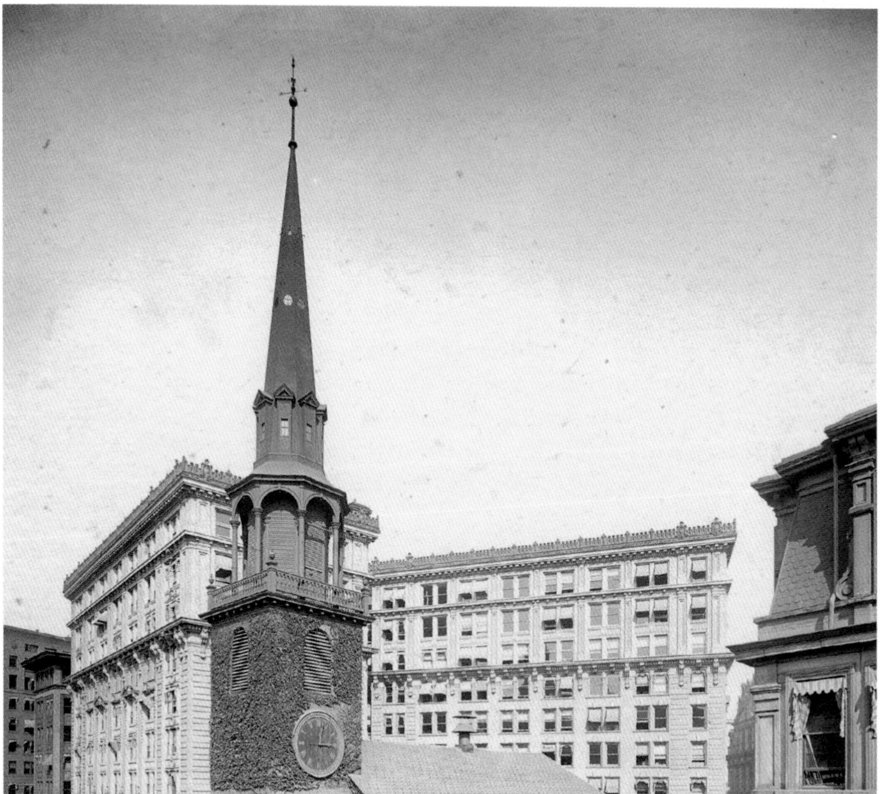

OLD SOUTH MEETING HOUSE
COURTESY LIBRARY OF CONGRESS

Court, which ruled that the extra six feet were in violation. Thus, in 1903, the roof and its sculpture came down.

Ironically, when the Westminster itself came down in 1975, it was to be replaced by the skyscraping and height-changing John Hancock Building of sixty floors, which exceeded restrictions on both height and heft and also dwarfed its historical Copley Square brethren, like Trinity Church. There were other problems, too, as you will see.

Boston had been through a long period of stagnation during which the building of the Old Hancock in 1947 had been one of the few bright spots. But as the era of the "New Boston" took hold during the '60s, there was a call for lifting the height limits. This desire, of course, clashed with the desire to preserve the past. Compromise was called for. In 1960-1961, a committee of the Boston Society of Architects recommended a new master plan for Boston. Kevin Lynch, an MIT professor and member of the group, had a vision for a corridor where tall buildings could be built. It would run from the financial district west to the railroad yards along Boylston Street and was called the "High Spine" because it divided, spine-like, the historic Back Bay to its north from the South End to its south.

This High Spine allowed building without bulldozers. It was a chance for needed development to take place in an area that would not affect the old town that traditionalists wanted so badly to preserve. The High Spine now reaches to the Christian Science complex with its new development, while leaving alone the open space of Copley Square, the Public Garden, and the Common as well as the low-rise Back Bay of Olmsted and Eliot. It allowed Boston to be a new city on the current edge of growth and also a unique one with historic buildings and the brownstone and brick so beloved by tourist and Bostonian alike. It was a master stroke hidden in a clever compromise.

The first development built along this spine was the Prudential Center, and the next was the Hancock Tower. They were followed in time by 111 Huntington, a thirty-six-story glass and steel office building connected to the Prudential Center and its gallery of shops. It is sometimes called "The R2-D2 Building" because of its "droidish" crown, but the tower's space with its sixteen elevators and a location close to the arts and nightlife is in high demand. The High Spine also boasts 500 Boylston Street within Back Bay, but most of its towers are in the financial or theatre districts downtown, or along the waterfront.

All this lay yet ahead when the Hancock rose, covered in a skin of glass that reflected the sky, but also covered in controversy in the 1970s. Built upon the site of Hotel Westminster on the southwestern corner of Copley Square, it was a totally different 790-foot tower that violated all kinds of local code and zoning ordinances. It was too high, it was too big, and its monumental scale simply dwarfed the Boston of Richardson and McKim, making Trinity Church and the Boston Public Library look like miniatures—mere toys on its doorstep—as it appeared to glower down upon them in dismissal of their insignificance from its gargantuan heights.

And the fates were not done with the Hancock tower, nor were the realities of physics and engineering and gravity. Shocking humiliations lay ahead as windows popped out and plummeted to the street on such a scale that, by 1973, one-third of the original double-glazed openings that acted as windows were covered with sheets

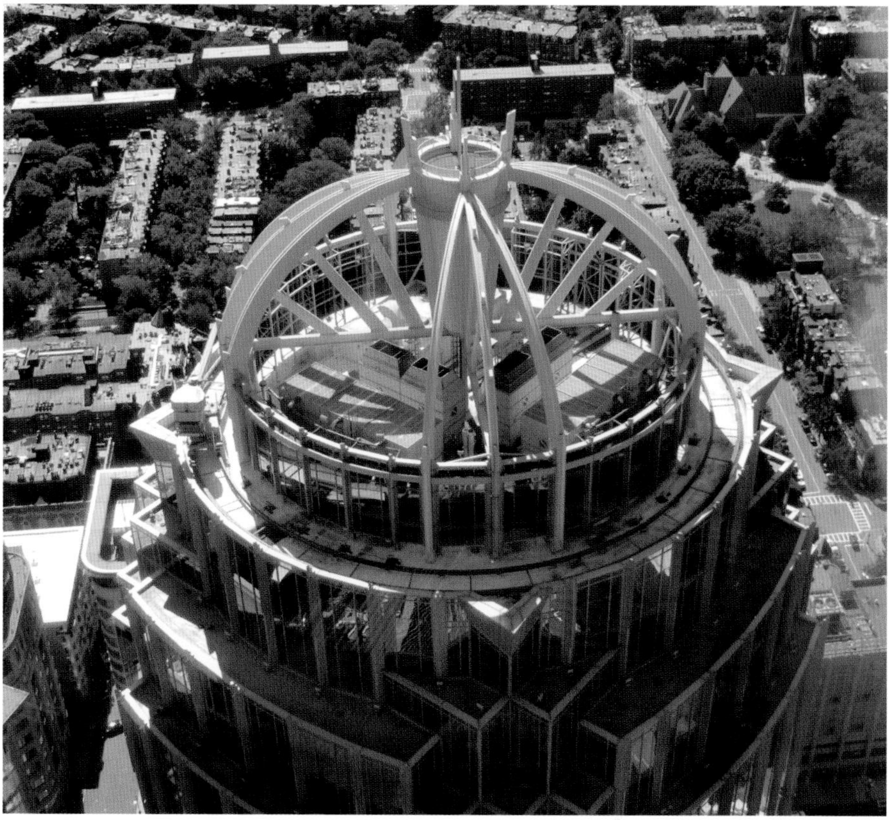

111 HUNTINGTON, VIEW FROM THE PRU
COURTESY AUTHOR

of plywood. Experts gave the reasons to those who cared, but to the public, this once gleaming shaft had become a tower of ridicule, a place to pass at one's peril lest panels of glass pulled by gravity descend upon them. It was mockingly called "The world's tallest plywood building."

It also had a problem with swaying in the wind, giving motion sickness to occupants of its highest floors. Solutions were sought, and once found, all 10,344 windows were replaced by a new type of glass, and mass dampers were placed in the building to reduce its motion in high winds.

Still, the building has its delights that come with its design and construction. The reflective glass acts like a mirror, capturing the reflection of neighboring buildings, like Trinity Church and others as well, with the changing of the seasons and even the time of day. A building like the Trinity, once made a meaningless miniature next to its giant new neighbor, was now part of the reflected glory of Boston's tallest—and proudest—building. The slender shape, the blue sheen of the surface as it almost blends into the sky, make it far less intrusive than would, say, a Prudential building on the same site.

One of the most fascinating times to look at the Hancock is during "blue hour," the period each morning and evening when the sun is well below the horizon and the indirect sunlight diffuses blue rays and makes it prominent while the longer wave red light passes directly into space. Photographers call it "sweet light." The building has a vertical notch on one side that catches the last light of the sky while much of the rest of the glass reflects the midnight blue darkness of the night sky and also the blueness of the morning light.

Admiring the building, author John Updike wrote:

> Now I am aware of loving only the Hancock Tower, which has had its missing panes restored and is again perfect, unoccupied, changeably blue, taking upon itself the insubstantial shapes of clouds, their porcelain gauze, their adamant dreaming. I reflect that all art, all beauty, is reflection.

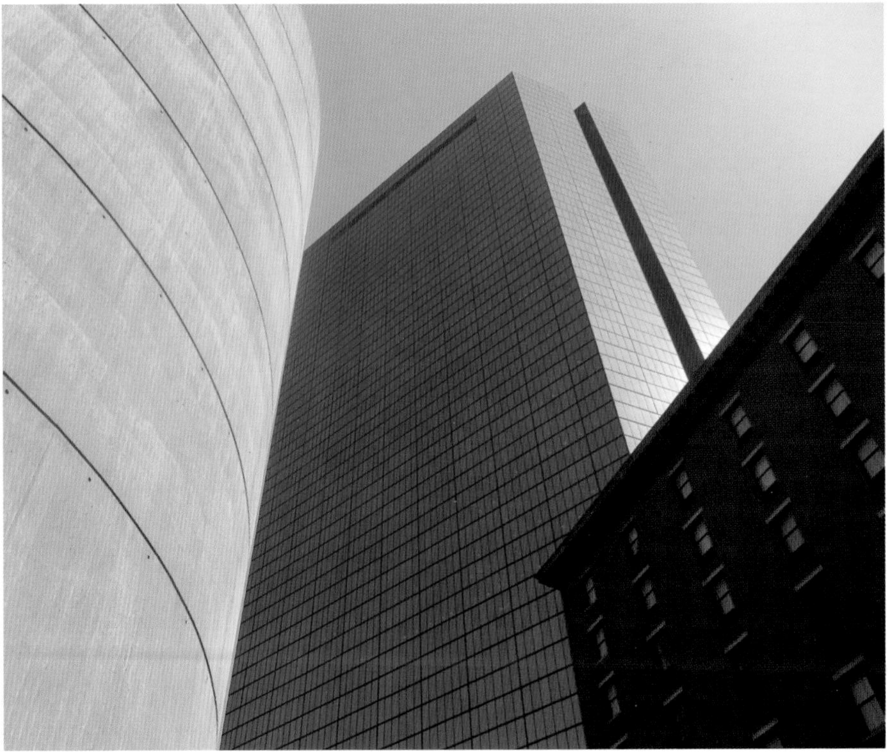

SUN'S BLUE RAYS MAKE HANCOCK STAND OUT
COURTESY AUTHOR

CHAPTER SEVEN

The Avenue of the Arts

Just as the Museum of Fine Arts led the parade of institutions up The Avenue of the Arts (Huntington Avenue) to the left of the Boston Public Library, other institutions fell in step and followed. Most of these were new; most had an artistic or educational bent or purpose.

Two of these were built on the same side of Huntington Avenue, had similar names, and were easily confused. The two stood just up Huntington from Copley Square, one on each side of West Newton Street across from one another, and both were behemoths of buildings. They were rivals as well, and both buildings were built in 1881. However, one had a short life span while the other endured for decades. Some readers will remember one, but few will even have heard of the other.

The New England Manufacturers' and Mechanics' Institute (established as a group in 1879) had formed in order to provide exhibition space for all the manufacturing and mechanical interests in New England, where there were none and was needed. The structure built in 1881 was by far the larger of the two buildings, providing 213,000 square feet of floor space on eight acres with a grand hall of 130,000 square feet. (The rival building had only a 90,000-square foot footprint.)

Governor Long opened the first exhibition in 1881, in company with all the governors, senators, and congressmen, plus mayors of the major cities in New England. During the winter, the New England Fair Building, as it was called, was used as a skating rink, and bicycle and pedestrian contests were also held there. In 1885, it was sold to the Metropolitan Horse Railroad for storage and repairs, but burned to the ground in a huge three-alarm fire in 1886 that caused eight deaths. The original building and its organization never quite turned a profit.

Across the street rose one of the first and most significant buildings on that part of Huntington Avenue. Known as the Mechanics Building, it was built in 1881 on Huntington Avenue at the corner of West Newton Street, not far from Copley Square. It was built by a group called the Massachusetts Charitable Mechanics Association (itself founded in 1795). They were rather like an early union or at least a relief society that helped struggling craftsmen, known that many years ago as "mechanics." Paul Revere, a silversmith, was one of the founders. (John Hancock might have his name on some important buildings of the neighborhood, but Paul, always in haste, got there first with this organization.)

The funds raised by the Association were used to offer relief to the families of mechanics who were in dire straits. They spent money, too, on things like education and libraries and, before Back Bay had been filled in, they came up with an unusual project. The Mechanics Association planned to set up a large building on a pier in the

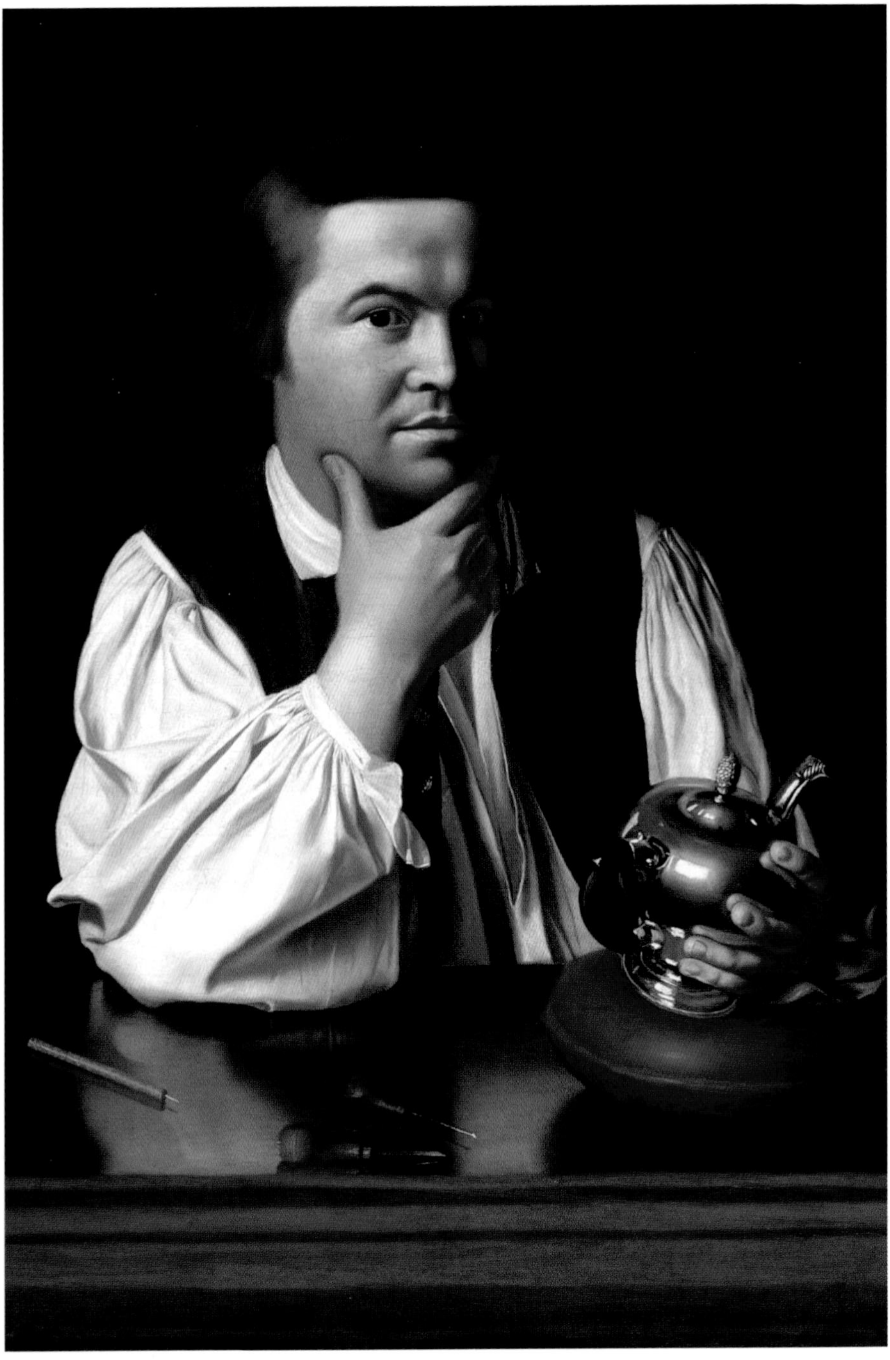

PAUL REVERE, BY COPLEY

middle of the bay. It would serve as their headquarters, but also be used for exhibitions and entertainment. It drew large crowds who went out on the pier, much as they did with other piers in other places, like Atlantic City's Steel Pier.

People called the building "the house on the water," and many went out there to see what was "playing." After the filling in was completed, the pier became West Newton Street and the wide street was first called "Avenue Number VI and later Huntington Avenue. The Bay filled, streets were built and named, and the Mechanics Building stood fast.

As we speak about the development in and around Copley Square, it is useful (but difficult) to remember that all of this land was water just before it was buildings and streets, and that the grand plan we see now had to come about gradually as institutions and buildings and avenues and streets came into existence.

With great religious institutions and later a great library in place at Copley Square, as well as a mighty museum, the Mechanics Building served other purposes. First it was used as the office and exhibition hall for its organization and also as the first amusement pier in the world. The Mechanics Building was a fine example of Victorian architecture. It had seating for 8,000 people and would serve for many decades as the city's location for exhibitions, shows, and fairs. When it was built, it was the only structure on Huntington Avenue beyond the railroad bridge.

And huge it was! If you were to stand at the corner of West Newton Street and Huntington and cast your eye along the length of the building, you would be looking along a frontage of 600 feet; look in the other direction along West Newton, and the walls of the property would rise for another 300 feet. It had a tower at that intersection octagonal in shape, ninety feet in height and forty feet in diameter. You could enter from the sidewalk on Huntington Avenue or from the carriage porch not far to the west, along the brick and stone wall of the building. And fortunate it was that the builders had chosen brick and stone, for the conflagration that felled the building across the street left the Mechanics Building virtually unscathed.

Beyond the tower were the administration building and an exhibition hall, where most people gathered in the spacious galleries and large basement. Next came the grand hall at the western end where 8,000 could gather. Here, too, were fine organs, including the famous Roosevelt organ.

In the administration building were offices, dining rooms upstairs, and another large hall on the third floor. In addition to the Grand Hall, which could seat 8,000 in the deepest end of the building, there was a Paul Revere Hall and two others. Grand Hall had balconies as well. It was so vast that it could hold events like track meets, water skiing, and fly casting. During the New England Sportsmen Show, thousands could watch Red Sox star Ted Williams, "The Splendid Spliter" as the tall thin star was called, compete in this fly-casting contest at appointed times and they could visit exhibits of camping and sports equipment as well as boats.

Someone like Williams brought out the hordes, of course, but once inside Mechanics Building, they were determined to have a good time, and that's what they did. Before cell phones and computer games and all that comes with modern society, it's hard to realize that the ordinary patron of that day enjoyed watching others compete at what

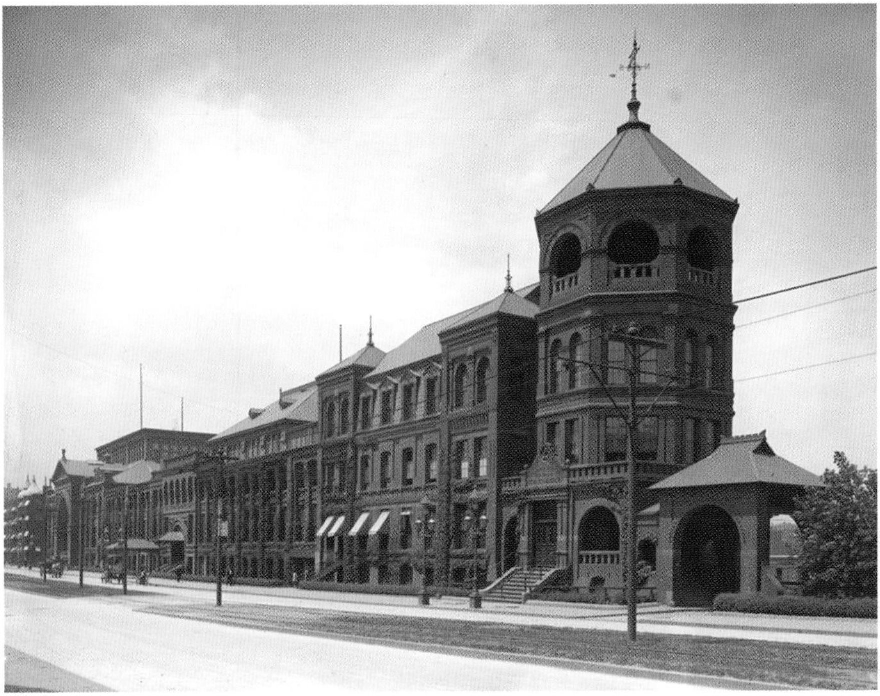

MECHANICS HALL
COURTESY BOSTON PUBLIC LIBRARY

they did best, and enjoyed looking at the equipment and paraphernalia that might allow them, too, to perform in the same areas to the extent of their own capabilities. That was what the Sportman's Show was about, and that was true of other activities also at the Mechanics Building.

Walking through the Mechanics Building was not like walking through T. D. Bank Garden or the Boston Convention and Exhibition Center. It was much older, of course, and you would move from one building to another. It was closer to walking through the old Boston Garden or perhaps Fenway Park. Perhaps the best word to describe each of those buildings is "quirky." But to some, that also made them more interesting than many modern buildings. Nothing about them was bland or vanilla. Roaming through the Mechanics Building was rather like discovering the charms of an antique, especially with its Victorian features like carved moldings and wide wooden arches.

It was also a bit mysterious. It was a huge and unique building with four halls of varying sizes along with smaller rooms and banquet facilities capable of feeding thousands of people at once. Nearest to Copley Square stood the tower, known by Shriners as the Aleppo Temple. That group rented the building for many years, using the offices and also the Grand Hall where they held ceremonies for large groups.

Apart from that were exhibitions connected to science and mechanics—inventions and new products like railway safety signals, a machine that cancelled postage stamps, trade shows, and annual events, like the Spring Flower Show, the Home Show, or the Dog Show. It was always busy, with lots of bookings right up to the end in 1958.

At that time in Boston history, everything was about renewal and the "New" Boston. The time was right for change, and it came in cascades, not as a trickle. The politics of the time called for it, and once it began there seemed no stopping the knocking down and building up of the New Boston.

After decades of blight, stemming from the administrations of James Michael Curley and his steady conflict with the state government who held control over Boston's spending, administrations, beginning especially with that of John Collins, knocked down parts of the city (West End, Scollay Square) and built them up (Government Center and the Prudential Center).

So, the Mechanics Building—historical masterpiece though it may have been—ran afoul of that movement. It was decidedly not new and was impressively in the way. The Prudential Center not only needed the railroad yards of the B&A, but it needed the land south of there, too. And that meant that the Mechanics Building had to go.

"Sidewalk superintendents" could look through protective peek holes in wooden walls and watch the pounding and pulverizing of this ancient lady as she gave way to the movement of the moment, leaving a cavity in her place that would soon be filled by a plaza and shops and apartments surrounding the fifty-two-story tower, a symbol of the new Boston. The Mechanics Building, an architectural gem, a place familiar to so many, was gone forever. One could be proud and nostalgic at the same time, but either way, Copley Square would never be quite the same again.

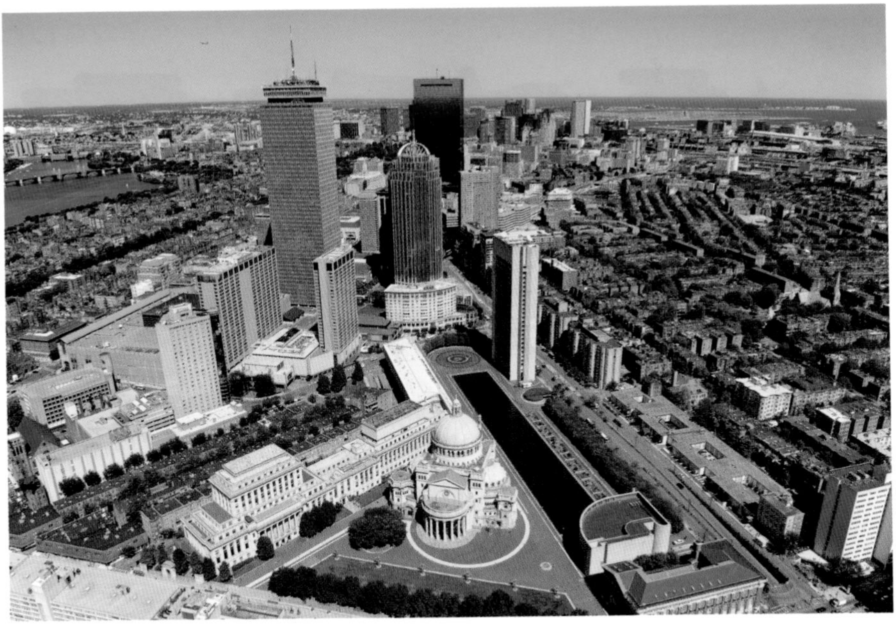

PRUDENTIAL ON SKYLINE
COURTESY AUTHOR

"Hallowed" it might become, "historic" would have its limits. We could keep the part of the past that fit with the future—like Trinity, the Old South and the Library—but other parts would be put to rest, like the Mechanics Building, S. S. Pierce, the old MFA, and the BAA clubhouse. Bostonians, as they always have, flinched and rolled and stood tall again as they moved forward but kept touch with their past.

The Mechanics Building was not the only place where sports activities took place on the Avenue of the Arts. Opposite Mechanics Building was Boston's National League baseball park. From 1871 to 1952, Boston had a National League team, and it played on the south side of the NY, New Haven & Hartford RR tracks through 1914, in one of three locations, all of them called the "South End Grounds."

The team had a number of nicknames. Four members had belonged to the famous Cincinnati Red Stockings who barnstormed the country during 1869-1870, winning most of their games and later called "The First Boys of Summer." The Boston entry called itself the Red Stockings, too, at first. Later they became the "Beaneaters," "Red Caps," "Rustlers," and "Doves." Shortly before leaving the South End they became

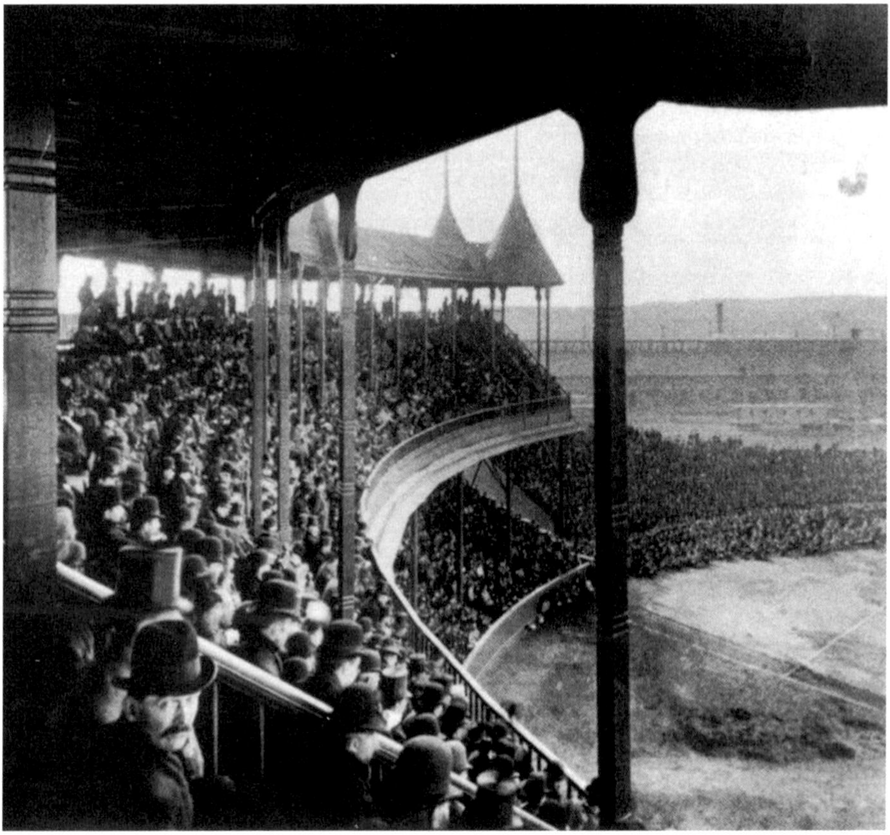

SOUTH END GROUNDS
COURTESY BOSTON PUBLIC LIBRARY

the "Braves." They won the World Series that year (1914) and moved to a new ball park at the present Boston University on the Charles River but only won one pennant there (1948) and moved from there in 1953 to Milwaukee. The team is now in Atlanta.

The first South End Grounds lasted from 1871–1887, replaced by one called the Grand Pavilion, which had a double-decked grandstand, and a "witch's cap" pavilion. It was destroyed in the Great Roxbury Fire of 1894. Ten weeks later, it was replaced by a smaller structure, so small that when the Braves began to win regularly in August 1914, they played their home games at the new Fenway Park.

The third park was located on the northeast corner of Columbus Avenue and Walpole Street just southwest of the current Carter Playground. It was also known over the years as Walpole Street Grounds, or at times Union Baseball Grounds and simply Boston Baseball Grounds. After the Braves left, the park was demolished. It had been located between the Northeastern University's parking lot on Columbus Avenue and Ruggles Station where there is a plaque.

For a time, the National and American League parks were separated only by the slim width of the steel ribbon of railroad tracks. World Series Championships would be won in the two parks on each side of the rails in 1914 and 1915 (as well as in other years of that decade by the Red Sox). The National League park was just across the tracks and south from the Huntington Avenue Grounds, home of the Red Sox before Fenway Park was built in 1912, and next to Northeastern University location of the final game of the first World Series in 1903, won by the Sox over the Pirates, with great help from pitchers Bill Dineen and Cy Young.

To the east end of the National League field—about where the Irvington Street Armory later stood—was an indoor bicycle racetrack, the Irvington Street Oval, where the first Boston Marathon ended. There were also athletic facilities on St. Botolph Street.

This was a unique and interesting part of the Huntington Avenue spreading out—the St. Botolph area. It was somewhat hidden and certainly not well known. The St. Botolph area is a neighborhood that was incubated in the overlooked area between the Back Bay and South End grids of streets and the railroad yards that shaped them. Its major thoroughfare, though a narrow one, was St. Botolph Street, which ran parallel to Huntington from Gainsborough Street east to Harcourt Street. It developed differently from either the Back Bay or the South End, the two areas between which it was sandwiched. Not only were the buildings different, but so was their usage, and even the kinds of people attracted to the small neighborhood were unique. Here was a case of geography and political events shaping history and the development of an area, such that the outcome was a district defined by the railroad tracks, held back by the economics of building upon that filled-in area, and shaped by the small area's ability to avoid being gulped into the maw of either the Back Bay or the South End. Thereby it makes an informative sociological study, one which survives to this day in almost the same form as it found itself in the pre-1900s development.

St. Botolph Street was laid out parallel to Huntington and lots were quickly sold at auction when the district first came on line. When the Mechanics Building was built, it was one of few structures on its side of the B&A tracks. However, during that decade, development reached west to West Chester Park (now Massachusetts Avenue). Along

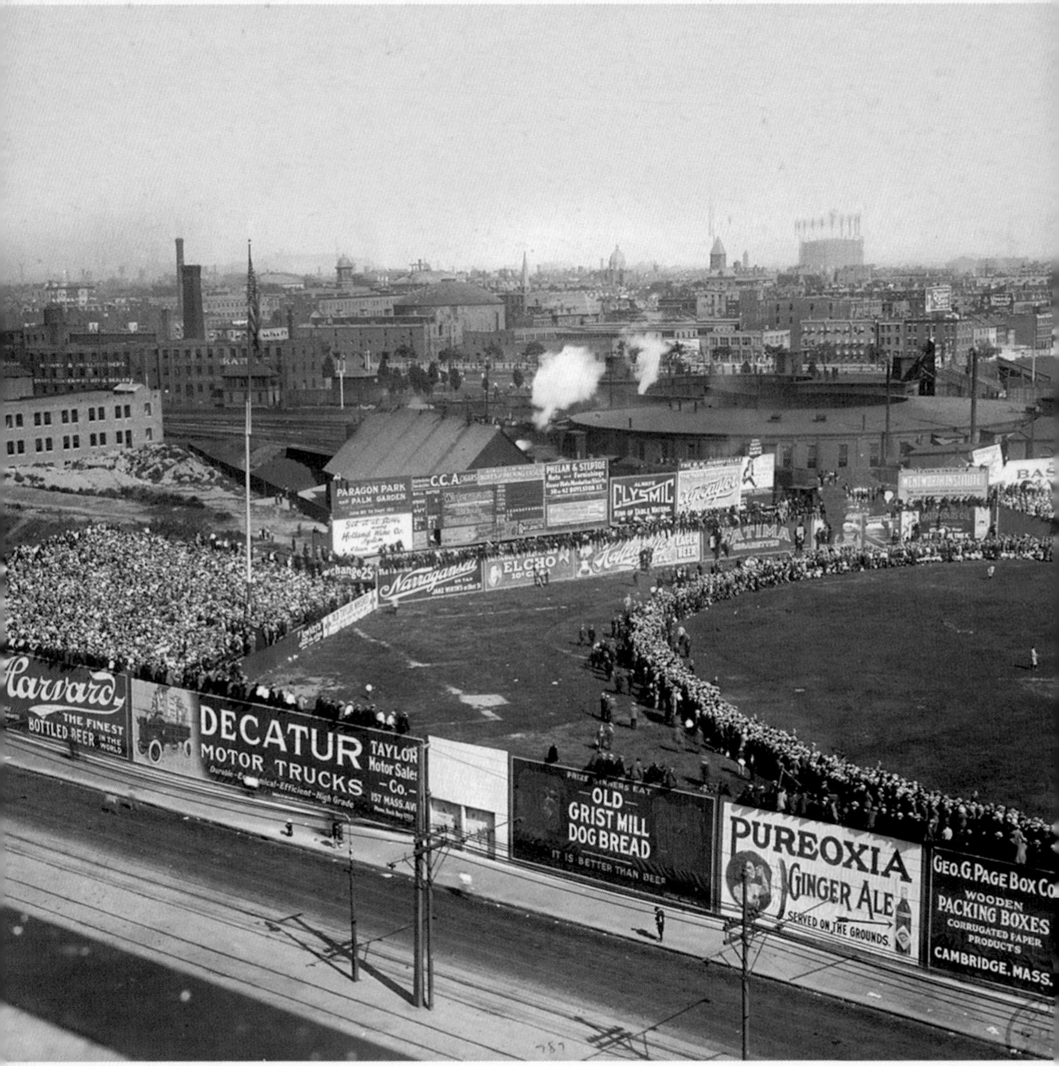
PARAGON PARK
PALM GARDEN
C.C.A.
PHELAN & STEPTOE
CLYSMIC
WENTWORTH INSTITUTE
FATIMA
LAGER BEER
ELCHO
Narragansett
Harvard
THE FINEST
BOTTLED BEER IN THE WORLD
DECATUR
MOTOR TRUCKS
TAYLOR
Motor Sales
-Co.-
157 MASS. AVE
PRIZE WINNERS EAT
OLD
GRIST MILL
DOG BREAD
IT IS BETTER THAN BEEF
PUREOXIA
GINGER ALE
SERVED ON THE GROUNDS.
GEO. G. PAGE BOX CO
WOODEN
PACKING BOXES
CORRUGATED PAPER
PRODUCTS
CAMBRIDGE, MASS.

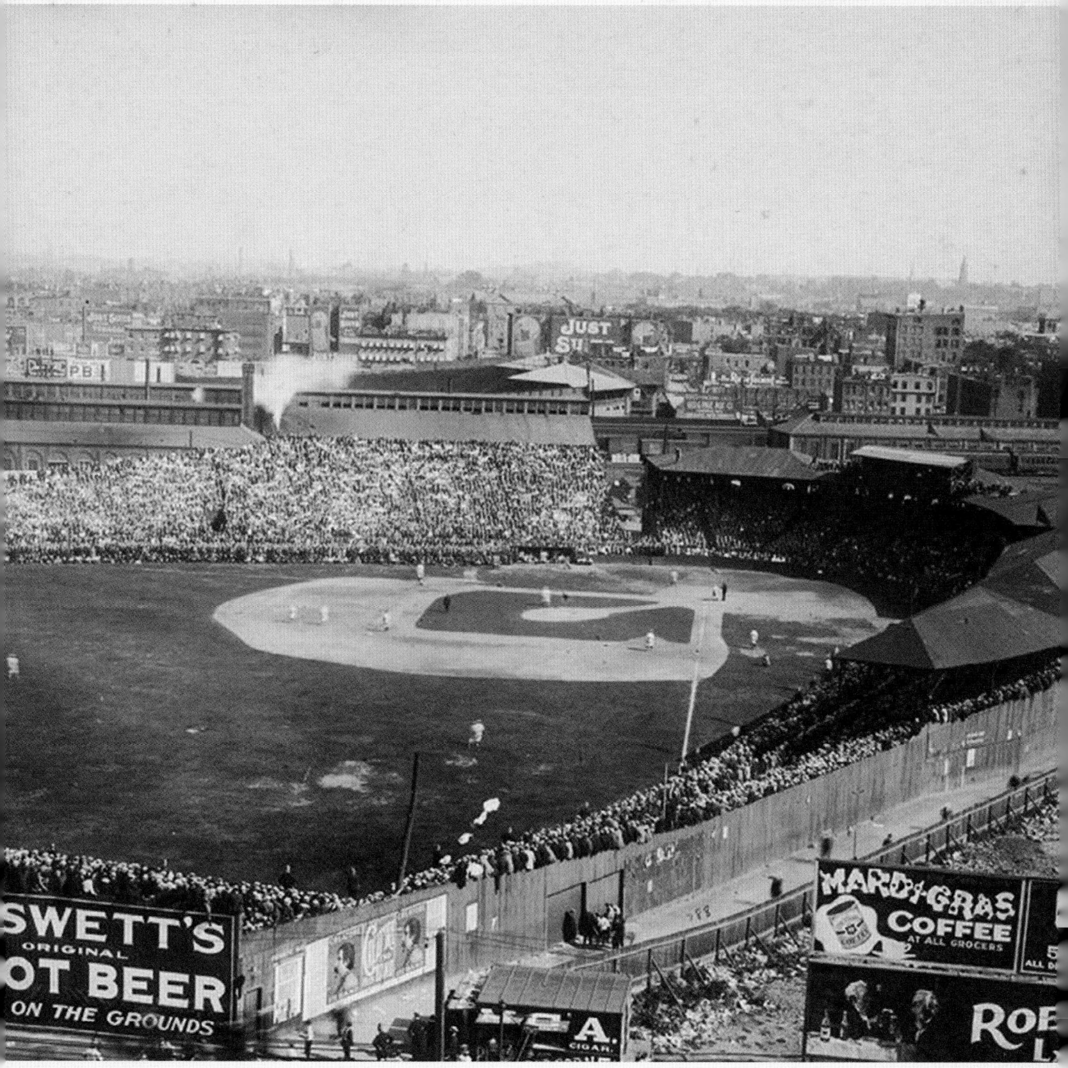

HUNTINGTON AVENUE GROUNDS

this stretch, houses were mostly walk-up apartment buildings of no particular distinction. The St. Botolph neighborhood, on the south side of Huntington, was laid out in 1880, somewhat later than Back Bay. That was because there had been a recession and real estate prices had fallen. Developers wanted to attract at least middle-class buyers and didn't want to sell at prices affordable to the lower classes.

St. Botolph Street was named for the patron saint of Boston, England, for which Boston, itself, had been named. Side streets in this neighborhood are alphabetical and were named for English places or peerages, except for Garrison, named for William Lloyd Garrison, the abolitionist. Often, one side of a street offered town houses while the other was lined with apartment houses, sometimes called "hotels." They were really "French flats" where each floor was sold or rented to one family, a cheaper way to house more people on small lots. These flats had radiator steam heat, gas lighting, coal-fired kitchen stoves, and full baths.

As mentioned, the land was filled in later than that of Back Bay. The main reason that it hadn't been developed earlier was that it was a triangle of territory between the two railroad yards, and that factor would keep it separated (and unique). It was close to many of the attractions of the city, yet not on the path to anywhere else. Thus it became different culturally and economically, with a hint of the Bohemian, rather a mixed use, an area populated by singles and retirees and people out of the mainstream. Haight-Asbury, you may think, but a century ahead of that enclave and hardly as permissive or off-beat. Still . . .

"St. Botolph," if we may call it that also had some unique institutions and industries. By the 1920s, the district had become respectable but not fashionable, and with the advent of streetcars and automobiles, many residents moved to the suburbs and it became a district of lodging houses.

The St. Botolph neighborhood was near Copley Square and the Mechanics Building, but also near athletic sites, such as the ones mentioned, but also the YMCA (then at Berkeley and Boylston), the Allen Gymnasium for women and children at St. Botolph and Garrison, and a Turkish bath near that gym. Allen Gym later became the Boston Music Society. Can't you just envision it as an area where young working class people (perhaps women) could avail themselves of athletic and artistic opportunities while working in an area removed only slightly from the business district? As a potential realtor, you no doubt would envision quick sales to people of this ilk—and you'd be right.

There was also light industry on this street. Harcourt Bindery, which bind valuable books to order, was famous for its craftsmanship as was Connick Stained Glass Studio, which has made thousands of stained glass windows, many of them for churches, including those of St. Patrick's Cathedral in New York. There have also been many artists' studios and some hotels that catered to retired people and singles. Both are located on Harcourt Street in the Franklin Building.

There is also a second stained glass manufacturer on St. Botolph Street (O'Duggan's), and there are schools in the neighborhood that concentrate on teaching various crafts, such as the Lowell School of Design and the George Vesper School of Art. Also on St. Botolph Street was Boston Arena (now Mathews Arena), built in 1911, though separated from the neighborhood by Massachusetts Avenue.

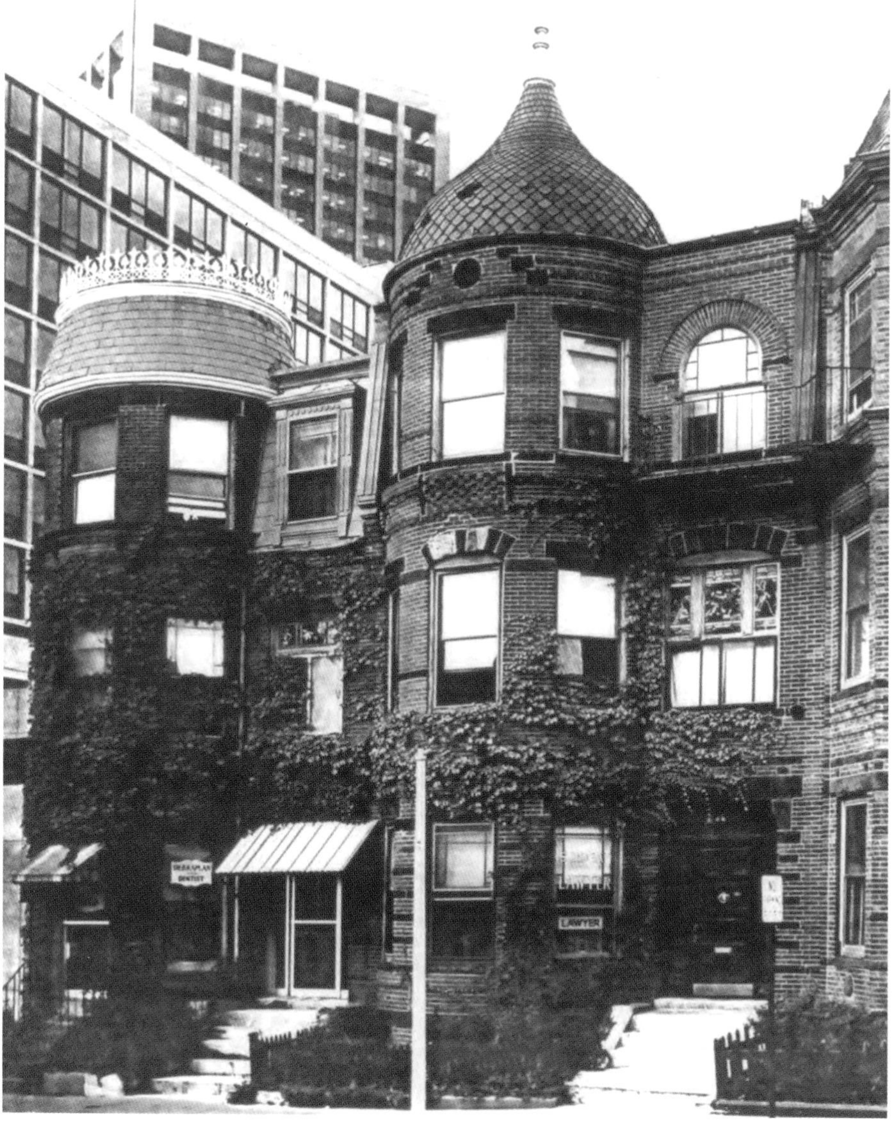

ST. BOTOLPH STREET NEIGHBORHOOD
COURTESY BOSTON LANDMARKS COMMISSION

There were medical establishments in the area as well. Harvard Medical School stood where the Boston Public Library's Johnson Building is now before moving to the Longwood area. The Massachusetts College of Pharmacy also wound up on Longwood Avenue, but was first located on Garrison Street near St. Botolph. Founded as the Massachusetts College of Pharmacy in 1823 by fourteen pharmacists, what is now MCPHS University is the oldest institution of higher education in Boston. In 2002, The Forsyth School for Dental Hygienists was also acquired and incorporated into the college, housing the school's Dental Hygiene program. Children's Hospital was on Huntington at Gainsborough before moving farther west to Longwood as well. Across the street was the Hospital for Women, which also moved.

Music and things musical hovered about the section near Huntington and Massachusetts Avenue that was often called "Uptown." Real estate was yet relatively cheap along the Avenue of the Arts, and plots of land were purchased by institutions promoting the arts and education, a theme that would continue west along the avenue and into the Back Bay Fens, later to be joined by those involving medicine in the Longwood area just beyond.

In the field of music, the Boston Symphony Orchestra built Symphony Hall in 1900, designed by McKim, Mead, and White who had also designed the Boston Public Library. The founder of the symphony was Henry Higginson, who was also a big financial supporter. He wanted to bring an acoustically excellent facility to Boston and hired a Harvard physicist to ensure that he got one. He did, and Henry was quite a cheerleader in rallying the populace to enjoy and support the orchestra. He was so successful that the subscriptions became hard to get, and were heirlooms in families who passed them on to the next generation. The Boston Pops sprang from the Symphony and played lighter fare, becoming known for its summer concerts on the esplanade and the facility in the Berkshires known as Tanglewood.

Higginson, a New Yorker by birth, nonetheless had some of the qualities of a Boston Brahim, especially his sense of *noblesse oblige*, his willingness to spend his fortune in support of the arts, and particularly the symphony.

Another musical institution in that area was the New England Conservatory, which moved from the South End to Huntington Avenue two years later.

Jordan Hall was built next to that, named for Eban Jordan, son of the founder of Jordan Marsh. Jordan was a benefactor of that building and of the Boston Opera House that stood across the street until 1958.

Chickering, famous piano makers, decided to move from Tremont Street in the South End and built a hall for chamber music near Huntington and Massachusetts Avenue. It soon became famous. It may have been the famed impresario P. T. Barnum who made Chickering famous. In 1850, Barnum arranged for a national tour by the famed singer Jenny Lind, the "Swedish Nightingale," a tour that would begin in Boston and that would use a Chickering grand piano designed especially for the tour. The piano was used in all ninety-three performances and must have made beautiful music, because at the end of the tour, Lind married Otto Goldschmidt, who had played it for each of those concerts.

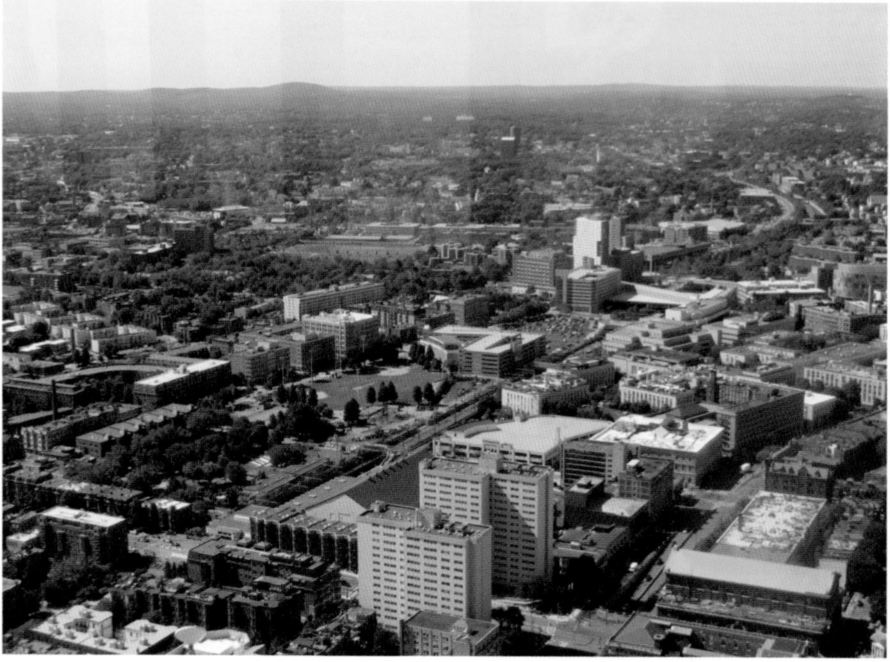

HUNTINGTON AVENUE WITH SYMPHONY HALL IN FOREGROUND (GREEN ROOF)

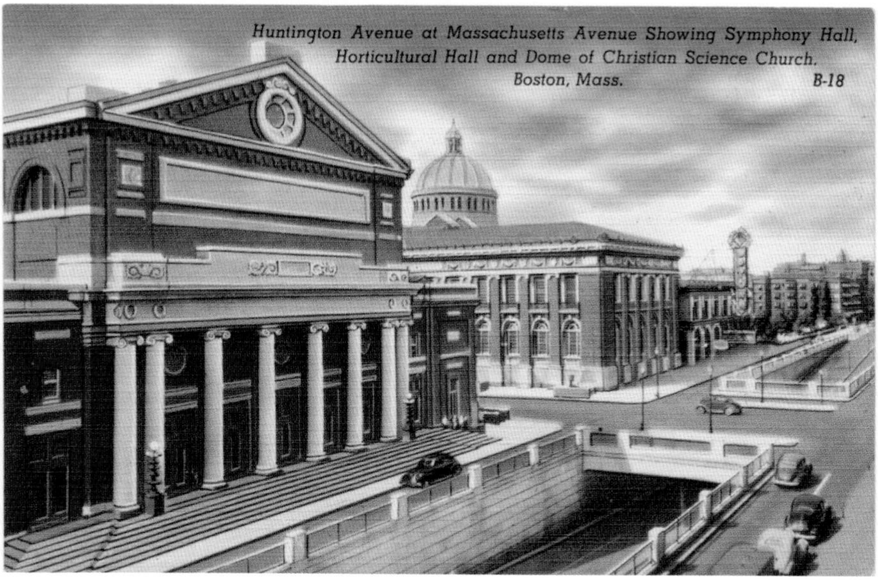

SYMPHONY HALL AND HORTICULTURAL HALL POSTCARD

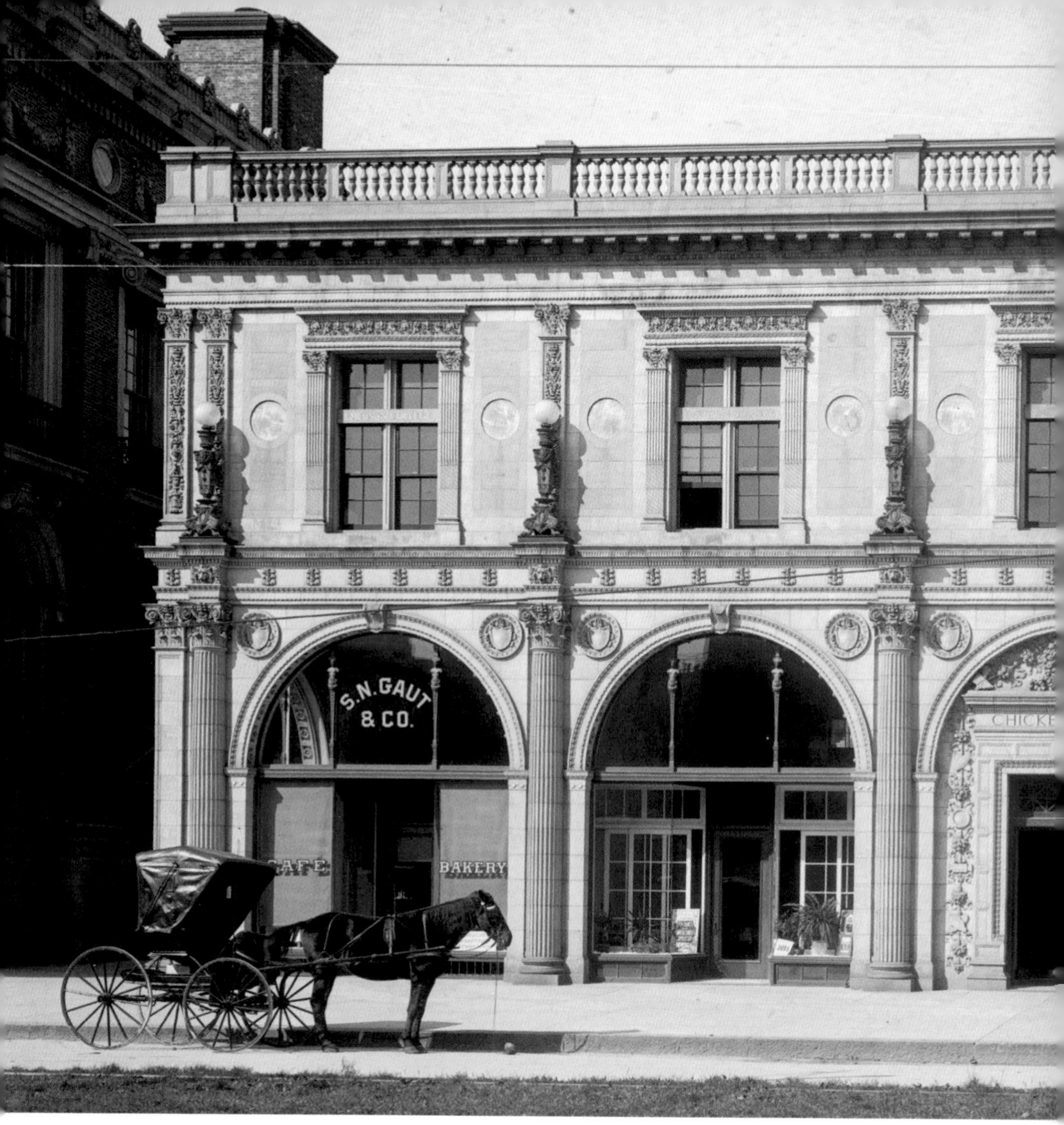

As a side, when the tour opened in New York, a recent immigrant from Germany managed to get a ticket and raced into the hall before anyone else, so that he could examine the piano, which had more interest for him than the singer. He spent so much time looking at the works of Chickering that he had to be led away so that the concert could begin. Two years later, he began his own company making excellent pianos. His name was Henry Steinway.

In 1911, Chickering Hall was replaced by the St. James Theatre, a playhouse that later became the Uptown Theatre, a movie house.

Next door was Horticultural Hall, built on land purchased and built upon in 1901 by the Massachusetts Horticultural Society, its third building. At its opening in 1901 (an opening that was ten days in length) thousands of members and visitors filled the hall, along with the fragrances and presence of azaleas, amaryllises, geraniums, gloxinias,

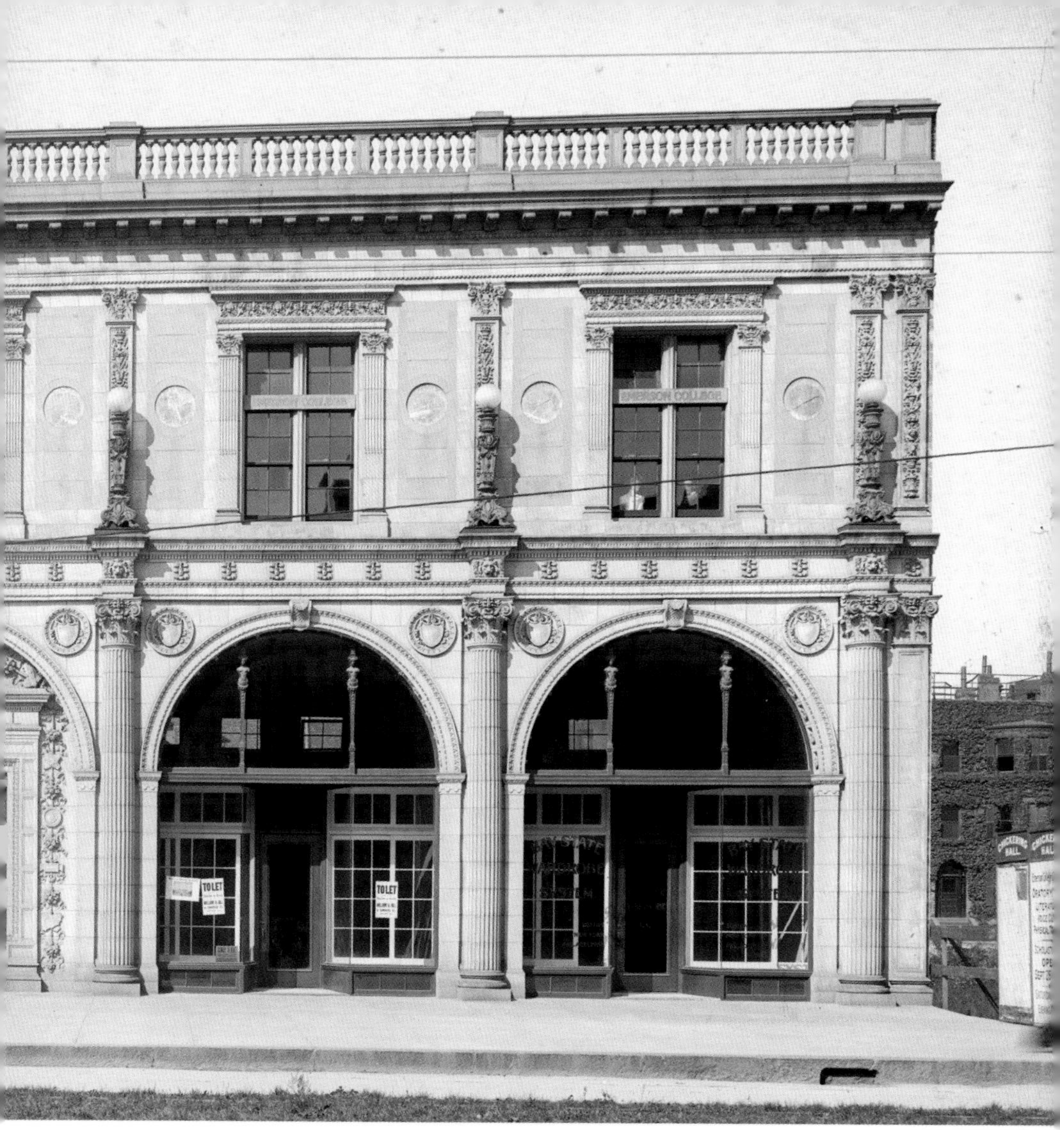

CHICKERING HALL, C. 1900
COURTESY DETROIT PUBLISHING

rhododendrons, jasmine, trumpet lilies, palms, wisteria, and a rare collection of 1,000 orchids. (The building was sold to the Christian Science Church in 1992.)

Also uptown is the Christian Science Center that has for years been set back from Huntington Avenue, occupying side streets like Falmouth and Norway. Its main building has been its temple, the first building of which was erected in 1894, but since evolving into seven structures. The huge, impressive, domed building that immediately catches the eye, came later, erected of granite and capable of seating 11,000 people. It reaches to 220 feet in height and is topped by a magnificent classical dome that has a chime of bells rung regularly with a pleasing tone. It is called The First Church of Christ, Scientists, or the Mother Church, endowed by its founder Mary Baker Eddy.

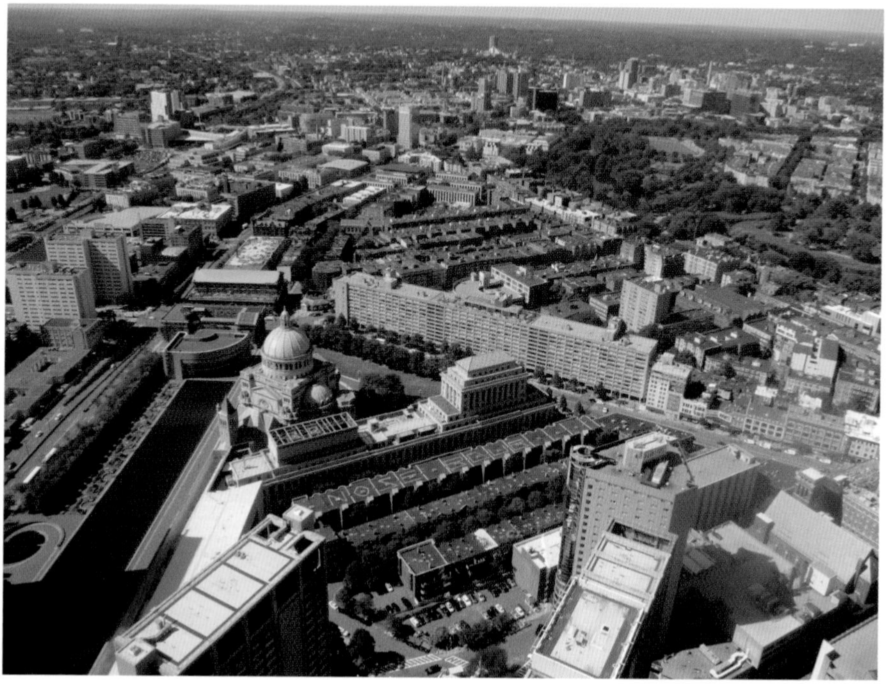

CHRISTIAN SCIENCE CENTER AND CHURCH
COURTESY AUTHOR

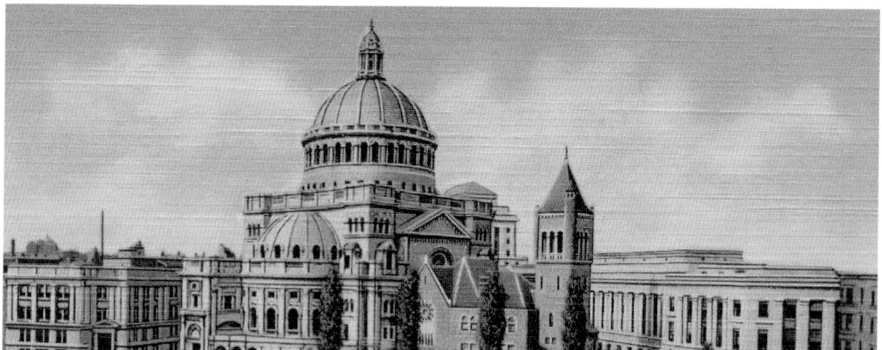

CHRISTIAN SCIENCE PUBLISHING SOCIETY POSTCARD

The eleven-story building that was once the Christian Science Publishing Society, a building with classical columns built in 1932, now houses the Marry Baker Eddy Library. By far the best-known and most attractive feature in this building (and perhaps in the whole center) is its mapparium. It is a hollowed-out globe of stained glass, with a glass bridge through its center. It allows visitors to walk through the center of the world whose map shows it as it was when the three-story globe was built.

This is now part of a fourteen-acre plaza designed in the 1960s by the architectural firm of I. M. Pei, along Huntington Avenue. It includes an administration building, a colonnade, reflecting pool, Reflection Hall, and a fountain. It has become a popular tourist attraction. While we speak of reflection, consider that this new open space provides a restatement or continuation of other such spaces, like Copley Square.

The long reflecting pool—ringed by modernist office buildings—is somewhat similar to the Government Center urban renewal project. But it adds new buildings of an attractive sort to the city and offers a new gathering space for activities.

Beyond the uptown crossing of Huntington and Massachusetts Avenue, the Avenue of the Arts welcomed bastions of Botonia such as the Opera House, Northeastern University, the Museum of Fine Arts, the Fenway, and the Longwood Medical Area.

The Opera House was, unfortunately, an institution fated to have a limited stay. It was erected after a long delay in 1909, benefited mainly by contributions from Eban Jordan, who did much for the arts in Boston. The Boston Opera Company provided the interior decorations for the building, which stood just west of Symphony Hall and the New England Conservatory of Music. It was described as a "perfect jewel-box of an opera house" at its opening of a performance of La Gioconda. When the BOC went bankrupt after six years, other local companies used it as did the Metropolitan Opera on a regular basis.

But the building and its business could not sustain themselves. Boston never became a great opera town. During the years of the 1930s and 1940s, the building fell into disuse and became shabby as well. Northeastern asked that it be demolished and, acting on its behalf, the Boston Redevelopent Authority did so, despite protests and demonstrations from opera lovers. Ironically, the building that had been declared "unsafe" withstood the efforts of two demolition companies to bring it down, and a larger wrecking derrick had to be procured to take down the walls.

Northeastern University appeared during that same turn-of-the-century era, holding its first classes in 1898 at the Huntington Avenue YMCA and known as the "Evening Institute for Younger Men." Adjacent to Northeastern and to its east, the Huntington YMCA, founded in 1912, was the first "Y" in an American city. One of its early functions was to provide homes to recent immigrants and sailors. The building, renovated in 2014, has long been a fixture on its site with the easily-recognizable, lit sign on its roof.

In addition to Northeastern, Huntington Avenue is the setting for Wentworth Institute of Technology at the intersection with Ruggles Street. A Boston businessman, Artioch Wentworth left an estate of $7 million, in 1903, to found such a school in Boston. The school expanded in the 1980s by acquiring the Ira Allen School and Boston Trade High School. Wentworh is one of six institutions of higher learning known collectively as the Colleges of the Fenway.

CHAPTER EIGHT

Back Bay Fens

It's fair to say that the people who ran Boston in the final quarter of the nineteenth century and on into the twentieth had a fair amount of vision as well as civic-mindedness. They had the same human frailties and faults as people have now, but we'd be well-served to have such leaders today.

Their problems were different, of course. They weren't troubled by Marathon bombers or drug dealers or people driving wildly with cell phones in their hands, bullying on the Internet, or troubles in the Middle East. Their problems were more fundamental. They had to worry about finding living space for all their people and ways to build solid ground where there had been marshland and water. Take your choice among the problems, but we must extend kudos for the attitudes of those times.

Having found a way to fill in land and build a new neighborhood in the Back Bay, while relieving to some extent the noxious odors and accompanying pestilence of the tidal mudflats, they were still not free from flooding, particularly in the lands just west of Back Bay where two streams, the Muddy River and Stony Brook, emptied their waters onto the flatlands of the Back Bay Fens and Roxbury where there had been severe flooding in 1873, despite putting these streams into culverts.

Sir Isaac Newton first formalized the axiom that for every action there's an opposite and equal reaction. In matters outside physics, the reaction may not be quite so equal, but with the filling of the Back Bay, a new problem did arise. The water in the Back Bay didn't just disappear when the land was filled in. It had to go somewhere else, especially during the rainy season. The streams that flowed into the Back Bay waters would now pose a danger of flooding onto the dry land during peak times of rainfall or melting.

The Muddy River and Stony Brook did overflow, and in as early as 1875, there was a proposal to make a storm water park west of Massachusetts Avenue to alleviate flooding or the potential of flooding. This area—the storm water park—would become the Back Bay Fens.

That vision we spoke of can sometimes be slowly acquired by learning from experience, and that happened in Boston where conservative and parochial attitudes were in place even then. Boston needed a savior, one knowledgeable about engineering and landscape management, hopefully one who could turn structural problems into urban greenery that would also provide solutions to the flooding problems. They had such a person close at hand, even though he was—gasp—in New York. Frederick Law Olmsted had been working in New York where he had designed Central Park and Prospect Park, two of his most fabled achievements.

Rather than signing up Olmsted at once, though, a three-man commission was formed in 1875, due to public pressure to develop a park system for the city. The commissioners knew about Olmsted's reputation and consulted him, but didn't come to an agreement with him right away. The Park Commission had been chosen after five years of discussion about the drainage problem in the Back Bay and the Fens in particular, so there had been no hurrying to this point.

The legislature of Massachusetts had given its mandate and the people of Boston, in a referendum, had approved going forward but steps to construct a park in the fens to improve drainage had been minimal and ineffective. The city had constructed a dam of rock-fill in the sluiceways to minimize flooding, but this created a stagnant pond that filled with sewage from the two streams and caused severe flooding during heavy rains or the backing up of high tides from the Charles.

In 1877, the city council authorized the acquisition of land and the laying out of a park in the unimproved portion of Back Bay. (This was the area west of today's Massachusetts Avenue and to the tidal flats south of Charlesgate.)

The Back Bay Fens was a noxious tidal swamp and creek left over from the times when the whole Back Bay was a shallow body of salt water. The sewage and swamp water that infiltrated the area created a serious health problem as well as a foul stench.

And, of course, another problem was the matter of flood control. Thousands of surrounding acres were drained by those two previously mentioned streams, and they tended to flood badly. Before the park could be constructed, the flooding and tidal fluctuations had to be eliminated.

What to do? The commission decided to hold a competition in order to choose a design for the area, and they asked Olmsted to judge the entries, since he was in the neighborhood. We don't know whether they realized it, but they were really asking Olmsted to look at these designs in the light of what he knew should be done. So, in effect, his own ideas were the standard against which the others would be judged.

He found that none of the plans addressed the major problem of flooding and so the winning design was never used. Instead, Olmsted was asked to work on it. They also wanted him to develop plans for a park system. He began and the assistants in his firm attacked the Fens part of his project in 1878, devising a plan that would solve the drainage problem as well as transforming the Back Bay area, or the Fens as he liked to call it, into a public park.

Olmsted submitted a plan with the help of his son, John C. Olmsted, called Proposed Improvement for Back Bay, and he then met with the city engineer and the superintendent of sewers. Those two men had in mind building a storage dam made of masonry to hold the overflow of the Muddy River, but Olmsted talked them out of it. On a grand scale, the Hoover Dam creates Lake Meade, an immense reservoir. Even on a small scale, this had no appeal for Olmsted. He wanted whatever work they did to be aesthetically pleasing and within the budget.

The idea proposed in Olmsted's report was to build a salt marsh park with sanitary improvements. He would do this in several steps beginning with the building of tidal gates at Charlesgate where the Fens flowed into the Charles River. Then he intercepted

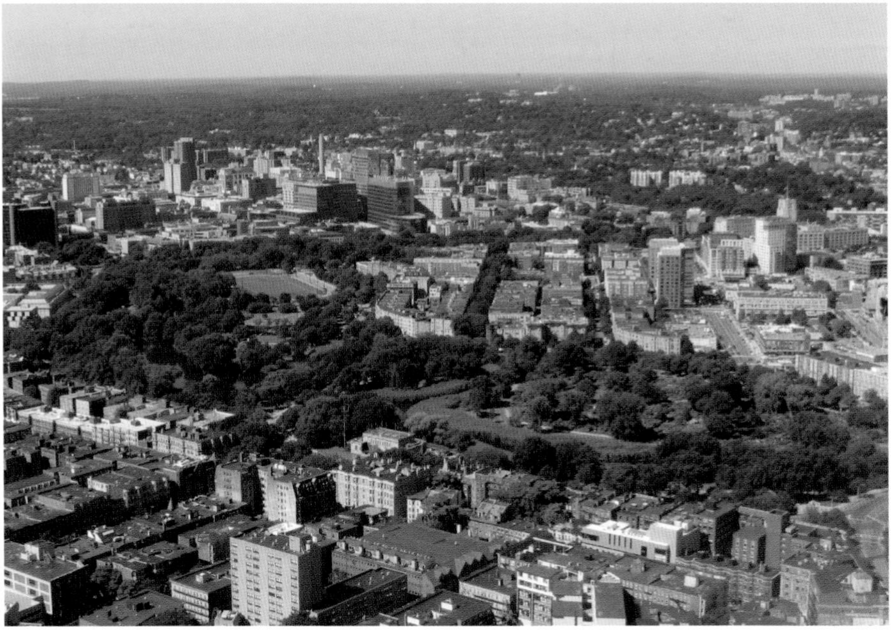

BACK BAY FENS
COURTESY AUTHOR

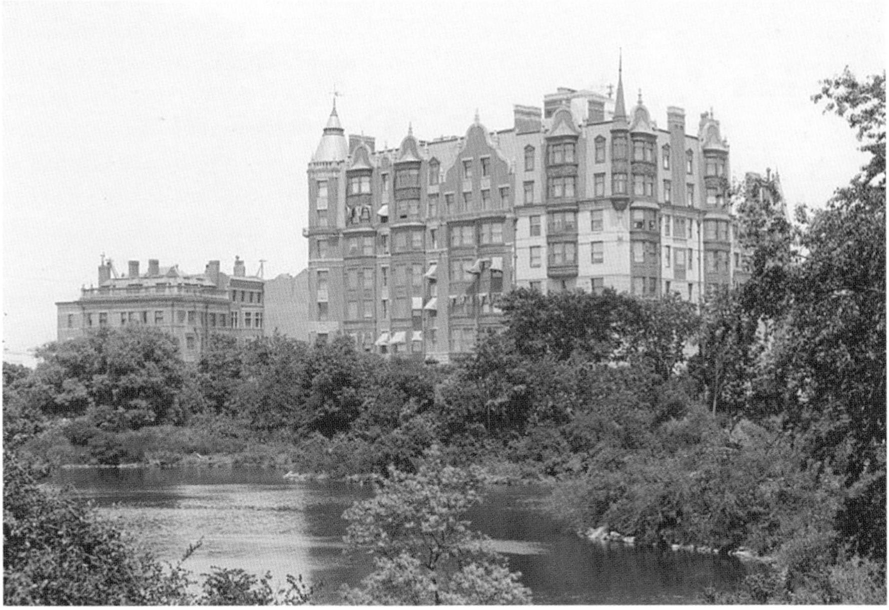

CHARLESGATE
COURTESY LIBRARY OF CONGRESS

the sewage with a large conduit that provided a run-off for both streams to run into the Charles. The tidal flow of salt water would be regulated.

He planned to let the Fens serve as a storage basin for excess water, so he planted vegetation that could withstand the water and continue to live. Then he filled in the land around the conduit. His project would be a big one, but it wouldn't look that way. It would look like ... a park!

His park had six approaches, which he called entrances, as well as paths for walking or riding horses and streets on both sides of the brook with bridges between them. Olmsted called it Back Bay Fens from a British term for a low, flat place, and the bridges of stone built from place to place across the stream, evoked a rural British look.

Muddy River approached the Fens from Jamaica Plain and Stony Brook from West Roxbury. Both emptied into the Charles at Charlesgate. The valley of Stony Brook, was the location of the tracks of the Boston & Providence RR. The flooding of the brook had cost the city dearly in flood control, and had caused the worst flood of all time in the city.

Improved culverts were built from Roxbury Crossing to the Muddy River, crossing under Huntington Avenue near today's Museum of Fine Arts. (Two stone buildings that contain valves remain. They are located behind the museum.) Upstream, channels were built toward Forest Hills to contain flooding in that area. Olmsted's conduit ran from this gatehouse to the Charles River, and another was made for the Muddy River.

Olmsted's Fens had pools and mudflats, marshes that were fully visible and some that were not. The soil itself was spongy. Olmsted didn't expect or want the waters of the Fens to be used by visitors. He wanted people to stay on the walks atop the banks. He placed plantings between the walks and the water to act as a kind of "fence." He said that the water would meander like a salt creek on the edge of a seaside meadow. But even though it would rise and fall with the tides, it wouldn't be enough to flood or to expose the mudflats with all their disagreeableness.

None of this was easy. In fact, most of it had never been done before—not in Boston and not anywhere else. This was a sizable space, and in some parts he had to dredge, while in others he had to fill—quite a balancing act, and far different than in Back Bay where they just dumped soil and smoothed it out. Piece of cake. Or at least a piece of sponge cake. Olmsted's plan required grading to specific contours, and to do this correctly, derricks had to be constructed that would do this specific job. Then they had to be floated out in the marshes to dig and fill. (Some of that "fill" was really people's garbage.)

Many things about Olmsted's work brought exclamation, and the Back Bay Fens was one of them. Putting a salt marsh inside a city would be novel indeed, but Olmsted pointed out that the marsh was appropriate because of the original and current conditions.

The plan proposed by Olmsted would look rather like the original landscape. But it would be a living system and it would take a lot of thought and a lot of work before it would look good enough to be part of a park system—a system that would be Olmsted's "Emerald Necklace." This would be no ordinary park or even a series of parks. He called it the "Green Ribbon," and that was perhaps a good name for it. It was a series of green spaces, extending from Boston Common across to the Public Garden and up the Commonwealth Avenue mall to Charlesgate and the Fens.

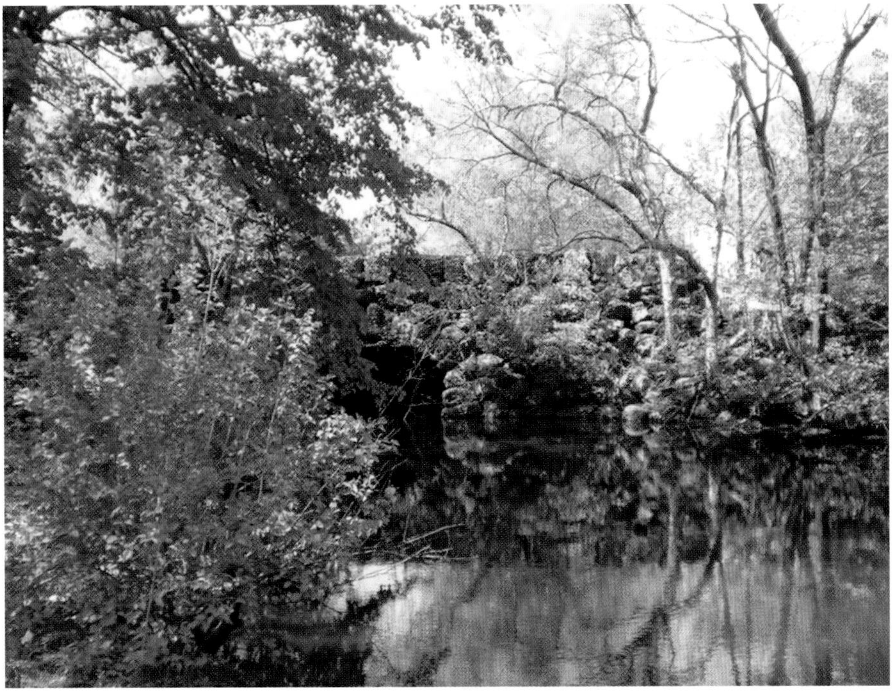

STONE BRIDGE, BACK BAY FENS

From there it extended out the Riverway to Brookline and on through a series of parks and green spaces to Jamaica Pond. The next park in the link would be the Arnold Arboretum and then Franklin Park. These were not that close, but Olmsted "connected" them by turning roads into parkways—making them wider and adding trees with lots of leaves. Olmsted's work showed vision and was based upon his unparalleled experience, and remains exemplary to this day. No other city has ever included such a jewel.

It took until 1895 to complete everything in the Fens, and when it was done, it was flushed twice a day by brackish tidewater. However, in 1910, a dam was built near the mouth of the Charles at Craigie Bridge where the Museum of Science sits now. That dam turned the Fens into a freshwater area. With the completion of his park, the area no longer flooded, but instead took the overflow from Muddy River and Stony Brook (as well as overflows from sewers and storm drains) and deposited it safely in the Charles.

Land in the center of the Fens was appropriated for the Museum of Fine Arts, which occupied its new building on Huntington Avenue in 1909. The Muddy River ran behind this land, and the classical building changed the fens from simply a landscape to a background for the structures on each side of it. One did not feel so much a part of a recreational area as of a visual one. Strolling through it, one could imagine himself providing human scale to a memorable postcard. As time went by, the Fens was less a pastoral greenery than an inner-city park overshadowed by buildings with high-rises a short distance away.

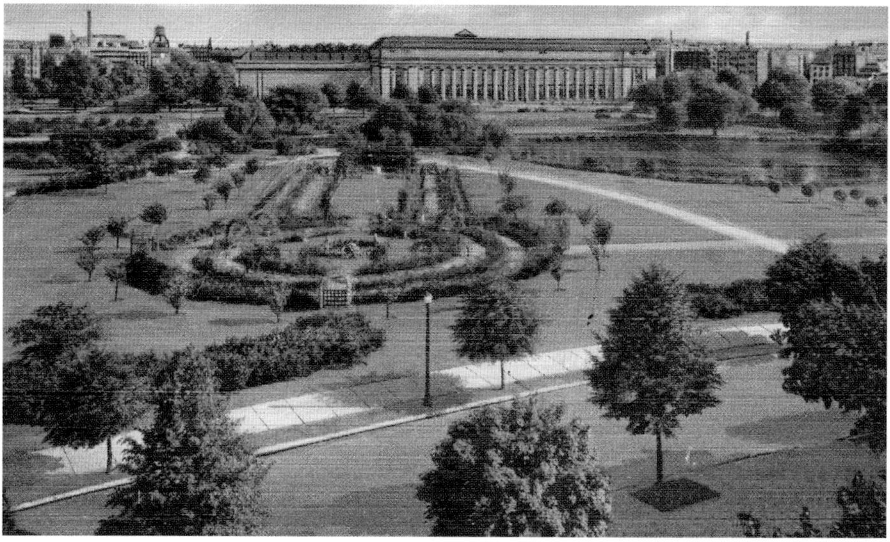

MUSEUM OF FINE ARTS FROM BACK BAY FENS POSTCARD

Today, the Fenway has changed greatly from the days of fens-building. No longer is it a marshy area used as a temporary storage basin for run-off water. The Fenway is now the home of many activities, from baseball to education. Much of what Olmsted designed has been overshadowed by highways and high-rises. But the green nucleus remains like a verdant oasis in a macadam-bound cityscape. There are apartment buildings on both sides, along with cultural institutions like the Museum of Fine Arts, the Isabella Stewart Gardner Museum, the Massachusetts Historical Society, and also educational institutions like Simmons, Emmanuel, Northeastern, and Wheelock. Fenway Park, built in 1912 and named for the area, is only a few blocks away, its light towers easily visible. There is also statuary, a Memorial Rose Garden, and the nation's first "victory garden," created way back in 1911.

One of Olmsted's "entrances" to the Fens was at Evans Way and Huntington Avenue. At that time, one could see southwest to Parker Street and the hills of Roxbury. The Boston Normal School occupied the site in 1872, along with Girls' High School and Girls' Latin School (both of which later relocated). The Normal School eventually evolved into the State College at Boston, and more recently the building became part of the Massachusetts College of Art and Design (called MassArt). It is one of the oldest art schools in the country (1873) and the only publicly funded free-standing art school in the US.

Next door to that is the Gardner Museum, then come Simmons and Emanuel Colleges. Across Brookline Avenue, where the Fenway becomes the Riverway, is Wheelock College a college for training teachers of young children. Also in that section between the Riverway and Brookline Avenue and opposite Beth Israel Hospital, is the

Winsor School. Mary Pickard Winsor founded it, at first as a six-month school for only her aunt's daughter and her friends. Mary Windsor had some credentials, having taught for a while at her mother's school in Winchester. The school began in a private home on Beacon Hill with eight young girls and grew into the school that bears her name. As of 1895, its graduates had begun to attend college, and today the grades taught run from five to twelve. In earlier times, it was known simply as "Miss Winsor's School" and it operated in a number of places until a group of parents asked her to direct a school that they'd planned to build. It would stand out from similar schools by having special advantages, like good light and ventilation, fire-proof construction, and the taking of sanitary precautions.

They bought land on the Fenway where a school was built with a library, science laboratories, art studios, and a gymnasium, and swimming tank. The school was named for her at the request of her students and alumnae. The school's motto was suggested by President Eliot of Harvard: "A sound mind in a sound body." The final graduating class at the school on Beacon Street presented the school with a lamp that has been since lit at every opening day and graduation. Winsor continued as director until 1922, preparing women to be self-sufficient and self-supporting.

A tall, yellow sandstone tower of 200 feet stands on the opposite side of Park Drive at the intersection of Brookline Avenue and Boylston Street. This is the Landmark Center, built in 1929 by Sears, Roebuck and Co. The art moderne building served as a retail and mail-order center that caused so much excitement that extra streetcars were put on to handle the opening crowds. It brought 1,200 new jobs, and a post office branch was opened inside the building to handle the mail order business.

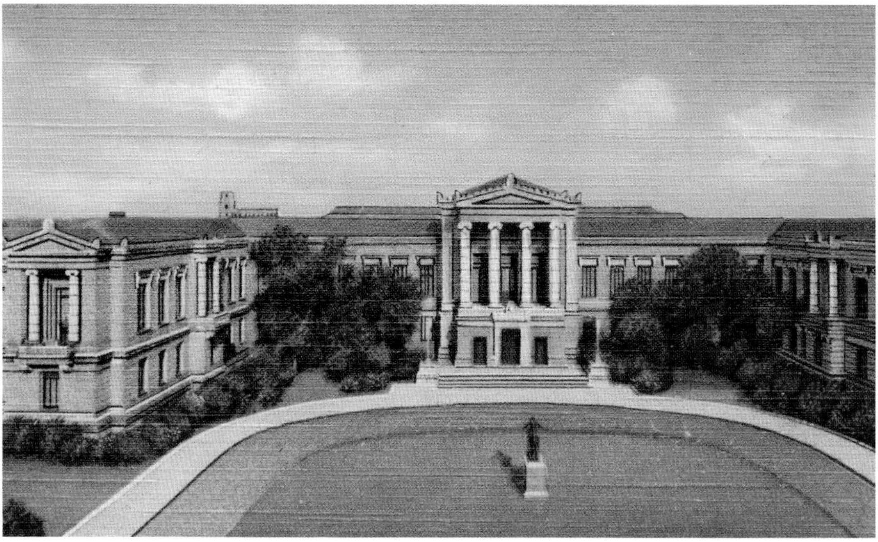

MFA FROM HUNTINGTON AVENUE

It is now a National Landmark. The Muddy River runs in a culvert beneath its parking lot and provides a border between Boston and Brookline. At this point, the Riverway runs west beyond Brookline Village, where there is one of several stone bridges designed by H. H. Richardson. Then there are a series of parks and ponds leading to Jamaica Pond. These were the last parts of the Emerald Necklace to be completed.

The Riverway appears to be a gladed, natural area that escaped development, but it's entirely man-made, as part of the Emerald Necklace. Olmsted had not been asked to design a park for this area, but suggested it as a continuation of his improvements in the Fens. It had become a source of mosquitoes and disease, and improvement was needed.

A major "jewel" in the chain would be the Arnold Arboretum, 265 acres of trees and shrubs collected via the gift of a whaling merchant, James Arnold, via his will. It would serve as both a park and a botanical laboratory. Franklin Park, beyond that, was nearly twice as big and had many natural features that Olmsted incorporated into his landscaping by which he was able to provide the illusion that a visitor was in a rural setting with no buildings and only the distant views of the Blue Hills and Arnold Arboretum.

But if Olmsted's work made Boston more aesthetically and naturally pleasing, then the artwork that graced its institutions contributed to its cultural supremacy, mainly along the Avenue of the Arts and particularly on the Fens and Fenway. There was now room for these cultural institutions, and the Back Bay had wealthy and acculturated people who would appreciate things like art and music.

When the MFA outgrew its home in Copley Square, it had bought twelve acres of land between Huntington Avenue and the Fens and opened its new building in 1909. Then they had to move in. If you've ever moved your household, then you know that it can be complicated and sometimes difficult. The museum, of course, had all those great collections and many of them were quite delicate as well. Moving everything was quite a task. This was well before the time of moving vans with shock absorbers, dollies, and padded crates. There was no bubble wrap, foam, or rubber cushions. The collection had to be hauled in horse-drawn wagons over bumpy roads, and only the great care of its workers and overseers ensured a successful transferral.

A wing was added on the Fens side in 1915, and the museum school was built to the west of the museum.

In addition to its collections from all over the world and all periods of history, the MFA has featured American artists, especially painters. John Singleton Copley, for whom the square was named, was a fine painter of portraits who spent much of his life in England. Much of his work hangs in the MFA, as does that of John Singer Sargent, who also spent time in England but returned to Boston from time to time and was known for his portrait of Isabella Stewart Gardner, which was risqué for its day.

Gilbert Stuart, too, has many paintings in the museum, and he also spent a lot of time in England. He painted Bostonians, but perhaps is known best for his portrait of Washington on the one dollar bill.

When the arts came to Boston, Bostonians were drawn to them and began to study painting. Many ladies used pastels and painted on china, while painters like Washington Allston became famous for landscapes. Allston was another who spent time in England,

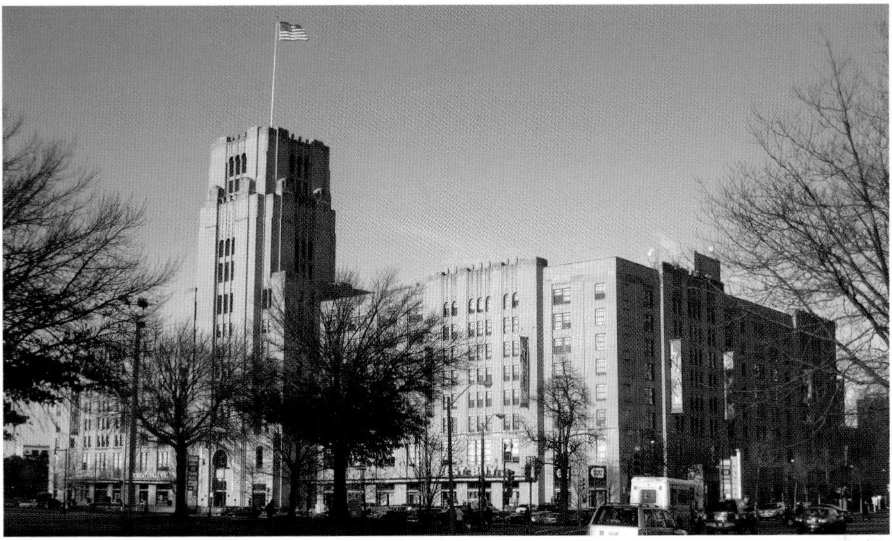

LANDMARK CENTER

but he lived in Cambridge as an older man and had great influence on American landscape painting. He is the only American to have a town named for him. (Allston is now part of Boston.)

Boston's first families made the major endowments to the MFA, but that handful of families didn't want to feel that it was their museum alone. They began a subscription program so that others could give in various amounts and feel that it was their museum as well. They were ahead of their time in this thinking about wide-spread "ownership."

One American associated with the arts was not an artist but a collector. Isabelle Stewart Gardner (she of the risqué portrait) built a palace on the Fenway to hold her works of art. "Mrs. Jack," as she was called in the press, was a connoisseur of the fine arts and made it desirable for other upper-class Bostonians to enjoy them as she did, even building this pleasure palace for that purpose.

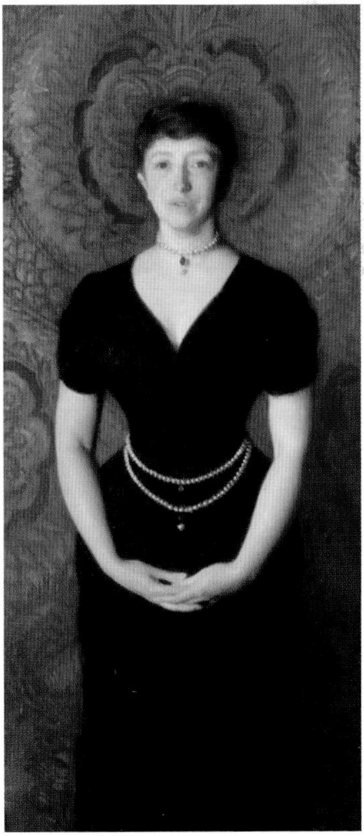

ISABELLA STEWART GARDNER

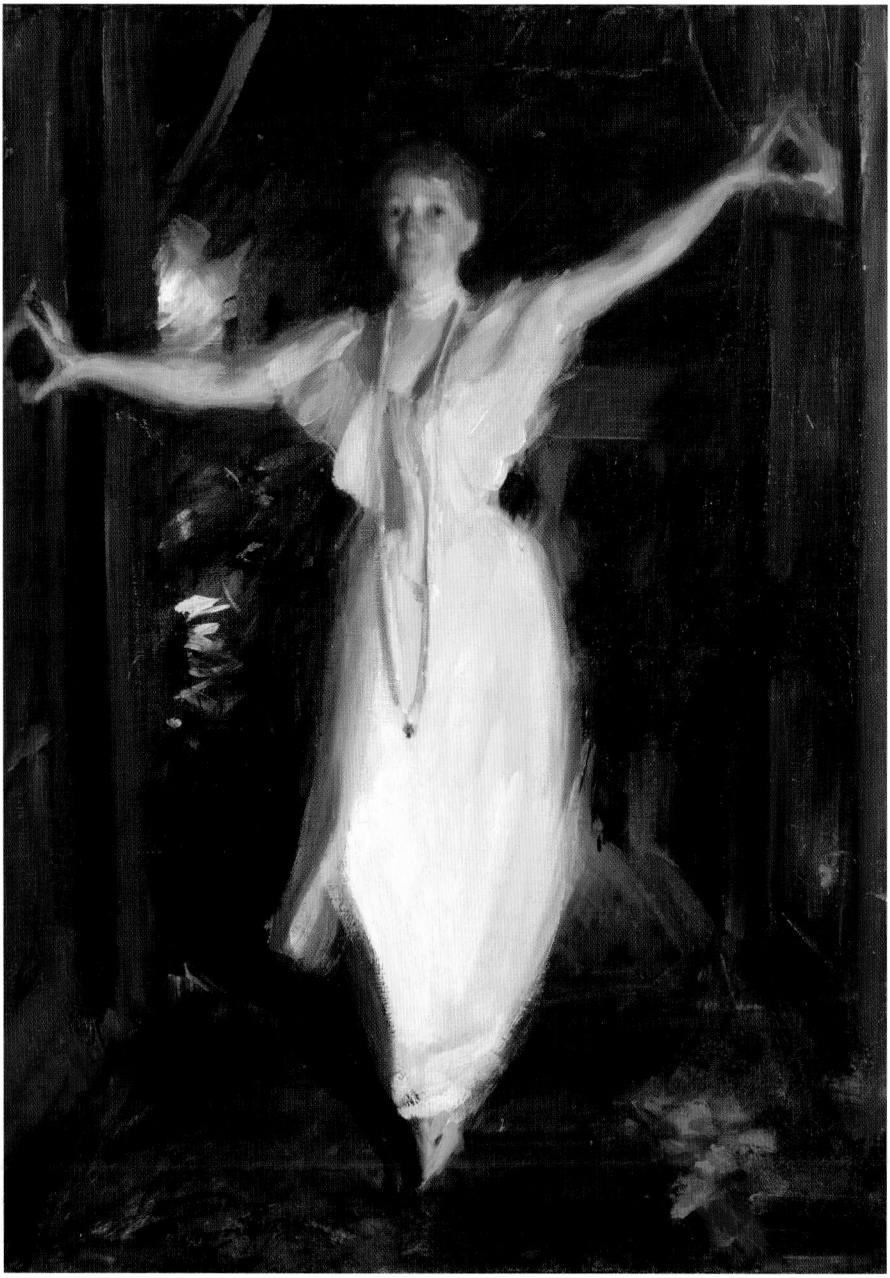

ISABELLA STEWART GARDNER

Isabella was great copy for the newspapers, often doing things that were considered outrageous. She loved to have fun—to sing, dance, converse with both men and women, and to flirt. She was skilled at all of these. One time she rented a pair of lion cubs and paraded down the street with them. Another time, when she and her husband were late for a distant engagement, she was able to get the railroad to lend them a train for their trip. She loved to ride fast horses, drive fast cars, and smoke cigarettes. Rather than sipping tea like a proper Bostonian lady, Isabella drank beer.

Though she married a Boston Brahmin, she was far from being one, although she did share that class's love for the arts. What she did not share was their love for anonymity.

When Isabella, daughter of a wealthy man in New York had married the wealthy Jack Gardner of Boston, the couple moved into a double home on Beacon Hill. But she was not just a wife on the arm of a prominent man. She pursued whatever interested her, and did so with abandon. Her major interest was in collecting artwork. She also entertained a lot and was often present at social gatherings among Boston's elite. She was a precursor of today's woman and certainly provided a model for any in her day who wished to be "liberated" or even "Bohemian."

Among her friends, as you might expect, were many artists, poets, writers, composers, and people who could provide stimulating conversations and new ideas—Henry James was one as were John Singer Sargent and George Santayana, the philosopher who wrote that those who cannot remember the past are condemned to repeat it. Isabella was not a repeater of the past. She and actress Sarah Bernhardt were mutual admirers. Isabella had so many unusual characteristics that Henry James used her as a hidden character in some of his novels.

Not all of her associates were artists or even from the top strata of society. She was friendly with minorities, gays, foreigners, and people of all classes, using her social skills, wit, and curiosity to expand her horizons. She traveled widely and once admired a palazzo in Italy, a home with a great collection of artworks that later became a museum. After seeing it, she wanted one like it and finally—at her husband's insistence, and when her father died, she was able to use her inheritance to collect things. Seeking and buying became a hobby. Then she would exhibit them for prestigious viewers at her home on Beacon Street. She studied art at Harvard with art historian Charles Eliot Norton. Her patronage of the arts and her bringing together of intellectuals and artists helped to make Boston a cultural center in America. She was generous as well. She gave to the Boston Public Library, New England Conservatory, and New England Home for Little Wanderers.

When her husband died, she followed through with their plan to build a house that was also a museum based on a fifteenth-century Venetian palazzo that she called Fenway Court, involving herself in every step of the planning and execution, especially the placement of items, for which she was very specific. Her collection spans thirty centuries and includes rare books and manuscripts as well as paintings and sculpture, many from the Italian Renaissance.

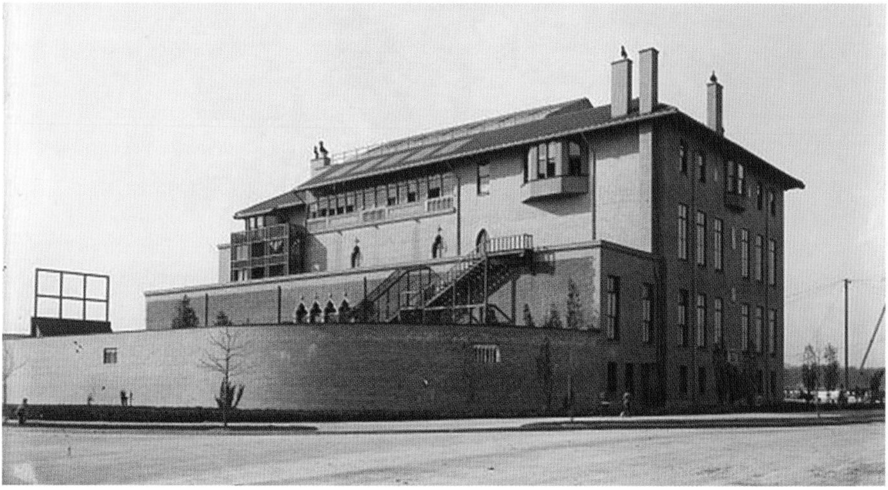

GARDNER MUSEUM
COURTESY LIBRARY OF CONGRESS

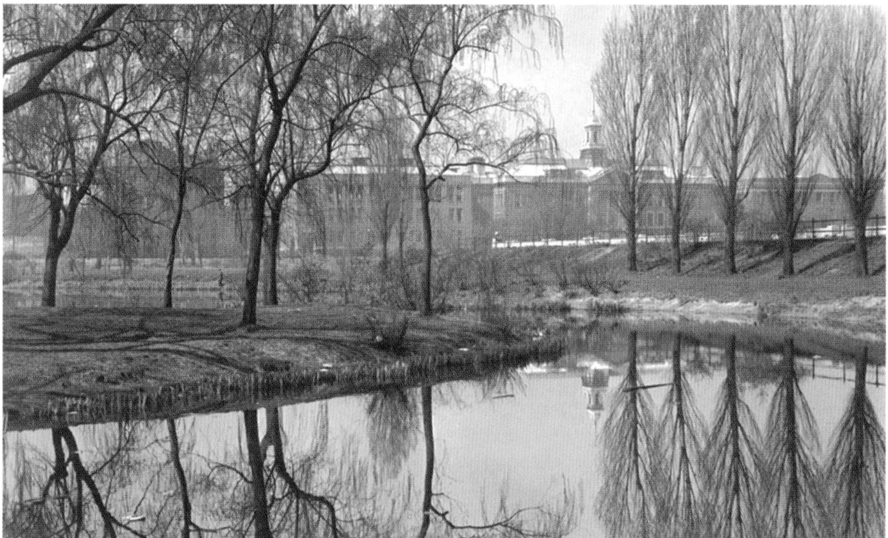

SIMMONS COLLEGE ON THE FENWAY, 1913
COURTESY BOSTON PUBLIC LIBRARY

The museum where she lived has an interior garden with a roof of glass and a garden often used for soirees, concerts, and plays. Her collection, indeed her arrangements, were definitely eclectic and unconventional, and she meant for them to stay that way. The plan was codified in her will, which left an endowment for future maintenance.

She used what was called her "palace" as a home where she had an apartment on the fourth floor. She frequently entertained, but had a grand opening on New Year's night of 1903, a gala to which she invited 150 guests to what was, of course, the event of the season.

"Mrs. Jack's Palace" or the Isabella Stewart Museum remained as she wished until 1990 when thieves made off with thirteen of the most valuable pieces, none of which have ever been retrieved. Due to the terms of her will and the need to leave her plan in place, the frames from the stolen paintings remain where they were before the theft.

The $250 million burglary is the largest art theft in history. It has altered the way she is remembered, since many people connect her name merely with the theft. The museum itself was renovated and expanded in 2012.

Next door is Simmons College, endowed through the will of John Simmons who made a lot of money selling men's clothes that were ready to wear, instead of made to order by tailors. Simmons used women seamstresses whom he came to know and sympathize with. Some of them, he felt, had good brains that were being wasted in the kind of work they did. He wanted to give them a way to use their brains to make their living. Simmons College was his answer starting in 1899.

Another college catering to females was built next down the Fenway—Emmanuel College—while across Brookline Avenue on the Riverway was Wheelock College, where young women learned to become teachers of children in their first years of school.

A block west of the Fens was Longwood Avenue, which became famous for medical schools, colleges, and hospitals. Located there are Massachusetts School of Pharmacy and Health Services, Harvard School of Public Health, Harvard School of Dental Medicine, and Harvard Medical School. There are also Children's Hospital Boston, Beth Israel Hospital, Deaconess Medical Center, Joslin Diabetes Center, Brigham and Women's Hospital, and Dana Farber Cancer Institute.

If you're going to have a district devoted to the arts and education, then you need a proud boulevard that befits it, and Boston would build a brand new one to connect the Longwood Medical area with the fens. It would be fitting for a Parisian-style city. Avenue Louis Pasteur even had a name that echoed Paris, as well as science and medicine, having been named for the French microbiologist. The avenue would be lined with impressive classical buildings that bespoke education, medicine, and art. Avenue Louis Pasteur was a Boston masterstroke. One of the exceptional buildings was the latest incarnation of Boston Latin School—a Georgian revival building. "Latin" had been the first public school in the US, with its beginnings on School Street in Boston where the old City Hall stands now, and moving from there to Montgomery Street in the South End where a dingy old building that it shared with Boston English was proclaimed at this early date as one of America's finest school buildings.

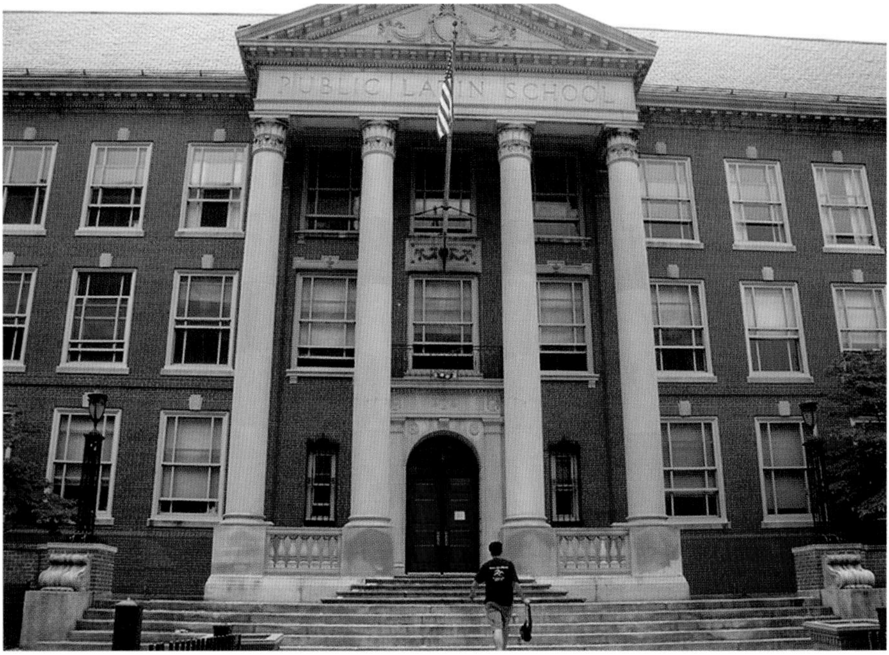

BOSTON LATIN SCHOOL

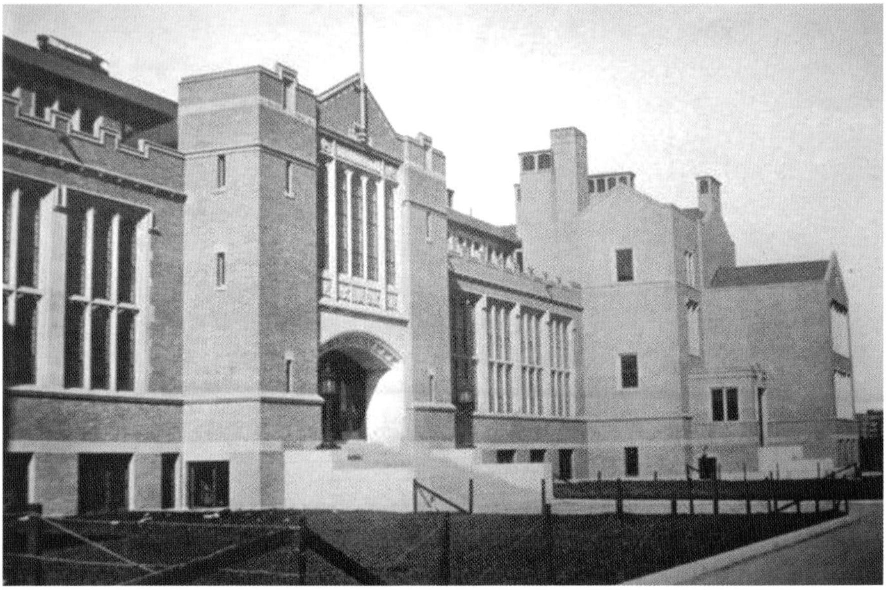

BOSTON ENGLISH HIGH, AVENUE, LOUIS PASTEUR
COURTESY CITY OF BOSTON ARCHIVES

As times change, Boston seems to capture these moments of change in some pre-ordained way. From there the school moved to Avenue Louis Pasteur with Boston English across the street for a time. (It occupied a building that was once the High School of Commerce). These two schools, so old, and so fabled, were also classical opponents in sports and their new proximity, after they had shared a building, brought the notion of rivalry just a step further. Consider, for a moment, how traditions come to be. We have here the preface.

Boston Latin, from the beginning, served almost as a prep school for Harvard. It continues to send many graduates there or to other Ivy League schools, but actually, Latin pre-dates Harvard by a year, having been formed in 1635. Its graduates then had Harvard to graduate to. Four Harvard presidents, as many Massachusetts governors and five signers of the Declaration of Independence have been produced by the school. On the other hand, Ben Franklin went there but dropped out, but Ben never did color between the lines.

These days, however, more in keeping with the way tradition is supposed to flow, ninety-nine percent of Latin graduates are accepted at four-year colleges—usually by more than one such school.

The Avenue Louis Pasteur is less than a half-mile long, but wide and impressive, lined at one time, with not only Boston Latin but Boston English, in a place now occupied by Harvard Medical School's modern addition and tower, and whose otherwise classical buildings line three sides of the "Great White Quadrangle," on Longwood Avenue where it moved from Copley Square in 1906. The quadrangle begins across from the entrance to Avenue Louis Pasteur, so looking in that direction gives one a long vista of classical buildings.

On Longwood Avenue, Harvard Medical occupies five marble buildings. The Avenue, where its other building is located, has at its foot Simmons College, the Isabella Stewart Gardner Museum, and Emmanuel College. A stroll or drive down this corridor, allows one to understand why Boston is often called "The Athens of America." Could it have been otherwise named? Harvard, Boston Latin, the Gardners, the MFA, all tie together with the Brahmin love for education and support of the arts and institutions of culture. All are well-represented here.

The sloping avenue intersects with the Fenway, and across from that intersection is Park Drive, the mostly two-lane street that runs from Charlesgate along the northern side of the fens and then turns right for Brookline Avenue and Beacon Street. It is mostly lined with older apartment houses, but on the fens side, there has been an open stadium built in 1918. For many years, the Boston Public Schools (even Latin and English) used it for competitive sports, mainly football. Recently, it has been renovated and renamed Roberto Clemente Field after the great right fielder and humanitarian.

Closer to the northern end of Park Drive, across from the Landmark Center at the intersection of Brookline Avenue and Boylston Street, the past is quickly becoming the future as large developments of housing, business, and retail establishments rise at both sides of Brookline and Boylston, including high-rise buildings that will fundamentally change the area close to Fenway Park.

Fenway Park, closer to the Kenmore end of Brookline Avenue, was built in 1912, replacing the Huntington Avenue Grounds as home for the Red Sox. Its presence has had a profound effect on the Kenmore Square-Fenway area for many years. All spring and summer it beckons huge crowds to the area for baseball, but also for concerts and other events.

On the day before it opened, the *Titanic* sank, crowding the ball game off the front pages. The Red Sox, nonetheless, won their opener in eleven innings over the New York Highlanders (later Yankees) and went on to win 105 games and the World Series in a thrilling seven-game set at Fenway vs. John McGraw's vaunted but hated Giants. The Giants had been but three outs from baseball Valhalla when they blew the Series by dropping an outfield fly in game seven, inning ten, and an infield popup that let the Sox tie the game after the Giants had slipped into the lead in the top of that inning with their ace, Christy Mathewson, on the hill to settle the Sox.

The deciding run scored on a sacrifice fly. The Giants had scored a run in the top of the 10th inning to lead, 2-1, and seemingly secure the title. Instead, the Red Sox' two runs off the Giants' ace Christy Mathewson in the bottom of the inning reversed the outcome. Highlanders and Giants or no, the Sox were then king of the hill, A-Number-One, top of the heap.

There seems to be some kind of symbolism in the rise of the Red Sox with the sinking of an invincible ship, even looking at this then-new ballpark that would remain forever iconic and old-worldish along with other icons like the CITGO sign nearby, a park that would represent this dowdy old-world city as it found its way into the future both as an Elysian Field sport and a team with uncanny ability to rise phoenix-like from burnt embers to heroes and champions. Trying to fit this, piece-by-piece into some jigsaw of meaning is almost hopeless, but placing it within the Boston idiom of sports and heroism somehow seems to fit.

Another curiosity about the Red Sox made itself known in the summer of 2014. The defending World Champions were having a sub-par season and, halfway through, were in last place. It didn't seem to matter as far as attendance was concerned. Tickets continued to sell well. Theorists said it was because the team and the park with its Green Monster and Citgo sign are tourist attractions and even a mediocre team won't keep spectators away.

In keeping with traditions and with Boston ways of doing things, most readers know that the north-south streets of the Back Bay (Arlington-Hereford), are alphabetical, but in the West Fenway area, the streets are named for cities and towns in Scotland that appear in Robert Burns's literary work. Enough names were selected by the Burns Memorial Association of Boston to continue from Hereford to the end of the alphabet, but not all were used. Some near Fenway Park were: Ipswich, Jersey, Kilmarnock, Landsdowne, Peterborough and Queensberry. These are the trivia that a surprising number of Bostonians are onto, though outsiders would find it difficult to understand why.

On one of those streets, near Fenway Park, is a 1905 building made in the arts and craft style that was popular at that time. It is an artist's cooperative on Ipswich Street called Fenway Studios, and it fits in with the promotion of the arts that is associated with Back Bay—in fact, its original incarnation was on Harcourt Street near St. Botolph

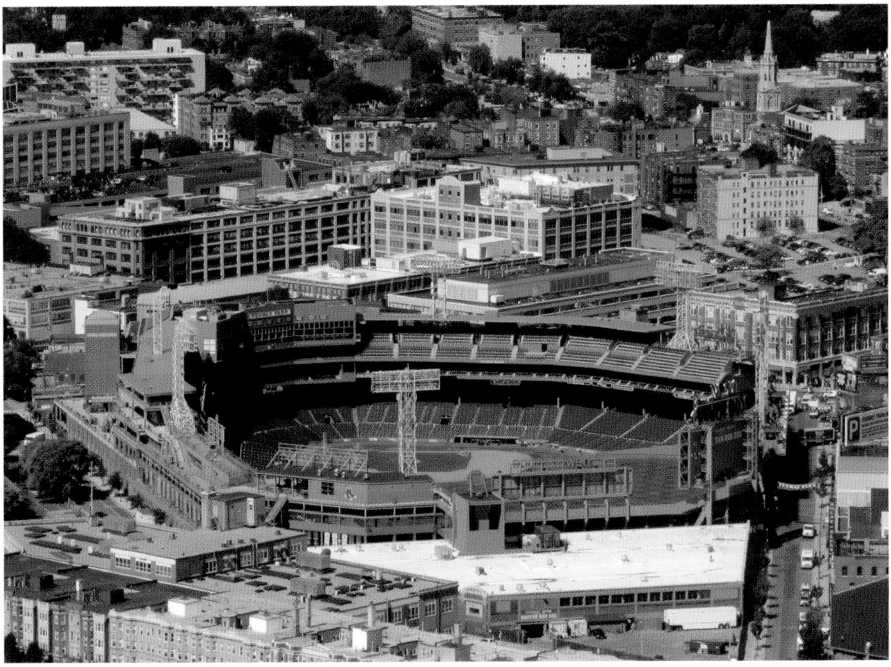

FENWAY PARK
COURTESY AUTHOR

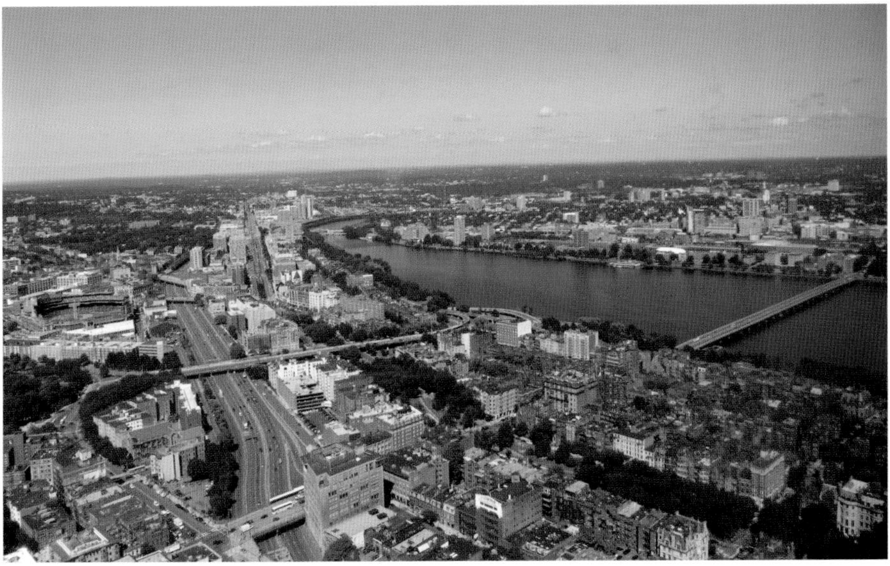

FENWAY, TURNPIKE, BOWKER, COMMONWEALTH AVENUE
COURTESY AUTHOR

where so many artists found homes and studios. This old building has a unique feature, however—all forty-six of its studios have twelve-foot windows with northern light. Also, it's the oldest of artist studios in the country and is a National Historic Landmark.

From the old to the new: Development and the promise of it have increased in the Fenway/Kenmore area recently. Start with the renovation of the Landmark Center, which has plans to add residential units and a Wegman's grocery store—the first in Boston. There's also the Hotel Commonwealth which was built on the former site of the once-popular Rathskeller bar. A large apartment building, the "Trilogy" was completed at Boylston and Brookline and another high-rise, 1330 Boylston was completed. A former Howard Johnson motel is being upgraded and changed into one called "The Verb," and other high-end housing will be built on that street, changing the mostly commercial area dramatically. There are plans, too, to build above the Massachusetts Turnpike that runs behind Fenway Park.

Boylston Street begins at its intersection with Brookline Avenue and Park Drive and runs east toward Copley Square. As it crosses the fens, the building for the Massachusetts Historical Society sits on the right. This is the eighth building for the Society and places it near the Christian Science Center and the Museum of Fine Arts. It has been here since 1899. To its north is Charlesgate.

The term is instructive. The area is the gate between the Charles River and the Back Bay Fens. It is the point at which Back Bay touches Olmsted's "Emerald Necklace," and an important contact point between the seaward-bound Charles River and the flooded and noxious hinterland fed by the Muddy River. Charlesgate was considered by some to be the crown jewel of this plan since it served as a kind of barrier between the neighborhood of Kenmore/Fenway and the open seascape represented by the Charles and its tidal flows.

But the "crown jewel" lost its luster as time went on. Some used the word "progress" to describe what happened to the area west of Massachusetts Avenue to Charlesgate and beyond. It became blighted and increasingly choked with more and more vehicular traffic. Major highways like Storrow Drive and the Massachusetts Turnpike brought traffic to and through the area in overwhelming quantities.

Just as Muddy River and Stoney Brook had brought excess water to the area in years past, floods that were beyond the capability of the natural infrastructure, so now, with so many vehicles entering this gateway area, the impulse was to get them in and out more quickly. The municipal fathers forgot the mission of their forebears to beautify Boston with greenery and a park system.

One glaring remnant of this rush to action is the Bowker Overpass meant to connect Storrow Drive traffic to Boylston Street and Park Drive, a nexus less immediate in retrospect than it seemed at the time. The building of the Bowker, which amounted more to a physical barrier separating Back Bay from the Kenmore/Fenway area than a modern shuttle of traffic that relieved backup on Storrow Drive, Bowker Overpass said to Bostonians, "We have here a modern city where cars have to be able to move quickly from one place to another, and that trumps any arcane notions about Emerald Necklaces or pastoral visions. One cannot be both modern and green, and modern is more important"—or at least that's this author's interpretation of what happened.

The end chapter may not, however, have been written. The "modern" overpass has come near to the end of its life span and will have to be either renovated or replaced. For those who wish to promote the greenness of the area, there will come an opportunity to redo the narrowing and rerouting of the Muddy River and revive a neighborhood that needs revitalization. The Friends of Charlesgate do not wish to see the overpass revitalized, but would have it removed with traffic routed in different ways.

CHAPTER NINE

Kenmore

By 1882, the filling in of the Back Bay had proceeded as far as Charlesgate and then, by 1890, beyond that to the present Kenmore Square. The area where Beacon Street and Brookline Avenue now meet was then just a spit of land surrounded by salt marshes, an area where the Muddy River met the Charles, known as Sewall's Point. It was named for its owner, the once-notorious Judge Samuel Sewall. He had presided over many of the witchcraft trials of the seventeenth century, but had later repented of the harm he had done, became an abolitionist, and was a promoter of equal rights for women.

Sewall's Point had been connected to Beacon Hill via the fifty-foot wide Mill Dam, which enclosed the waters of the Charles in 1814. But as the Back Bay was gradually filled in, the filling reached Sewall's Point, now part of Boston. It had been part of Brookline until 1874, at which time Brookline voted to become a municipality, separate from Boston, while at the same time Allston/Brighton was annexed by Boston.

By 1890, the filling had created new land around Sewall's Point where Beacon Street met Commonwealth Avenue. It was renamed Governor's Square.

When it came time for Frederick Law Olmsted to extend Commonwealth Avenue and its mall west of Massachusetts Avenue in the 1880s, he faced a major problem, but this time it wasn't a water problem. The current path of Commonwealth Avenue would bring it head on into the tracks and rail yards of the Boston & Worcester RR.

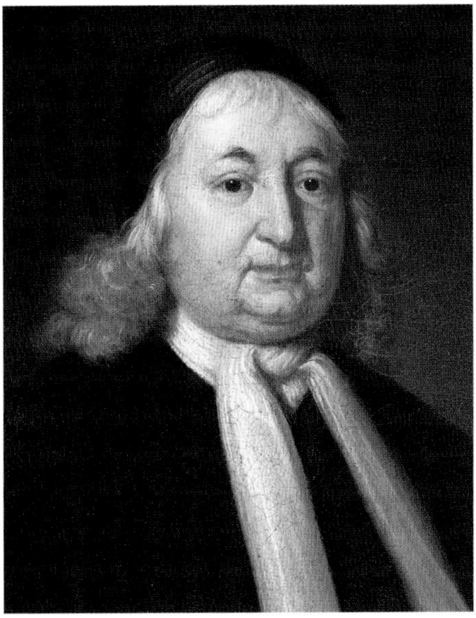

SAMUEL SEWALL

He didn't want to deal with an overpass that would spoil the stately elegance of his street. So what he chose to do was to jog to the right about twenty degrees.

That meant that Commonwealth would intersect with Beacon Street at Governor's (later Kenmore) Square. As a result the grid of streets between there and the river as well as those between Commonwealth and the Fens would

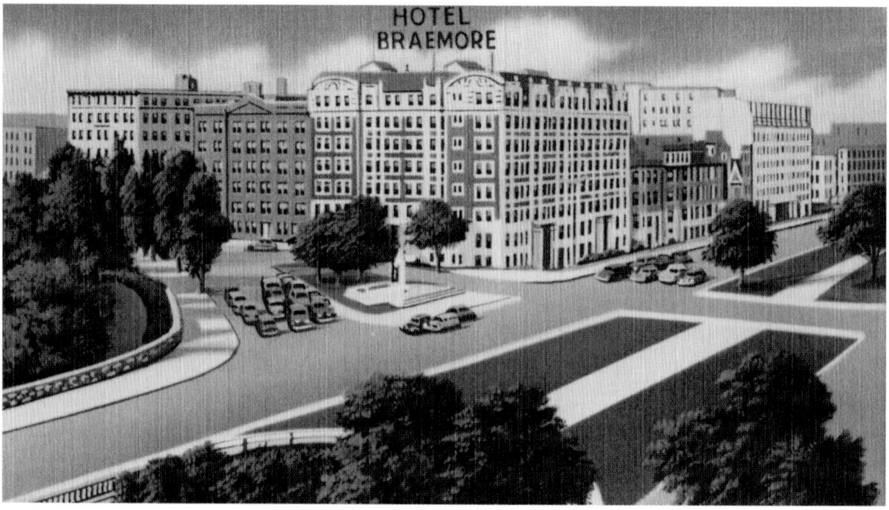

HOTEL BRAEMORE AT CHARLESGATE POSTCARD

have their own separate street patterns. The intersection of the two major streets also meant that Kenmore Square would become a hub of transportation. That did happen, and Kenmore also became the busiest square in the city.

What it didn't become was high-priced real estate. When the Charlesgate-Fenway area was filled in, it looked as though it would become expensive residential real estate like that of the Back Bay, but that never happened. Neither Charlesgate nor the Kenmore area would equal the Back Bay in property values, and more than anything else, the area would cater to students and educational institutions. The year 1907 saw twenty-two such institutions in and around the Fenway, including nine colleges or universities. The residential buildings that were erected were required, however, to have high quality frontage (as determined by a Board) so that they would have the right look to fit in along the park and parkways of the fens district.

The crossing of transportation spokes at the square brought people there from many directions, principally from the west (Brighton, Newton, Watertown) and the southwest (Brookline, Roxbury). Not only roads, but railroads met there, as did the subway, so that many people passed through or stopped there, leading in time to an influx of hotels.

Those railroads and trolleys and indeed, the many hotels would lead to Kenmore Square becoming known as "the Gateway to Boston," a transient area for businessmen from the west. The hotels appeared over a period of time—places like the Buckminster, Shelton, Braemore, Somerset, Myles Standish, and the Kenmore, which gave its name and the name of the side street next to it to the square. Kenmore Square became a stopping-over point, and the hotels gave it a certain luster. It even had that Commonwealth Avenue Parisian look that Bostonians had become rather fond of and that allowed travelers to believe they were in pursuit of something important and that the treatment they received at these hotels was something that was their due.

The square had the boulevard Commonwealth approaching from the downtown direction and intersecting with other streets of importance that could shuffle a rider or driver of a wagon into the right channel to head to outlying towns, reaching them through verdant vales and leafy lanes created only because Boston was a singular place that recognized its significance and was ready to celebrate it by presenting itself as a model for other places.

Transportation hubs have to be centrally located, and originally, the Boylston Street subway stop (Kenmore) was in the square and the entrance to the underground tracks lie just east of it. Later, the subway entrance was moved west to Blandford Street, and the former station became a bus kiosk. (In 2007, the MBTA renovated the Green Line station as well as the Yawkey Way Commuter Rail Station, almost unknowingly recalling the area's foundation as a commuter crossroads).

Another means of transportation, fully suited to the "Gateway" title, was the automobile. Car salesrooms and automotive businesses opened on the north side of this crossroads-square. One such dealer that left its mark, and whose building is still there, was the Peerless dealership at 660 Beacon Street, established in 1910.

When one thinks or looks back on automobiles of the pre-World War I era, Packard comes to mind, or the Stanley Steamer, perhaps the Lincoln and Ford, but Peerless, made in Cleveland, had not always made cars. However, in 1910, was one of "the three Ps": Packard, Pierce-Arrow, and Peerless. One of its models was the Peerless Limousine, said to be "Planned and built on attractive lines calculated to please the most refined tastes;" it seated five people. Passengers had the luxury of electric reading lights, armrests, and a speaking tube to communicate with the driver." The driver was extra. Peerless, indeed. But it was the building at 660 Beacon that attracted interest, more than the car. The building was six stories, and was leased to Peerless from 1910 to 1930. Red brick and limestone, it had a fancy showroom with mahogany furniture and chandeliers. Upstairs,

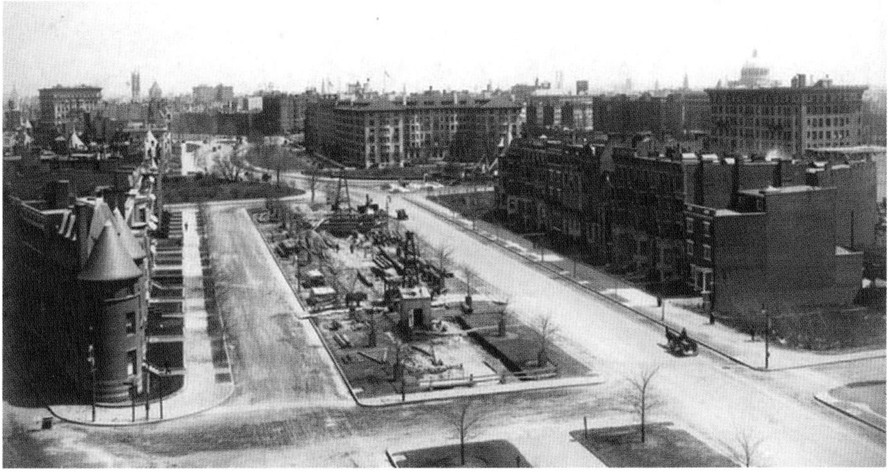

KENMORE SQUARE, 1912
COURTESY BOSTON PUBLIC LIBRARY

above the showroom, were offices and a stockroom, while repairs were done on the third and fourth floors. Floor five was devoted to making tops or repairing them, while the top floor had a painting department. There were four elevators.

Peerless was replaced in the building by Cities Service Oil Co. in 1940. The "Cities Service Building" had a super service station, as they called it, and a salesroom on the ground floor, then three floors of parking and two for corporate headquarters. On August 9 of that year, a large neon sign first appeared, high above the roof. It was 90' x 75' with the words "Cities Service," but was replaced by the present CITGO sign in 1965. The new sign used the same frame, and John C. Brink, maker of signs, claimed that it was the largest sign in New England.

The sign was turned off in 1973 during the oil crisis and again from 1979-1982. But when Citgo announced its plan to demolish the sign the following year, public protests made them change their mind. Those who wanted the sign to remain called it a fine example of urban neon art and as "Boston as baked beans." Two other times (2004 and 2010) saw the lights go out, but only to be replaced by LEDs.

Marathoners look forward to the sight of the sign as they near their destination and Red Sox players view it as a target beyond the green monster in left field even though it's 1,200 feet away. They read CITGO as "SEE-IT-GO"'. Even expectant mothers at Beth Israel Hospital on Brookline Avenue have been known to use its pulsing flash in the night sky to time their contractions as their time of delivery draws near. Seen on Red Sox telecasts around the country and world, the CITGO sign in Kenmore Square has become an image representing Boston.

Johnny Kelley, a Boston University student who lived at the Myles Standish, recalled a moment in 1957 when he was leading the marathon into Kenmore Square and felt the pressure of the moment. As the sign and then the square drew nigh, he said he felt "... a qualified 'Whew!' The race was almost done, and yet that crucial mile remained," he told a magazine years later: "Those thousands of fans, [including] BU students—many of them my friends from Myles Standish dorm or classes—I couldn't let them down at this penultimate moment!"

From his digs on Bay State Road, Kelley would have been among hundreds of BU students who lived in brownstones that had been bought and converted to dorms when the college began to boom with the post-World War II influx of GI Bill students that went hand in hand with shrinking real estate prices, even in the Back Bay. By the mid-1960s, many of the hotels were in the hands of schools or businesses.

The Buckminster Hotel, which has become something of a landmark for the rounded corner of Beacon Street and Brookline Avenue, was known for more than its hotel function. A good-sized betting operation was run from there over a long period.

One would have liked to be a fly on the wall when first baseman Chick Gandil of the Chicago White Sox met in a room of the Hotel Buckminster at the juncture of Brookline Avenue and Beacon Street with gambler Joseph "Sport" Sullivan to plan the throwing of the 1919 World Series as featured in the film *Eight Men Out*.

Later, in 1934, three men were arrested when more than 2,000 betting slips were recovered from the betting pool they were running out of the hotel along with horse-betting syndicates.

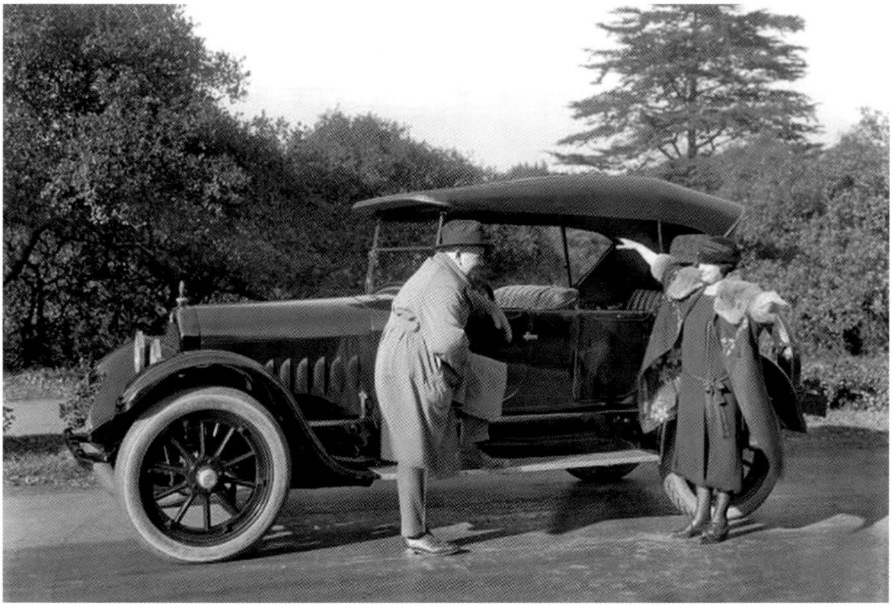

1920 PEERLESS LIMOUSINE CO.
VINTAGE EVERYDAY

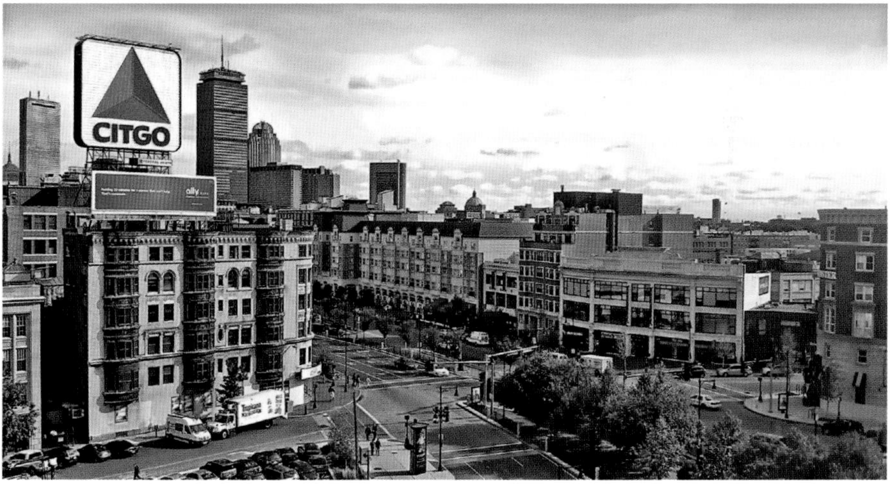

KENMORE WITH CITGO SIGN
COURTESY HENRY HAN

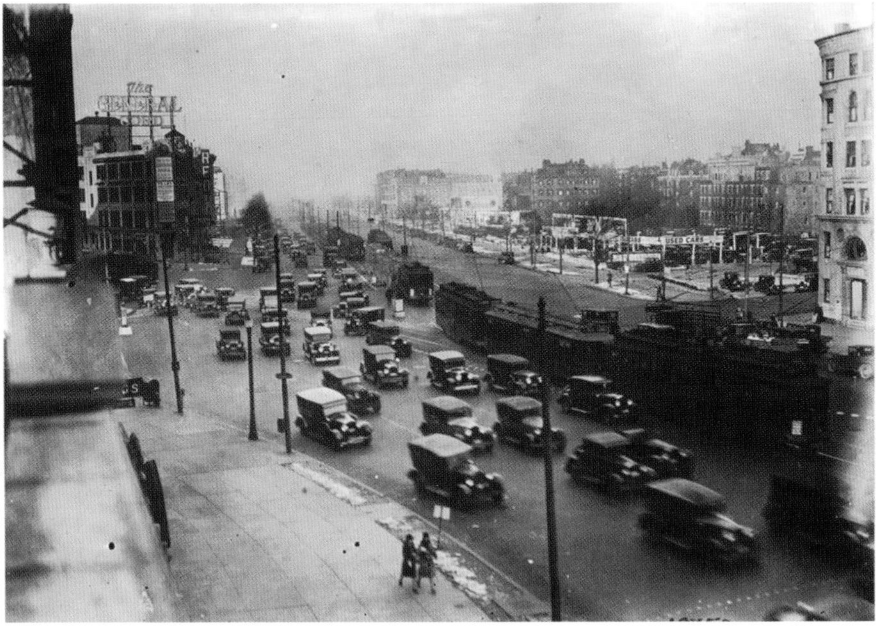

KENMORE NEAR HOTEL BUCKMINSTER, 1920S

For many years, beginning in 1929, the Buckminster was host to a radio station (WNAC). It used an antenna that was actually strapped to the roof with a clothesline. Along with a station in New York, WNAC took part in the first network broadcast of all time, after which the two stations joined together as the Yankee Network. John Shepard, the owner, later established a regional network of hometown stations and began the Yankee News Service in March 1934, the first independent news roundup on radio. WNAC-TV began broadcasting in 1948 and remained at the site until late in the 1960s, though the hotel became the St. George. WNAC became WRKO.

During World War II, however, the hotel had been used as a military barracks for the Army Emergency Relief Administration, as a drop off place for gifts to servicemen, and temporarily as a prison for a German submarine crew and Italian prisoners. After the war, it became a transient hotel until 1962, and during part of that time, the popular jazz club Storyville occupied the basement. Storied performers like Billie Holiday, Louis Armstrong, and Sarah Vaughan were featured. It then became the "Colonnade Room," and for many years after the war a Howard Johnson's was located in the front of the building.

Another popular Kenmore Square sign sat atop the Buckminster from 1939 to 1982—White Fuel operated an animated neon sign that, during World War II, promoted US Defense Bonds. It depicted a plane that appears to be sky-writing a huge letter "V" for Victory and then the words "Keep 'em flying" in red neon followed by "Buy U.S. Defense Bonds and Stamps" in gold neon. The White Fuel Company had a retail store across the square that sold household appliances.

The hotel that's probably most associated with the square is the Kenmore, which began in 1916 as an apartment hotel for long-term residents. It stood (and the building still stands) on Commonwealth Avenue at the corner of Kenmore Street (for whom the subway station and square are named) and was advertised as the "Hotel Kenmore." It doubled in size in 1925 by adding land and tearing down buildings. It was thus able to add 150 more rooms, a large dining room and café as well as a banquet hall. In 1926, the hotel also added the Hotel Wadsworth, behind it on West Newbury Street and Kenmore Streets, connecting the two via a walkway and using the Wadsworth for long-term apartments.

The Kenmore was not only an elegant hotel, but an important one as well. It had 400 rooms and many services for its guests, but was also the center of professional baseball, being only three blocks from Fenway Park. While the Braves were still in Boston (and just up Commonwealth Avenue where BU now has athletic facilities) all fourteen visiting ball clubs in both leagues stayed at the Kenmore while in Boston. Even many Red Sox players stayed there upon returning from spring training before finding permanent housing.

Team owners often used banquet and meeting rooms to conduct business, and many trades and personnel decisions were made there. The fabled Casey Stengel, who managed the Braves and later the Yankees, was known for his late-night gatherings where he held court for reporters and others. Even the Gridiron Club, a football organization, held its dinners there. In the early years of the American Football League, teams playing the Patriots stayed there, too.

In later times, newer hotels cut into the Kenmore's business, and in 1966, it was sold to the Cambridge School (later Grahm Junior College), which bought a number of properties around the square. They used it for dorms. Grahm closed in 1979, selling its properties to Boston University. It turned both the Kenmore (then the Kenmore Abbey) and the Wadsworth to senior and special needs housing.

Another memorable building stood on Bay State Road, behind Kenmore Square and overlooking the river. It was eight stories high and had 132 apartments of two or three rooms. Owned originally by the Sheraton Corporation, it was sold and renamed the "Shelton." Ted Williams lived there as did actress Jeannette MacDonald and playwright Eugene O'Neill. The Shelton, too, had a radio station, WBMS,

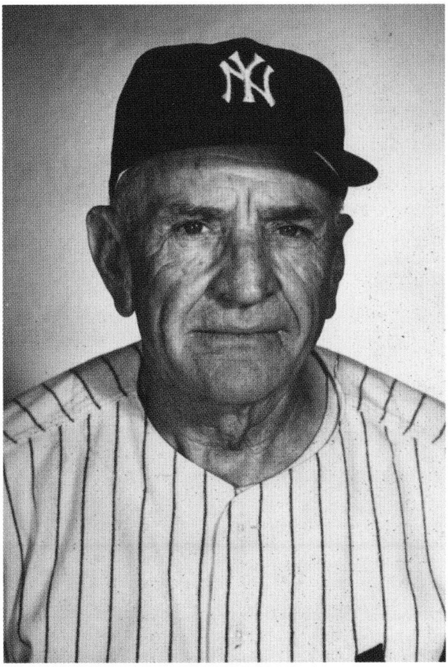

CASEY STENGEL, 1953

and had Boston's first African-American host, Sabby Lewis, as well as Mayor James Michael Curley, who gave political commentary. In 1954, BU bought it, along with many other Kenmore-area buildings. It was used as a women's dormitory.

On the south side of Commonwealth at the corner of Charlesgate West, stood the Braemore, built as a luxury hotel during World War One. It had an unlucky history, with several deaths, a fire, and the disappearance of a famous patron, but also a tip of $300,000 to a doorman by a wealthy New Yorker for his hard work and honesty. The building is now the Braemore Condominiums. Like many hotels and other buildings around the square, the exterior is largely as it was, the interior adjusted to new, but similar use.

Reality came in with a bite in 1962 when a torrential rain flooded the subway station and tracks at Kenmore, and required the closing of the station and transporting of passengers by shuttle bus for a week. People were quick to remember that the whole area had once been a swamp and that the Muddy River and Charles River were close neighbors, never quite safely held at arm's length. This was easy to recall if you were being rescued by rowboat in this "Muddy River Revenge."

The student population that dominated the area for a time, and still has an influence, created a demand for fast-food places, small shops, a laundromat, and nighttime entertainment which, over the years, turned Kenmore Square into a kind of Times Square in terms of bombast and sleaze, and also a place for memorable neon signs.

The college students who populated the area in the final decades of the twentieth century brought rock 'n' roll bands, loud music and night clubs. The one that drew the most attention was "The Rathskeller"—called "The Rat," which attracted top groups and gave starts to local talent. It was the focus of the punk rock scene and the club lasted from 1974 to 1997 when it was sold, being demolished in the year 2000 in favor of the new Hotel Commonwealth—a sea change that highlighted the gentrification of the square.

There were other clubs offering music, too, as well as youth-oriented businesses like music stores, late night restaurants, pizza places, a karate school, and a place that sold socks and t-shirts. Many of the patrons were BU students, and the administration was concerned about the crime, drugs, drinking, and general decline of the area. BU began to buy up property, beginning with the Peerless building in 1983, which it converted into one of the biggest book stores in the country.

Along with civic groups, it worked on a plan to revitalize the area. The university partnered with developers to buy the buildings on the south side of the square between "The Rat" and the International House of Pancakes. After the demolition of those buildings, the Hotel Commonwealth was built there, opening in 2003, with retail on its street level and 149 rooms above. Two upscale restaurants, Eastern Standard, and the Island Creek Oyster Bar became very popular. Curiously, the person who is executive chef at one and co-owner of the other is Jeremy Sewall, a descendant of Judge Samuel Sewall, original owner of Sewall's Point, where Kenmore Square began.

The square has changed in other ways recently. The entrance to the square's subway station is now up against the façade of the hotel, and its bus terminal has acquired a modern-looking canopy. However, foot traffic through the square continues at a high level due to events at Fenway Park and the restaurants and bars that are now on the streets near the ballpark as much as in the square, bringing people to both areas. Sidewalks

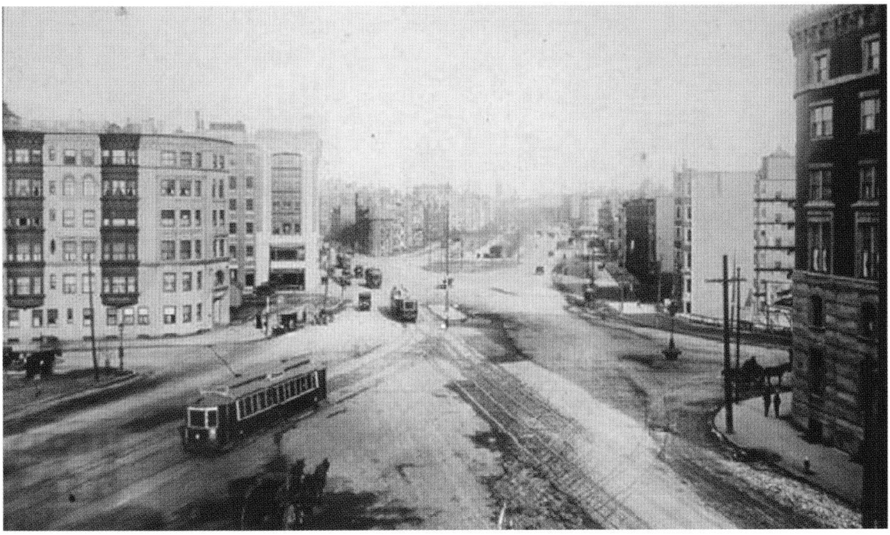

KENMORE SQUARE, 1910s

have been widened, crosswalks and traffic islands added, making the square safer to cross. But crowds still gather on Patriot's Day to watch the runners approach their final mile or so to Boylston Street and the finish line.

But perhaps the most apparent, and welcome, impact of the joint revitalization effort has been in pedestrian safety. Sidewalks were widened, trees planted, and stoplights added and wide, bright crosswalks and islands installed, making a stroll across the square significantly less stressful than it used to be. Underground, the MBTA still thrives. Where once streetcar tracks began their trek down Beacon Street toward Cleveland Circle, the C Branch of the Green Line continues below ground to St. Mary's Street and Audubon Circle. Other trolleys continue and emerge for the B line on Commonwealth Avenue, though buses now run on the A line to Watertown. There is also the Riverside Line with a "Fenway Park" and a "Longwood" stop, and the Purple Line (commuter rail) runs alongside the Massachusetts Turnpike.

Down that same Brookline Avenue to the southwest are Landsdowne Street and Yawkey Way and the familiar edifice of Fenway Park, pennants flying from its banner years, particularly the recent World Championships in 2004, 2007, 2013. An hour or so before game time, those streets fill with people seeking souvenirs, sausages, or last-minute tickets ,which are hard to find. At the ends of games, those same crowds will empty onto the streets and many will head for Kenmore Square's or Landsdowne Street's bars and restaurants, but especially for the T station, which will slowly disperse them toward their various destinations, usually after long waits in line.

Some may be staying at those hotels around the square, including opposing teams. In years past, Red Sox players, like Babe Ruth and Ted Williams, stayed at hotels in the square and would walk to the games. These days, celebrities tend to stay out of the public's way for the most part, but you could run into almost anyone in Kenmore Square.

CHAPTER TEN

Olmsted and His Work

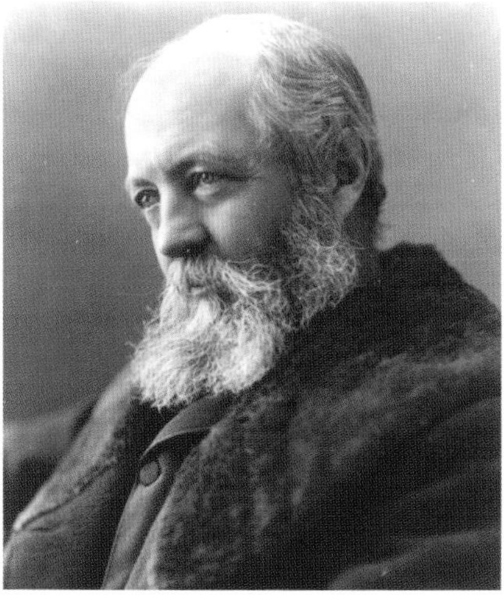

FREDERICK LAW OLMSTED
OLMSTEAD PAPERS PROJECT

It seems that we each have our role to play before passing the baton to the one[s] who will move our work forward. Such was the case with Frederick Law Olmsted who played such a central role in saving the Back Bay from the vicissitudes of flooding and who made the Back Bay Fens into an aesthetic and green area, miraculously part of an urban setting. His work, however, was a long-term stopgap that had to be supplemented. Luckily, or perhaps due to forethought, he had put in place an organization that produced people who could take the next step and the one after.

Those steps led inevitably to the 1910 dam at the Craigie Bridge that turned the salt-water basin to a fresh-water one, but which, in its turn, required further improvements in the form of still another dam at the Zakim-Bunker Hill Bridge, which improved the Charles River Basin and its water yet again until—who knows what will yet be required and who will arise to answer it?

You can't, however, write a history of Boston, and especially of the Back Bay, without prominent mention of Frederick Law Olmsted who designed so many of the green spaces, particularly the Emerald Necklace, and perhaps more importantly, the Back Bay Fens where his work alleviated flooding. Beyond those changes, however, the landscape gardening firm that he began made many other innovations and improvements, including the land along the Charles River, called the Embankment, and later the Esplanade.

Olmsted, himself, had a varied background before he arrived in Boston, having followed a number of careers and having success in each of them. Born in Hartford, he missed attending Yale because of a severe case of sumac poisoning (rather ironic for a future landscape gardener), but served as a farmer, a sailor in the China trade, a clerk, and—perhaps most notably—he became the superintendent of New York's Central Park and architect-in-chief of the park's construction that bears his special mark of roadways that run at various levels and allow the safe intersection of motor roads and

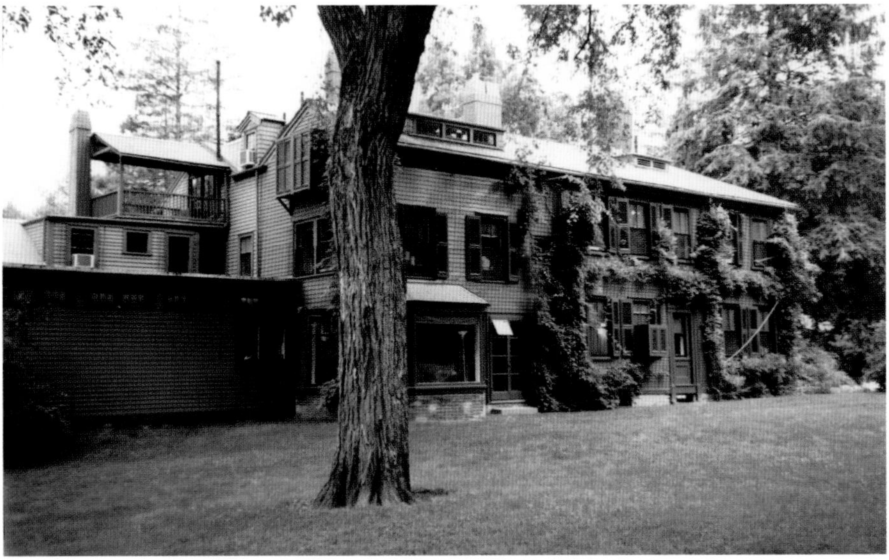

OLMSTED NATIONAL HISTORIC SITE, BROOKLINE
COURTESY GR BOST BUILDINGS

walking paths. Olmsted not only created numerous city parks around the country, he also conceived of entire systems of parks and interconnecting parkways to connect certain cities to green spaces. In 1883, Olmsted established what is considered to be the first full-time landscape architecture firm in Brookline, Massachusetts. He called the home and office compound Fairsted, and it is now the restored Frederick Law Olmsted National Historic Site. From there Olmsted designed Boston's Emerald Necklace, the campuses of Stanford University and the University of Chicago, as well as the parts of the 1893 World's Fair in Chicago, among many other projects.

The next of his "varied" careers was as head of the US Sanitary Commission—the forerunner of the American Red Cross, which would have looked good on anyone's resume, but to someone like Olmsted, this was simply a bagatelle. His last job was even a greater departure for the Easterner. He was hired to manage the extensive Mariposa gold mining estate in California, out where the buffalo roam—or used to anyway. He found the Wild West quite unlike the places he was used to, but was a good manager and resolutely fearless. He was even able to break a strike that became violent, and to prosper in spite of it. His gold-mining operation brought in about $25,000 a month, but the parent company went bankrupt and he picked up the latest telegram asking him to come east again, and he joined Calvert Vaux in designing Prospect Park in Brooklyn, a venture that turned into one of his greatest forays into park and landscape planning.

All this was more than just a career for our Frederick Law. It came close to being a crusade if you substituted naturalism for religion. In addition to designing for urban life, Olmsted was almost Rooseveltian in his efforts to preserve areas of natural beauty for future public enjoyment. He headed a commission to preserve Yosemite Valley and also led the effort to establish the Niagara Reservation, along with Calvert Vaux, in 1887. He was involved in protecting America's greatest resources.

The 550 projects that his firm engaged in between 1872 and 1895 were college quadrangles and campuses, and residential communities—a wide spread of ventures indeed. In addition to Central Park and Prospect Park, his best-known projects include the country's first and oldest coordinated system of public parks and parkways in Buffalo, New York; the country's oldest state park, the Niagara Reservation in Niagara Falls, New York; Mount Royal Park in Montreal, the Grand Necklace of Parks in Milwaukee, Wisconsin; Cherokee Park and the entire parks and parkway system in Louisville, Kentucky; as well as Forest Park in Springfield, Massachusetts, featuring America's first public "wading pool." Then, too, there was the George Washington Vanderbilt II Biltmore Estate in Asheville, North Carolina; the master plans for the University of California, Berkeley, and Stanford University near Palo Alto, California. And in Washington, DC, he worked on the landscape surrounding the United States Capitol building.

As a journalist, he wrote extensively about the failures of the slavery-based economy of the South where only the owners of large plantations prospered and most white people lived at far lower levels than those in the North. He wrote:

> The citizens of the cotton States, as a whole, are poor. They work little, and that little, badly; they earn little, they sell little; they buy little, and they have little—very little—of the common comforts and consolations of civilized life. Their destitution is not material only; it is intellectual and it is moral. They were neither generous nor hospitable and their talk was not that of evenly courageous men.

Unlike many of his era, Olmsted believed in and fought to achieve egalitarian ideas such as making the green spaces available to all, regardless of class. He was also an early leader in America's conservation movement.

The Back Bay, which he did not build, but certainly influenced, was not at all a classless endeavor. Both the pricing of properties and the regulations were meant to preserve property values, and did that quite well for a long period of time. Back Bay remains today the largest intact Victorian neighborhood in the US—even though the days of the townhouse (superior to those of Beacon Hill by the end of the nineteenth century) passed quickly when people began to move to the suburbs with the availability of cars. In addition, fewer people were looking for jobs as domestic servants in this area.

However, the housing stock remained largely as it was, though uses went from single-family ownership to apartments and offices, and then to condominiums and student housing. The residential streets like Beacon, Marlboro, and Commonwealth Avenue look much the same as they did, with most of the brownstone rows of three- and four-story buildings looking uniform in their architecture, though the original architects were often different for each building. The architectural uniformity has placed the area on the National Register of Historic Places.

Perhaps as many as ninety percent of these Back Bay properties are now condominiums. Values have remained the highest in the city as well, though demand for real estate has fluctuated from time to time. People with sufficient wealth to live in the Back Bay are also able to work within short distances or at least just a few subway stops away. Empty-nesters have also moved there to enjoy those things planned many years ago—namely the arts and entertainment, beautiful buildings, and especially the parks and green spaces and views of the river. Unlike their ancestors, however, today's residents enjoy the modern-day additions of balconies and roof gardens. The effects cast by Olmsted and his colleagues can still be felt today. Olmsted's work runs through Back Bay with his Emerald Necklace running from the Common and Public Garden, down the mall at Commonwealth Avenue to Charlesgate and the Fens, but also along the Charles River.

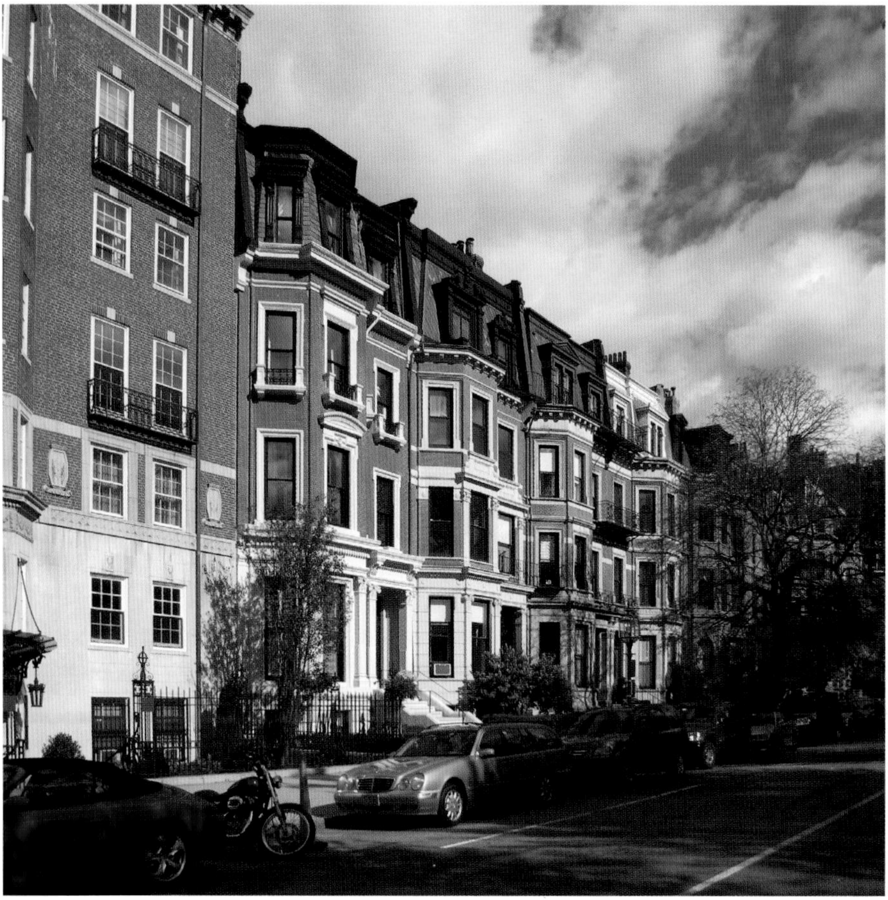

COMMONWEALTH AVENUE BROWNSTONES

CHAPTER ELEVEN

The Boston Common and Public Garden

The Emerald Necklace begins with the Boston Common and the Public Garden, two areas that were already begun when Olmsted began work on the rest of it. Olmsted's firm, under his sons, did make contributions later. However, the Boston Common goes back much further than that. It was used first by a lone settler, William Blaxton, who lived on Beacon Hill and used the Common for an apple orchard. When the Puritans under John Winthrop came to Charlestown across the river, they had trouble with the drinking water and Blaxton invited them to join him. That 1634 settlement didn't work out for long. The Puritans stayed; Blaxton left.

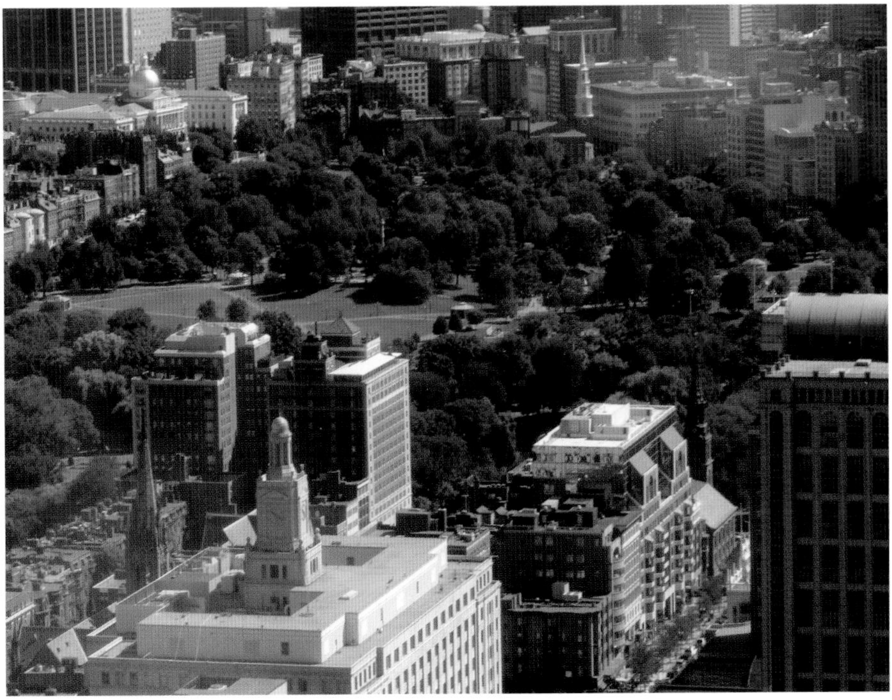

STATE HOUSE AND BOSTON COMMON
COURTESY AUTHOR

The Puritanss first used the Common to graze their cattle and sheep, but it was never used exclusively for that purpose. Each family paid a fee for its grazing privileges, but some of the wealthier people allowed too many animals in and the space became overgrazed, so restrictions were placed, allowing a total of only seventy milk cows (four sheep could be substituted for a cow). Even at that, the common's regular use for grazing would be short-lived. The fifty-acre space, the first public park in America, was also used for public gatherings, parades, and even a graveyard. And it had an oak tree that served as a gallows where Quakers, such as Mary Dyer, were hanged.

During the Revolution, British soldiers drilled and camped there. By 1830, cows no longer could chomp on the grass. They were banned. Practically everything about the Common and later the Public Garden was the first in the country.

The Common, just below the State House, has remained a walking area and gathering space. In recent years, the Frog Pond has served for ice skating in the winter, and there is a prominent bandstand along with sculptures and fountains.

At the western end of the Common was a swampy area known as "the round marsh," which, after the filling of the Back Bay, would become the Public Garden. Before the filling, the land was given by the city to owners of rope-walks whose buildings had been lost in a fire. When the new rope-walks, too, burned a few years later, the owners decided not to rebuild but to sell the land, which had increased in value. Many people objected to this and, in 1824, the administration of Mayor Josiah Quincy bought the land the city had given away earlier. They paid $55,000 for land that had once been theirs. The city council then proposed selling it, but the citizens vetoed this idea.

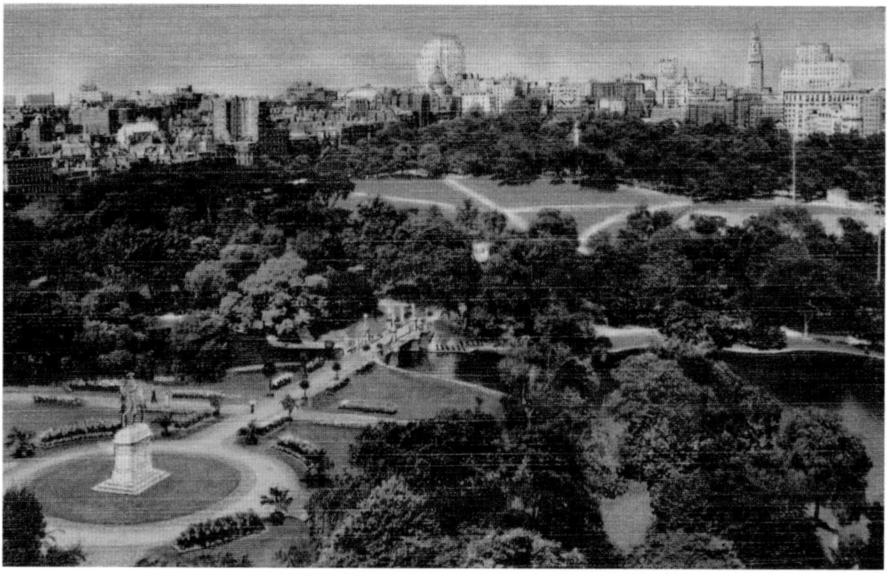

PUB GARDEN/BOSTON COMMON POSTCARD

For a number of years, various plans were proposed, including the building of a city hall on the land at Arlington Street. Events and people would decide otherwise.

Just as the name of Olmsted is known to many with only a casual knowledge of Boston history, others who contributed to the greening of the city and preservation of parklands, received little notice and are mostly forgotten. Such is the case with Horace Gray. Probably this was because Gray was scion of a Brahmin family whose members achieved many things but, like most of their ilk, shied away from public notoriety. Brahmins did not want their names carved into public buildings, even the ones they had financed. They held to the idea that a person's name should be in the news at birth, death, and marriage—only.

Gray's family, like that of many of his peers, had made its wealth mostly in international shipping and trade. His father, "Old Billy" Gray, owned more than sixty square-rigged vessels and had become, perhaps, the wealthiest man in the country. During the Revolution, he had made a fortune in privateering. He later added to it by trading with Russia and the East Indies, and had then gone into politics as a Jeffersonian Democrat, rising to the rank of lieutenant governor of Massachusetts.

They had lived in Salem but, in 1809, had moved to Summer Street in downtown Boston. Horace Gray, the fifth son, earned an MA from Harvard in 1819 and joined his father's mercantile firm. Upon his father's death, he inherited the Summer Street mansion and married, raising a son Horace Jr., who would become chief justice of the Massachusetts Supreme Court and then an associate justice of the US Supreme Court. A son from a second wife, John Chipman Gray, became a law professor at Harvard and a leading legal scholar. (Horace's obituary, in 1873, mentioned the achievement of his son, the Supreme Court judge, but stated only that Horace had been a merchant.) In fact, he had been much more, and his successes had been in the civic realm of which he never bragged. The home at Summer and Kingston Streets was next to that of Jack and Isabella Stewart Gardner, who had one of the finest gardens in Boston, though not as fine as that of Horace with his prize camellias and other exotica.

Despite his business successes and many directorships in banks, insurance companies, and the iron industry, Horace's great love was for horticulture and landscape design. He was an early Brahmin in the shift from making money to using it for public amelioration. He would combine his love of horticulture with his public spirit to become the leader and major financial supporter of the effort to turn the swampy area west of Boston Common into the park that became the Public Garden. Thus he is known as "The Father of the Boston Public Garden" (but only among the cognoscenti).

In the fall of 1837, Gray and his associates petitioned the Boston City Council to use the twenty-four acres of swampy land to create a botanical garden—the first in the US. They were granted permission, but could have no buildings other than a tool house and greenhouse. The land was leased to Gray and his fellow horticulturists incorporated in 1839 with an investment of $50,000.

Changing swampland into parkland is no easy task, as we have seen in the Fens. Since it was a lowland, steps had first to be taken to alleviate flooding. Under the guidance of an English gardener, a boardwalk was built and plants and trees were set out. They also took an existing building that had been used by a circus and converted it to a conservatory where exotic plants and birds were raised. It had four galleries, each for a different kind of plant. Gray imported the first tulips into America at this time.

The Public Garden became popular with the people, and Gray was its chief supporter for most of a decade.

During that time he also began an endeavor in Brighton where he bought 100 acres on which he erected three grape houses that were the largest in the country, and in this temperate climate grew a number of varieties of foreign grapes. However, he had to sell it and also cease support of the Public Garden when he suffered financial reverses at the end of the 1840s. The city then took over the public garden. In the next decade, Gray and citizen groups opposed attempts by the city to sell the land, until, in 1859, an agreement that the land be forever devoted to public use was passed by the state and ratified by Boston's citizens by an overwhelming margin.

Following that, many of the features with which we are now familiar began to be installed. A lake was finished and a wrought iron fence placed around the perimeter. A small peninsula was created within the lake, but it became a kind of "Lovers' Lane" and so was converted into an island. Flower beds and paths were laid out according to the plan of architect George F. Meacham, selected in a competition. His plan called for a city hall to be built there, but fortunately, the location on School Street was chosen instead.

Next came four fountains, and the bridge across the lagoon, which opened in 1867 as the world's shortest functioning suspension bridge. (It was converted in 1921 to a girder bridge and the suspension system is now only decorative.) There were also Thomas Ball's equestrian statue of George Washington and the Ether Monument. Swan boats (more later) were introduced in 1877.

Among the statuary are those of Edward Everett Hale at the Charles Street gate, Wendell Phillips (pastor of Trinity Church) on the south walk, Thomas Cass and Charles Sumner's statues are also on that walk, along with that of Tadeusz Kosciuszko.

A memorial to those people from Massachusetts who died in the terror attacks of 9/11 is located near Arlington and Newbury Streets. Favorite among the younger set are the bronzes representing the ducks from Make Way for Ducklings, near the gate at Charles and Beacon Streets.

However, the flower collections and 1,500 trees fulfilled the original purpose of Gray and the others. Each spring there are new beds of flowers along the paths. Those on the central path are rotated on a schedule throughout the year. Plantings are transferred from the fourteen greenhouses the city keeps at Franklin Park. The trees are of many species from around the world. Notable are the weeping willows along the lagoon, elms, horse chestnuts, beeches, redwoods, and ginkgoes. They designed vibrant floral patterns in the Garden that utilized new techniques of collecting, hybridizing, and propagating plants. With access to showy annuals and greenhouse-grown plants, they bedded the Garden with colorful displays and planted exotic imported trees. George Meacham used these new techniques to win the public design competition held for the Garden, for which he received a $100 prize.

In the early days, some complained that the unnatural combinations of colorful plants were garish beyond the bounds of good taste. Now Boston calls the Public Garden one of its greatest attractions.

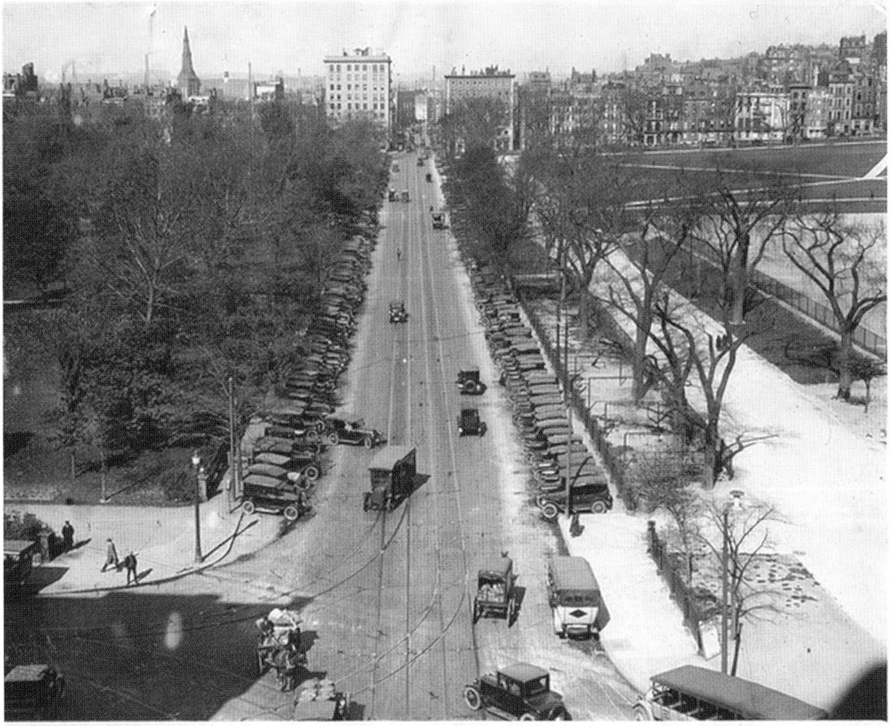

CHARLES STREET

A major disruption took place in 1897 affecting both parks. America's first subway was dug along Tremont and Boylston Streets, with an inclined entrance along Boylston near Charles. In 1914, the subway was extended west along Boylston and a strip of the Public Garden forty feet wide was lost. The story of the Swan Boats began in 1877 when Robert Paget was granted a boat for hire license by the City of Boston. It had become traditional to row small boats on the lagoon of the Public Garden in the summers, but Robert's idea was different. It would be a catamaran driven by bicycle power. A paddle wheel would be hidden beneath the boat and pedaled by its driver. The mechanics would be hidden by a façade made to look like a swan.

The swan came to mind because Robert, an opera fan, enjoyed *Lohengrin*, an opera based on a medieval German story about a knight who crosses a river in a boat pulled by a swan in order to defend Princess Elsa, the heroine of the tale.

Paget lived only a year after his boats first set sail. He was forty-two. His wife, Julia, had four children to care for and decided to continue the business herself, a singularly unusual thing for a young woman to do in that era, and one where she had to jump through many administrative and bureaucratic hoops, like getting signatures from community business leaders attesting to her ability to run a business—a task required for several years. In the 1870s, the glass ceiling placed a roof even above the swan boats.

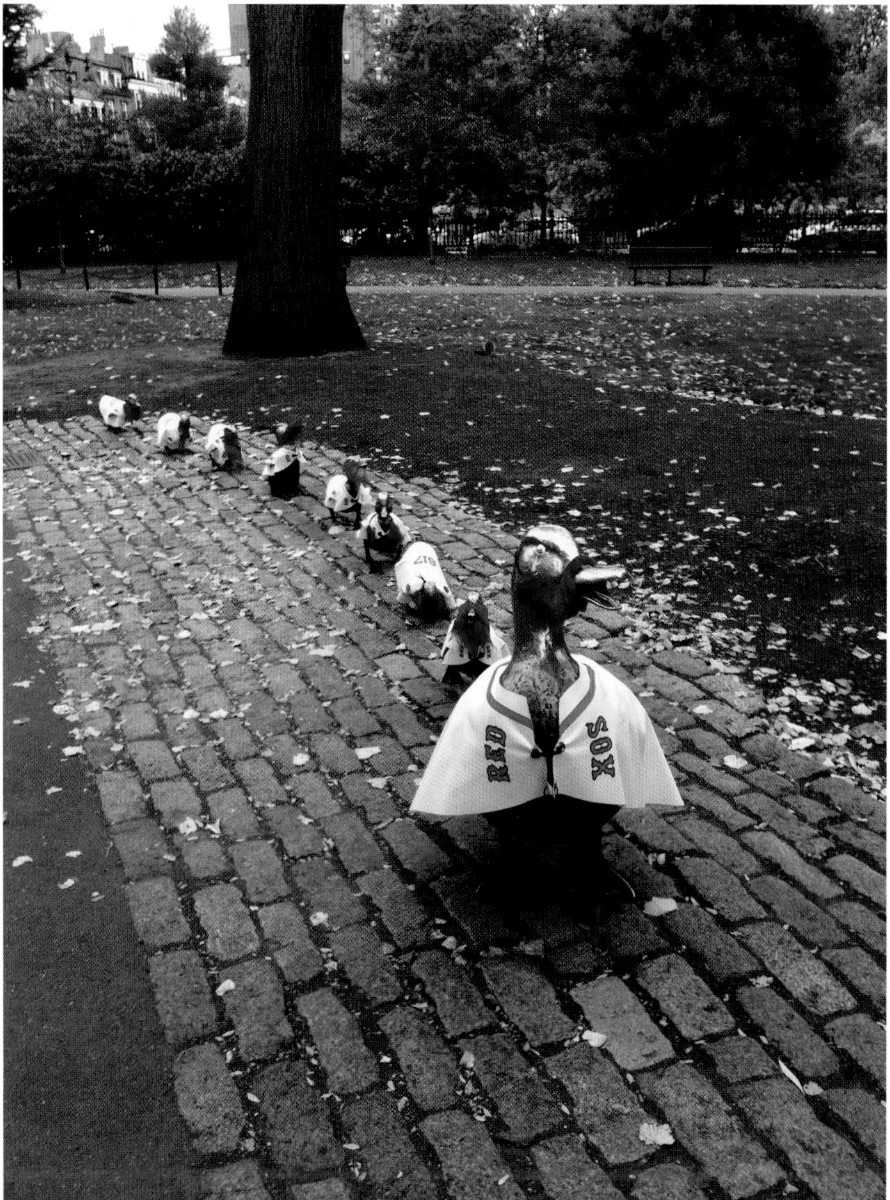

MAKE WAY FOR DUCKLINGS SCULPTURE

The boats, nonetheless, became increasingly popular. At first the boat could only hold eight passengers, but they grew to include up to twenty.

Julia's youngest son, John, began to build larger boats in 1918. His first boat is still used, one among six. John and his wife, Ella, raised six children who all have worked on the boats. When John died in 1969, after fifty years on the boats, his son, Paul took over, along with his wife Marilyn, extending a family tradition that nears 140 years. Youngsters love to ride on the boats, but they are not alone. A sail on a Swan Boat gives a fine view of the Public Garden, its lagoon and trees and flowers, as well as its famous bridge—all this in the middle of a large city.

One local newspaper reporter, in speaking of the charms of Boston wrote:

> The Swan Boats are cruising and the ducks are chasing peanuts. It will be just that way for a hundred springs from now, we hope. The New Boston is here and maybe someday there will be a new, New Boston, but good old Boston, like the Swan Boats, quietly glides on forever.

Old Boston went through a serious period of decline in the twentieth century that lasted until the 1960s, and its parks, including the Common and Public Garden suffered from neglect. In 1970, a volunteer group, the Friends of the Public Garden, formed and presented a plan for improving it. However, it had first to fight off another challenge from developers who wanted to build tall skyscrapers on Boylston Street, opposite the Garden and casting shadows onto it. This group and others helped to defeat the plan. The Friends, along with the mayor's office and the Park Department jointly manage the Public Garden which, in 1987, was made a National Historic Landmark.

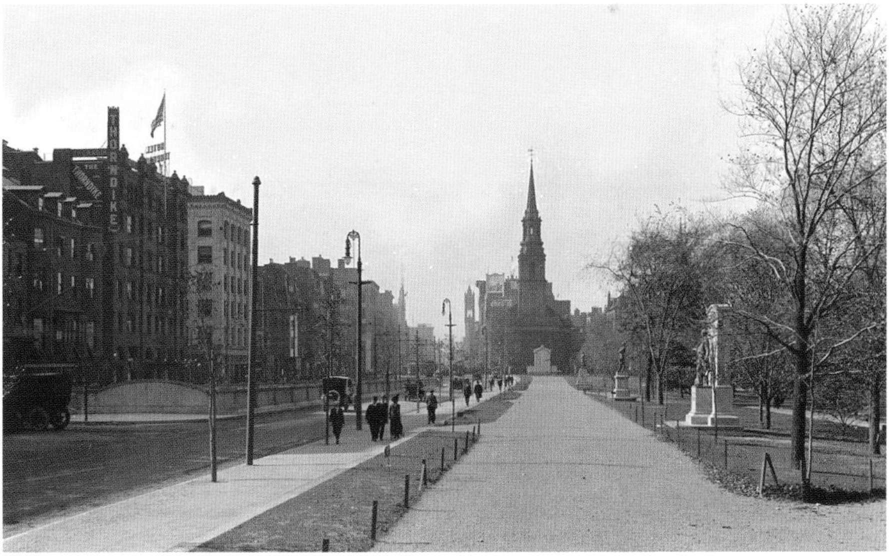

SUBWAY ENTRANCE, BOYLSTON AT ARLINGTON

CHAPTER TWELVE

The Commonwealth Avenue Mall

The Emerald Necklace begins with the Boston Common and Public Garden and then extends through the greenness of the Commonwealth Avenue Mall to Charelesgate and the Fenway/Riverway and on to Jamaica Pond, the Arnold Arboretum and Franklin Park. No other city has such a park system, and Boston was lucky to have the right person (Olmsted) and talented associates who helped to make Boston a green city. Olmsted and his associates brought a lot to Boston, but the Common and Public Garden, and in fact the mall, were not Olmsted originals. They were in place and he or his disciples improved them, so the end result was good.

Stepping smartly across Arlington Street toward the broad beginning of Commonwealth begins an adventure in architectural history that presents the viewer (and the Bostonian) with an outstanding depiction of the architecture that prevailed in the last part of the nineteenth century.

The broad avenue was the conception of Arthur Gilles, who, it is said, was inspired by the great Parisian boulevards of that same era and, if so, was successful in creating a Boston version of those fine avenues.

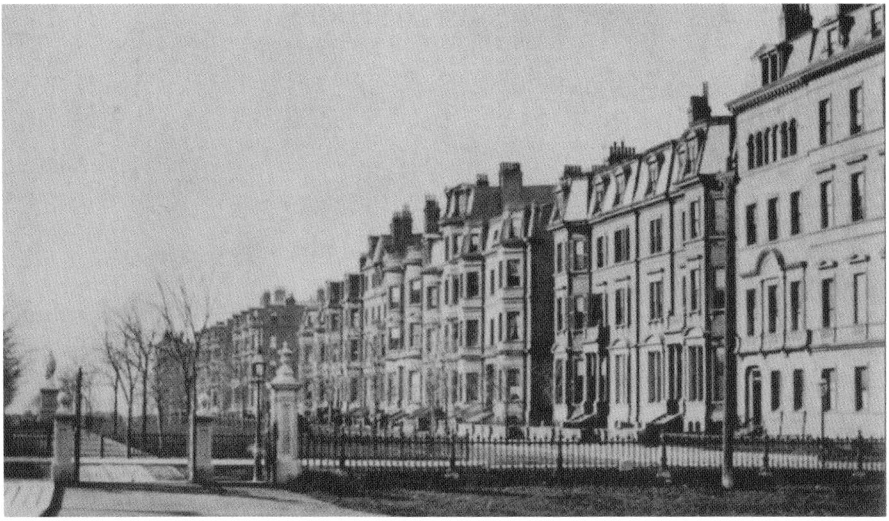

COMMONWEALTH AVENUE NEAR ARLINGTON

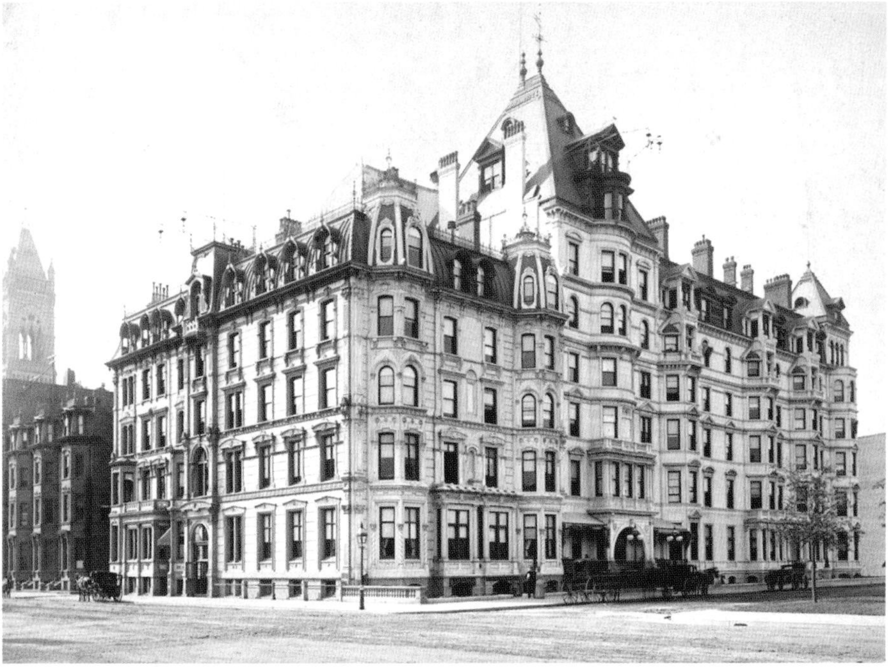

HOTEL VENDOME

Some called it a "grand allée of shade trees" that plunged straight through the heart of Back Bay as it connected the Public Garden with the Back Bay Fens. Winston Churchill called it "the grandest boulevard in North America." In an advisory role, Olmsted suggested that the trees that had been planted be replaced by American elms. The City Council thought that would bring about public protest from uprooting of trees, so they demurred and other shade trees with a mixture of elms were added instead. Olmsted insisted that the trees be planted in two single rows, and today they're a key part of the mall—along with the walkways, the benches, and magnificent sculptures.

Three blocks to the west on Clarendon Street is another building on the National Register of Historic Places, designed by the same Henry Hobson Richardson who later designed Trinity Church, a stone's throw distant from it. The Brattle Street Church, later the First Baptist Church, also was erected in the style that became known as Richardson Romanesque. It was just after the completion of this building that he won the contest to design Trinity that led to all his sketch-waving and breakfast table announcements. The church opened in 1875. Seven years later the First Baptist congregation bought it.

The building has ivy-covered walls and a prominent tower, visible at the time from Copley Square for which it was called "the northeast corner." Its distinctive tower has carvings by French sculptor Frédéric Auguste Bartholdi.

If the name seems familiar, it was he who created the Statue of Liberty, a New York Harbor fixture. For a while, when New York was slow about providing funding for its pedestal, Betholdi considered placing the statue on Boston's harbor islands.

Betholdi's frieze represents four sacraments and he used famous people like Longfellow, Hawthorne, and Lincoln for the faces. Some critics were harsh about the sculpture, some even calling the building "The Church of the Holy Beablowers" for the angelic trumpeters of Bertholdi's making. The name stuck.

The Commonwealth Avenue mall has a row of statuary that begins with Alexander Hamilton near Arlington Street, one that has a story connected with it is the statue of Leif Eriksson, near Charlesgate East. Leif's statue is shading his eyes, perhaps trying to see beyond the Bowker overpass to regain the view he had before it was built that even let him "see" the Charles. He alone among the statues faces away from Boston, his back turned on the city. This Eriksson looks less like the pillaging, plundering Viking the real Leif was. He looks instead like a noble, handsome adventurer.

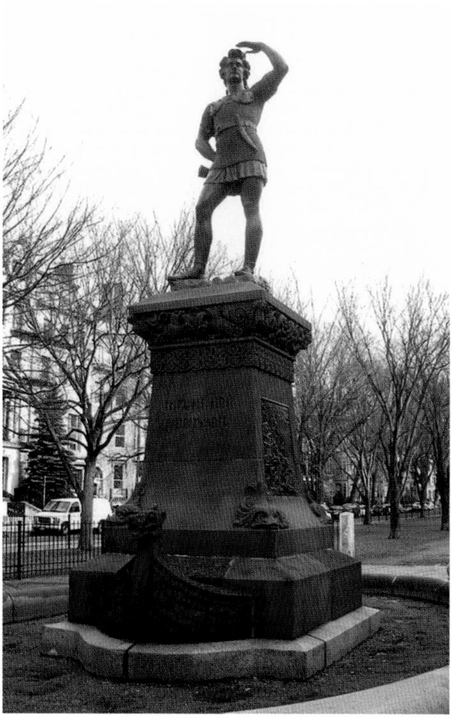

STATUE OF LEIF ERICSON

The statue was commissioned by Eric Horsberg, a chemistry professor at Harvard who had invented a type of baking soda that was commercially successful, really a useful breakthrough that especially helped people who were traveling west and also military units during the Civil War.

Horsford is recalled, however, for something quite different. He was a strong believer that the Vikings were the first Europeans to settle in North America. In fact, he subscribed to the views of those who said that the Viking settlement called "Norumbega" had been inland from the mouth of the Charles River. Finding Norumbega became an obsession with Horsford. He even dug up some items he said had come from the settlement and published his findings. There was interest in his theories at the time, but they have been largely cast aside. Horsford built a tower in Weston where he believed the fort had been all those many years before. This tower stands across the Charles from where Norumbega amusement park was built. The word "Norumbega," a corruption of Norwegian and Indian terms, has in recent times, been associated primarily with the park and its Totem Pole ballroom.

The statue, financed by Horsford, was the brainchild of a Norwegian violinist named Ole Bull. He, too, was deeply into the notion that the Vikings had settled in New England and proposed placing a statue of Eriksson on the Commonwealth Avenue Mall. Horsford met Bull at the home of a mutual friend in Cambridge, a neighbor of

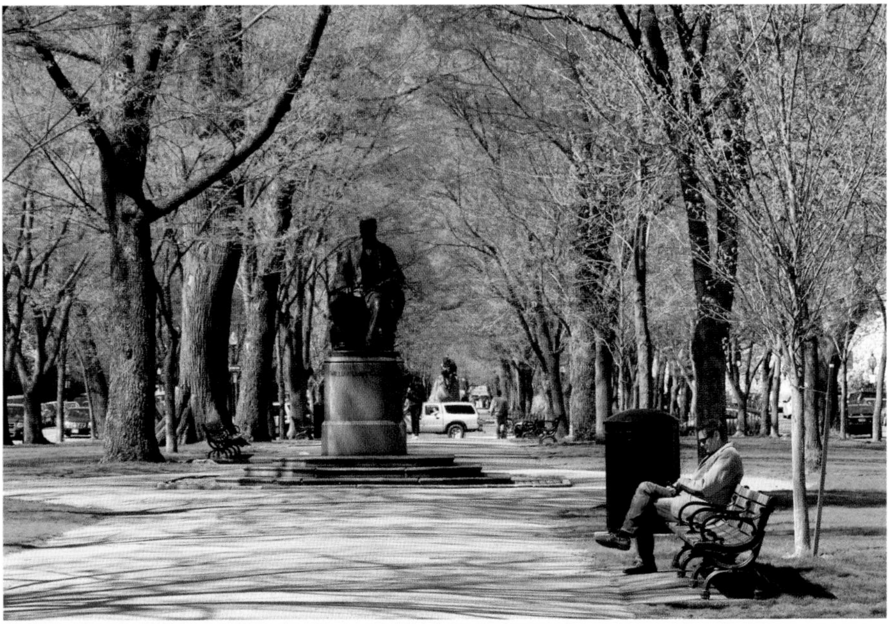

COMMONWEALTH AVENUE MALL

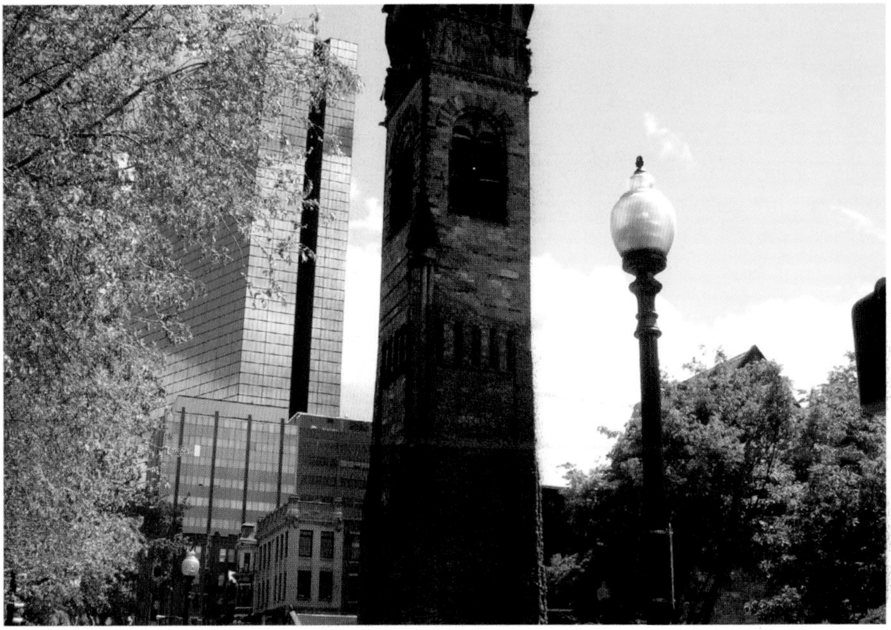

FIRST BAPTIST CHURCH
COURTESY BOSTON PUBLIC LIBRARY

Horsford's, the poet Henry Wadsworth Longfellow. It was sculpted by Ann Whitney and erected in 1887. One might note that the statue has outlasted the theories of Horsford and the others. Also along the mall, at Dartmouth Street, the widest of the cross streets except for Massachusetts Avenue, stood the Hotel Vendome. With its Mansard roof, the French Second Empire-style building, built in 1871, was the best hotel in town for many years, and a landmark on the southwest corner that fit well with the houses of similar age on Commonwealth Avenue.

It aged, however, while newer, more modern hotels were built, and toward the end of the 1960s, renovations were being made. But before they could be completed, a fire destroyed a large section. The fire took the lives of nine fire-fighters when some of the building fell in after the fire had been extinguished. A memorial to the fallen firefighters stands on the Commonwealth Avenue Mall at Dartmouth. The section that had been destroyed was replaced, and the building is being rented as apartments, offices, and retail.

CHAPTER THIRTEEN

The Esplanade

The river's edge was not the first thing considered when Back Bay was filled in during the years from 1857 to 1890 and beyond. The Charles was still tidal when this filling took place, and it wasn't until the 1880s that the easternmost part of the Esplanade, known as Charlesbank, was built on the filled-in land to the north of Charles Street, a north-south thoroughfare at the bottom of Beacon Hill. When Olmsted designed it, his main goals were to provide access to the waterfront via a wide promenade with many benches, and to provide recreational activities for everyone. He even devised an outdoor gymnasium of sorts near today's Massachusetts General Hospital.

Charles bank was then only a strip of land along the river, but things would change much in the years ahead. For one thing, a dam would be built across the river that would change the river from a tidal estuary to a fresh-water estuary. The dam would create a broad basin in which the water levels remained fairly steady.

The eventual wide improvements that came to the shores of the Charles are due mainly to Charles Eliot, who had apprenticed at the Olmsted firm. He envisioned a water park along the southern bank of the river. After he had formed the Metropolitan District Commission (MDC), it acquired much of the land along the river. Eliot had

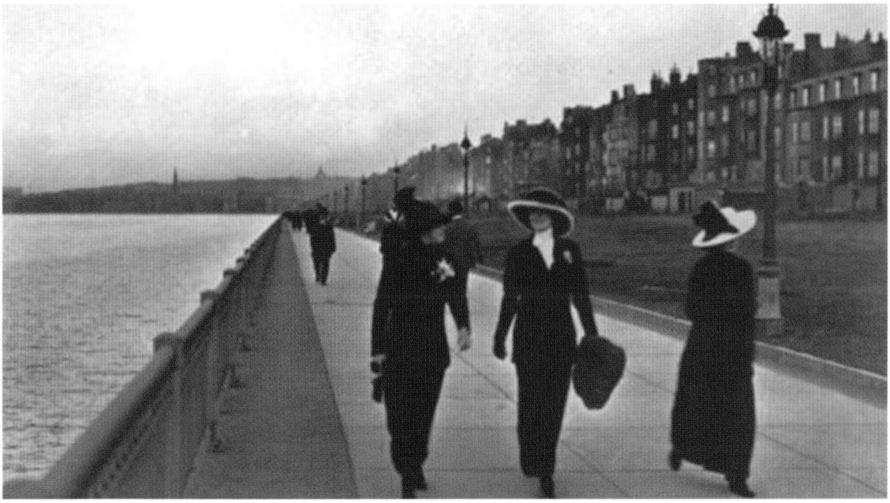

EMBANKMENT, WOMEN WALKING
COURTESY ARCHIVES, DEPARTMENT OF CONSERVATION

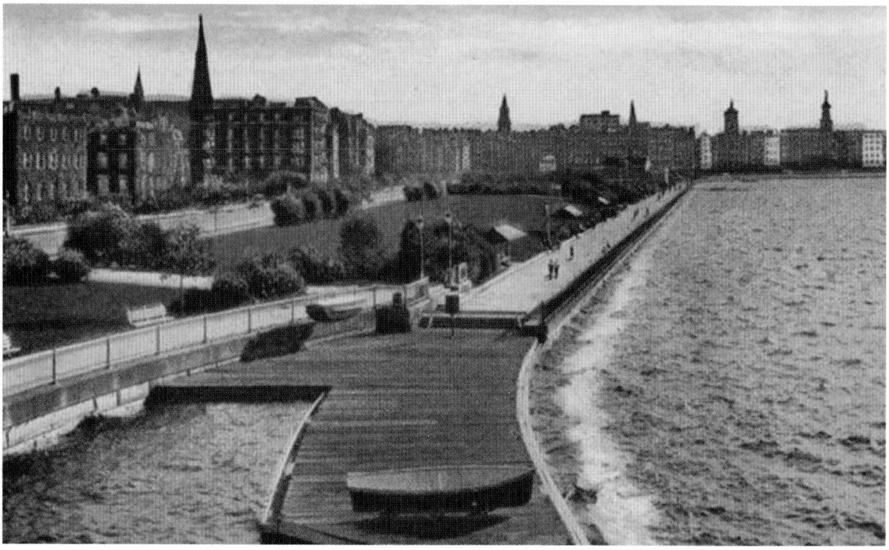

ESPLANADE, DOCK

admired such a park in Hamburg, Germany, one with trees and boats and a lagoon, and he tried to get one built in Boston. Before such a park could make sense, the river had to be dammed, and Eliot was unable to overcome the resistance to that before he died in 1895. It would be left to others.

The one who did the most to bring this about was banker James Jackson Storrow who lived on Beacon Hill. His neighbors were against the plan, but Storrow was fighting for fresh air and beautiful open spaces. With the help of his influential friends in tapping legislators on the shoulders or twisting the arms of those who could make things happen, the legislature finally gave its approval.

The dam was finished on June 30, 1910, just in time to hold a celebration on Independence Day. So, on the Fourth of July, a tradition began with an outstanding two-hour display of fireworks watched by thousands who stood or sat on the new Boston Embankment (later called the Esplanade) an area that had once been all tidal flats. The narrow strip of land at Charlesbank could now be transformed into a 100 foot-long swath of grass that ran two miles from the Longfellow Bridge west to the Muddy River at Charlesgate. It was fronted by a steep granite seawall—a wall that seemed to make sense at the time.

It was no easier then to please the public than it is now. They had suffered through the stench of the mudflats and then the lack of a complete plan for the riverfront. Now they had the dam that made it pleasant to live on Beacon or adjoining streets, and there was an attempt, at least, to make use of the land along the river for recreation.

But the Esplanade had no amenities, not even shade trees, and was little used but greatly criticized. High hopes shrank to bitter disappointment. Improvements were made a few at a time, including the planting of numerous shade trees. But Storrow's influence had not run its course. After his death, his widow, Helen Osborne Storrow, offered $1 million of his legacy for improvements, a gift she would give if the government matched her donation. Nearly $4 million was raised in all, and playgrounds, beaches, and boat landings were added.

Improvements during the late 1920s and 1930s were designed by Arthur Shurcliff, disciple of Charles Eliot, who widened and lengthened the area. Shurcliff added the first lagoon, boat landings, plazas, playgrounds, and the Music Oval, including a temporary band shell. There was also a large lawn for summer concerts given by Arthur Fiedler, a violinist from the Boston Symphony Orchestra (BSO). In 1924, he formed an orchestra to play chamber music called the Boston Sinfonietta, made up of members of the BSO, and it was in 1929 that he began the series of free outdoor concerts. Six years later, he was appointed the eighteenth conductor of the Boston Pops orchestra, a group known for its playing of popular light classical music. During his tenure, the Boston Pops made more recordings than any orchestra in the world, most of them for RCA Victor, with sales of over $50 million. Fiedler is readily connected with the Esplanade and the Hatch Shell (1941).

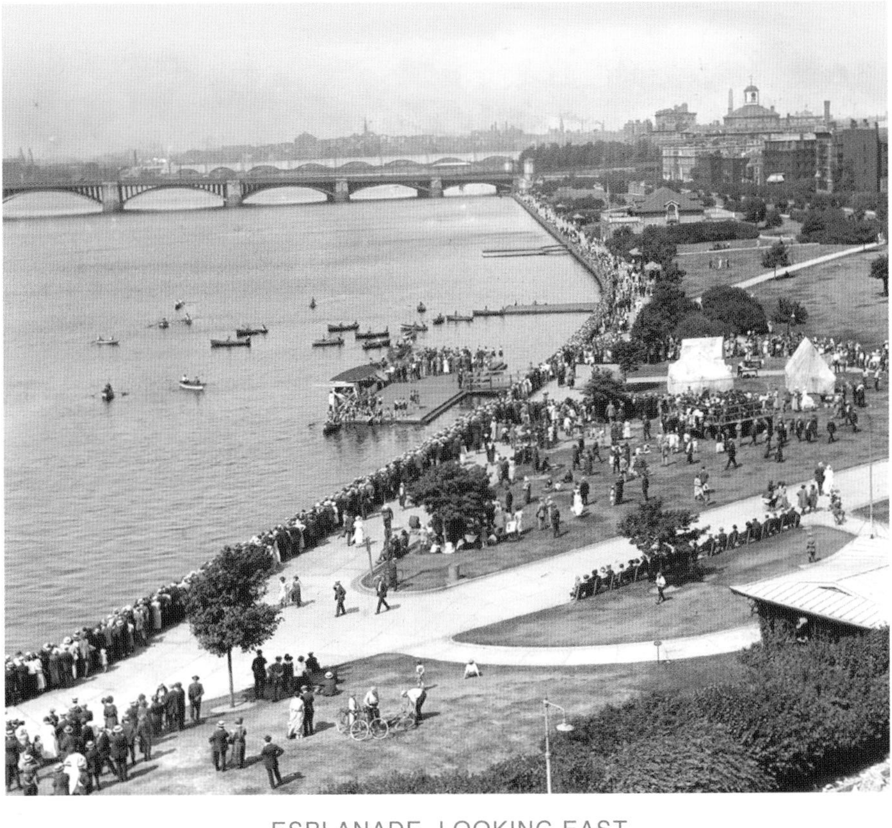

ESPLANADE, LOOKING EAST

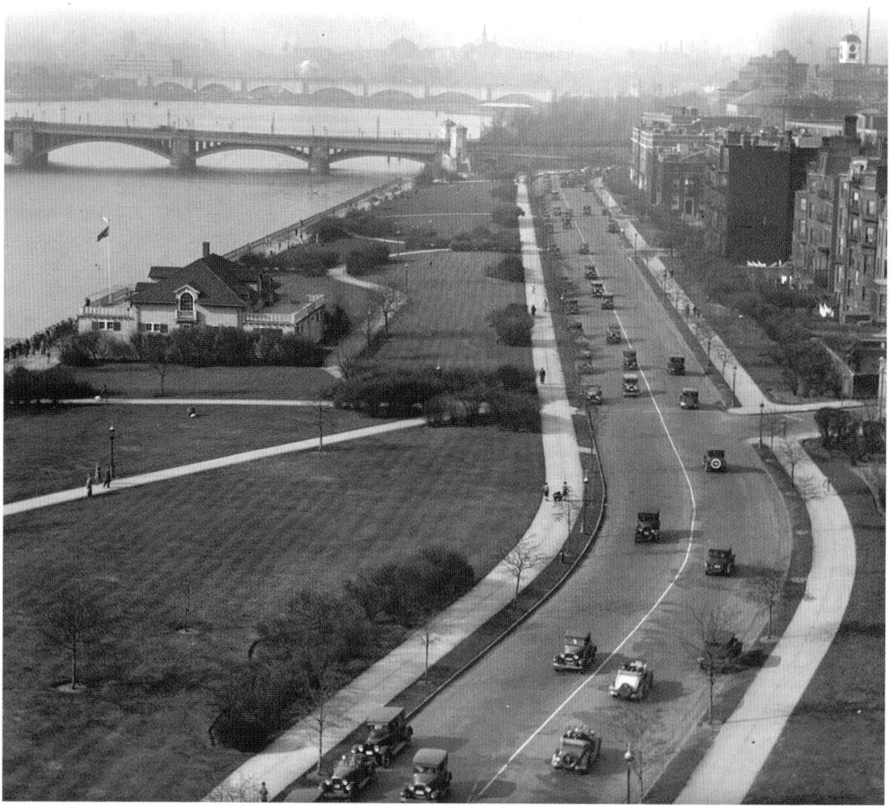

ESPLANADE, WITH TRAFFIC

The summer concerts, especially the one on the Fourth of July, gave the area status and later fame, but there were other enhancements during the 1920s and 1930s. One seemingly minor change that made a great difference had to do with the stone facing where the land met the Charles. There was hope, you will recall, for a lot of boats and boating, but the steep granite facing created strong waves that made it difficult to sail there. These were replaced by gentler edging of stone that now made boating possible. Sailing on the Charles began in the 1930s, and the boathouse on the Esplanade was built in 1941. Community Boating (1946) was the country's first public boating program. In all the years since, it has allowed thousands to learn to sail on the Charles.

These enhancements made the Esplanade a more pleasant place, but more trouble lay ahead. The legislature wanted to put a new highway through the Esplanade in order to move traffic in and out to the suburbs where so many people had moved. It would run along the Charles, and, of course, there was opposition to disturbing what was at last the pastoral, pleasant area that so many now enjoyed. A fierce battle took place in the legislature. It voted to eliminate some of the parkland, but mitigated this by adding land on the river side of Storrow Drive, a parkway of which Storrow himself, would have been unlikely to approve. For all the gifts and benefits the Storrows bestowed, the unloved highway is what most often recalls their name.

The aging Arthur Shurcliff was once again called upon to redesign the Esplanade along with his son, Sidney. More filled-in land was created to make up for what was taken for the road and its approaches. Most of this new land was a long island built out into the river and connected by several bridges. As the roadbed was dug, the land that was scraped out could be used for new land. A tunnel was also built near Berkeley Street so that the Music Oval needn't be disturbed. Land was also taken from the Charlesbank section for ramps and to expand Charles Street Circle near the Longfellow Bridge. At the western end of Charlesbank, adjacent to this, baseball fields, a swimming pool, and new paths and trees were added, while the end, near Craigie Bridge with its playground, remained much the same.

Storrow Drive opened in 1951, but was not well-designed, having sharp curves and narrow lanes, numerous underpasses, some of which flooded. Despite signs warning of clearance heights, trucks frequently got caught in the narrow passages. One time, a truck carrying a cargo of scissors disgorged the sharp steel objects, resulting in more than thirty cars getting flats—two of them four flat tires—backing the road up for all of a long afternoon.

More recently, the overpass at Clarendon Street was called by *Travel and Leisure* the most dangerous bridge in America due to its shortcomings. It appears to be a tunnel, but because it bears the weight of overhead traffic, it is classified as a bridge.

The magazine said:

> This double-deck roadway abutting Back Bay has been a headache practically since it opened in 1951. The problem: the pavement of the upper deck is too thick, straining the corroding steel beams that support the structure from underneath. Numerous rounds of costly interim repairs (most recently in 2 012–13) have kept the artery open, but they're merely stopgaps to extend its life through 2018 while longer-term solutions are weighed.

Resistance to Storrow Drive continued from the outset and still exists, but other improvements have been viewed more favorably. Bicycles were first allowed on the Esplanade in 1960, and in 1971–1978 the Dr. Paul Dudley White Bicycle Path was established along both sides of the river, reaching west to Watertown.

A new dam was built near the site of the present Bunker Hill—Zakim Bridge in 1978, and the last half-mile of parkland was created along both sides of the Charles between the old dam and Boston Harbor. The older dam (located where the Museum of Science is located) could not fully keep salt water from entering the basin during high tides. The new dam will do this and also keep water levels the same, even on tributaries like Muddy River.

The dam is also called "The Gridley Dam" for Richard Gridley who was General Washington's engineer while he was in Boston. It has three locks, one wider than the others, six pumps driven by six diesel engines moving 3.7 million gallons of water per minute, used when the tides from the harbor require moving excess water out of the river basin. It also has a walkway across the top that can be used by cyclists as well as pedestrians. On it is an artwork of chimes mounted on the railing that people can strike as they pass.

The Esplanade and the whole Charles River basin and Back Bay light up once a year on July 4 when the Pops plays at the Hatch Shell and millions of people watch them and the fireworks that follow. It's a national event. That kind of attention also comes when one of the Boston sports teams wins a championship and parades from the Prudential Center through the Back Bay and much of the city using Duck Tour boats to plunge into and emerge from the Charles.

After all, Back Bay began as part of the Charles River, did it not?

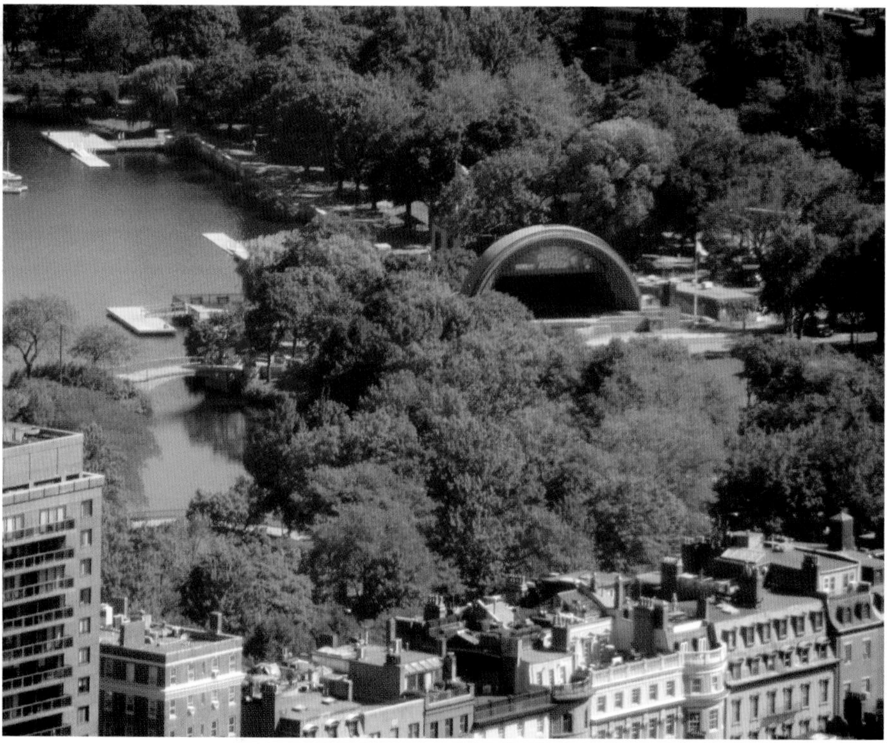

HATCH SHELL
COURTESY AUTHOR

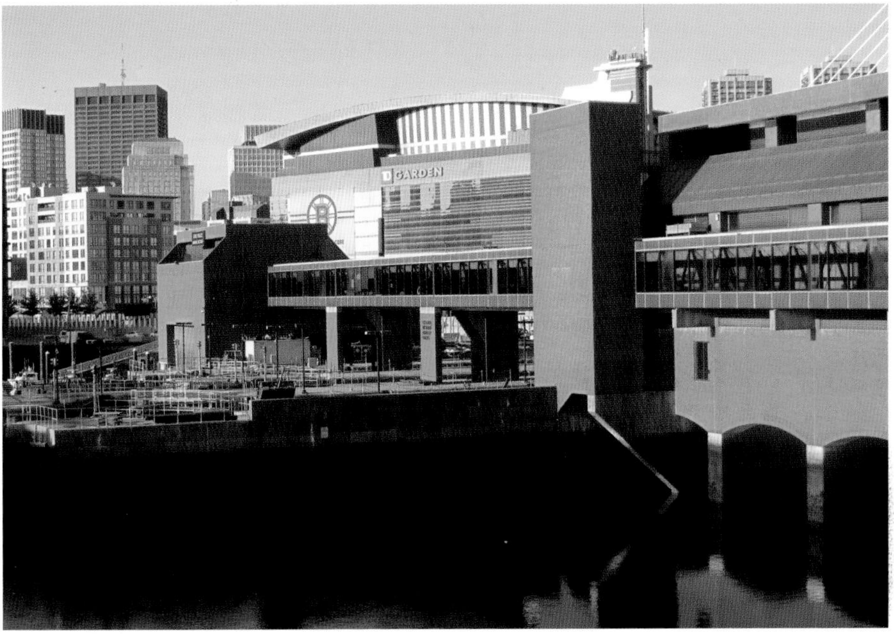

DAM NEAR TD BANK GARDEN
COURTESY AUTHOR

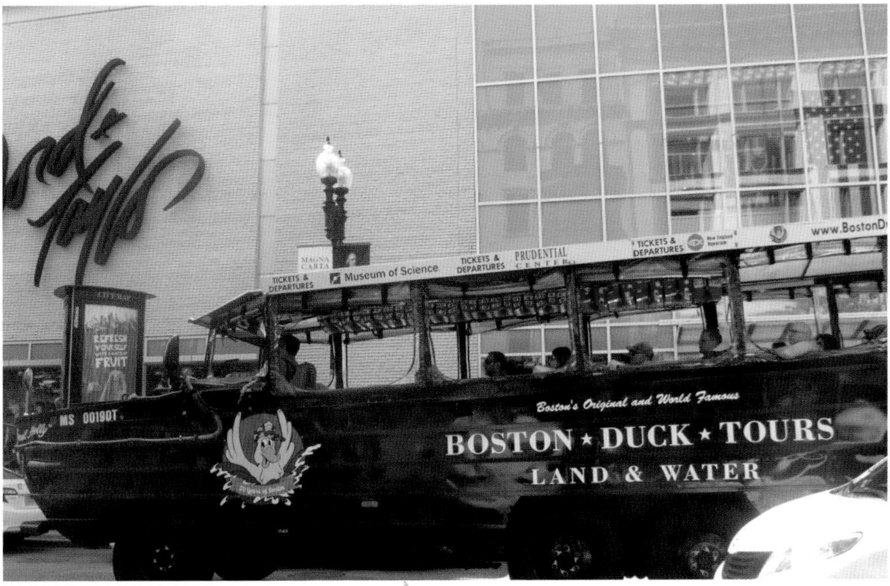

BOSTON DUCK TOURS VEHICLE
COURTESY AUTHOR

Bibliography

Adams, Ann Jensen. "The Birth of a Style." *The Art Bulletin* Vol. 62, No. 3 (September 1980)

Bacon, Edwin M. *Boston Illustrated.* Boston: Houghton, 1891.

Baxton, Charles. *Boston and the Back Bay*. Boston: Reed and Co., 1884.

Cherubini, Penny. "Shaping Copley Square." *Back Bay Sun*, Nov. 8, 2011.

Cherubini, Penny. "Boylston Street Over the Years." *Back Bay Sun*, Sept. 6, 2011.

Clarke, Ted. *Beacon Hill, Back Bay and the Building of Boston's Golden Age*. Charleston, SC: The History Press, 2010.

Cox, Linda M. *The Charles River Esplanade: Our Boston Treasure.* Amherst, MA, University of Massachusetts, 2000.

Hall, Alexandra. "The New Brahmins." *Boston Magazine*, May 2004.

Ileran, Michael, Boston's "Changeful Times": Origins of Preservation & Planning in America. H-Urban, H-Net Reviews. May, 1999

Kenndy, Lawrence W. *Planning the City Upon a Hill: Boston Since 1630.* Amherst, MA: University of Massachusetts Press, 1992.

Leccese, Mark. "Love That Dirty Water," *Boston Magazine*, August 2000.

Mcmorrow, Paul. "Adjusting Boston's High Spine." *Globe*, January 29, 2013.

Parrow, William J. *Durham Street: The First Century, 1885-1995.* s.n., 1995.

Southworth, Susan, and Michael, *AIA Guide to Boston.* Guilford, CT: Globe-Pequot Press, 1992.

Travel & Leisure. "America's Most Dangerous Bridges." August 2013.

Whitehill, Walter Muir and Lawrenee Kennedy. *Boston: A Topographical History.* Cabridge, Harvard University Press, 2000.

Electronic Sources:

Green, Gloria, "Vikings on the Charles." http://needhamhistory.org/features/articles/vikings/.

The Greening of Boston, Boston.com.

www.boston.com/yourtown/cambridge/articles/2.

010/07/04/100_years_of_celebrating_the_fourth_of_july_at_esplanade/?page=1.

Society of Architectural Historians. Archipedia, http://sah-archipedia.org/detail%2Fcontent%2Fentries%2FMA-.

01-BB38.xml?q=agent%3A%22I.%20M.%20Pei%20and%20Partners%22.www.boston.com/yourtown/cambridge/articles/2.

010/07/04/100_years_of_celebrating_the_fourth_of_july_at_esplanade/?page=1.

Index